The State of Black America 1986

Published by **National Urban League, Inc.**

JANUARY 23, 1986

Edited by
James D. Williams
Director of Communications
National Urban League

ABOUT THE AUTHORS

<u>DR. BERNARD E. ANDERSON</u>: Visiting Fellow at the Woodrow Wilson School of Public and International Affairs, Princeton University. An internationally respected economist. Dr. Anderson graduated with highest honors from Livingstone College where he received his A.B. Degree. He received his Master's Degree in Economics at Michigan State University in 1961. He was awarded the Ph.D. in Business Applied Economics by the University of Pennsylvania. He is also the recipient of the L.H.D. (Honoris Causa) from Shaw University. He has served as a professor at the Wharton School of Finance and Commerce at the University of Pennsylvania, an instructor at Swarthmore College in Pennsylvania, and as Director of the Social Science Division of the Rockefeller Foundation. He is the author of several books including: <u>The Impact of Government Manpower Programs</u>; <u>OIC: A Decade of Community Based Manpower Services</u>; <u>Moving Ahead: Black Managers in American Business</u> (with Richard F. America). Dr. Anderson has also served as the Vice President of the Board of Directors of the Philadelphia Urban League and has been a frequent contributor to other editions of "<u>The State of Black America</u>".

<u>PROFESSOR JOHN O. CALMORE</u>: Associate Professor of Law, North Carolina Central University, School of Law, Durham, N.C. Professor Calmore has written extensively on housing discrimination and fair housing and in addition has served on the Board of Directors of the Fair Housing Congress of Southern California, and the National Housing Law Project based in Berkeley, CA. He earned his undergraduate degree at Stanford University and his law degree from the Harvard Law School. Professor Calmore's professional career began when he served as a Reginald Heber Smith Fellow, Western Center on Law and Poverty and Boston Legal Assistance Project. Subsequent positions included Regional Heber Smith Community Lawyer Fellow and Staff Attorney, Legal Aid Foundation of Los Angeles; Staff Attorney, National Housing Project, Berkeley; Director of Litigation, Legal Aid Foundation of Los Angeles; and Staff Attorney, Western Center on Law and Poverty.

<u>DR. ROBERT B. HILL</u>: Visiting Professor of Sociology at the University of Pennsylvania. Since 1981 he has been Senior Research Associate at the Bureau of Social Science Research, Inc. in Washington, D.C. Prior to joining BSSR, he was Director of Research for the National Urban League for about a decade. Dr. Hill received his Ph.D. in Sociology from Columbia University and his B.A. Degree in Sociology from the City College of New York. He has served on a number of high-level panels--the U.S. Census Bureau's Advisory Committee on the Black Population in the 1980 Census; the 1981 White House Conference on Aging; the 1980 White Conference on Families and the National Academy of Science's Committee on Child Development Research and Public Policy. He has also taught at the University of Maryland, Howard University, Morgan State, Princeton, NYU and Fordham University. His publications include: "<u>The Polls and Ethnic Minorities</u>" (1984); <u>Economic Policies and Black Progress</u> (1981); <u>Discrimination and Minority Youth Employment</u> (1980); <u>Informal Adoption Among Black Families</u> (1977); <u>The Strengths of Black Families</u> (1971), and various articles for the NUL's annual <u>State of Black America</u>.

<u>JOHN E. JACOB</u>: President and chief executive officer of the National Urban League, the nation's most respected community-based social service

and advocacy agency. He is author of a weekly newspaper column, "To Be Equal," distributed by the Copley News Service to over 600 newspapers and he has written articles on national issues for major publications. Mr. Jacob has been President of the NUL since January 1, 1982. Prior to that he was Executive Vice President of the National Urban League. Mr. Jacob began his Urban League career in 1965 as Director of Education and Youth Incentives at the Washington, DC Urban League and served in a number of important administrative positions, including Acting Executive Director and Director of Community Organizations Training in the Eastern Regional Office of the NUL. He serves as Vice Chairman of the Howard University Board of Trustees and serves on the boards of New York Telephone, the National Conference of Christians and Jews, the Local Initiatives Support Corporation, New York Foundation, Eisenhower Foundation, American Board of Family Practice, and Independent Sector. He is also a member of the Rockefeller University Council and holds honorary degrees from Old Dominion University, Fisk University and Lafayette College. A native of Houston, Texas, Mr. Jacob received his undergraduate and MSW degrees from Howard University. He has also served as Executive Director of the San Diego Urban League and as President of the Washington (DC) Urban League.

DR. JOYCE A. LADNER: Professor of Social Work, Howard University. One of the nation's leading experts on the sociology of the black family and sex roles, and race and ethnic relations, Dr. Ladner's career has included the authorship of over 60 articles for scholarly publications. She has also written for several general publications including Ebony, Essence, Black Enterprise and the New York Times Dr. Ladner has served as a consultant for several films, delivered lectures before groups as diverse as the Children's Defense Fund and the National Conference of Afro-American Writers, and chaired the Mayor's Blue Ribbon Panel on Teenage Pregnancy Prevention for the District of Columbia. She is the author of several books including "Tomorrow's Tomorrow: The Black Woman," (New York, Doubleday Publishing Co., 1971), and "Mixed Families: Adopting Across Racial Boundaries" (New York, Doubleday Publishing Co., 1977). She received her BA from Tougaloo College, and her MA and Ph.D. from Washington University. Dr. Ladner has also served a a Professor of Sociology at Hunter College and the Graduate Center, City University of New York, Visiting Fellow at the Metropolitan Applied Research Center, and as a Research Associate at the University of Dar es Salaam, Tanzania. At present, she is also an Adjunct Fellow at the Joint Center for Political Studies.

DR. GLENN C. LOURY: Professor of Public Policy at the John F. Kennedy School of Government at Harvard University. He is spending the current academic year as a member of the Institute for Advanced Study, Princeton. Dr. Loury received his Bachelor of Arts Degree in mathematics from Northwestern University in 1972 and the Ph.D. Degree in Economics from the Massachusetts Institute of Technology in 1976. He has served as an Associate Professor at Massachusetts University and as a Professor at the University of Michigan. Dr. Loury has also been a visiting scholar at Oxford University in England, Tel Aviv University in Israel, and the University of Stockholm. His numerous essays on the politics and economics of racial inequality in the U.S. have appeared in the New York Times, the Wall Street Journal, the Washington

Post, The New Republic, The Public Interest and other journals and publications. He has served as an economist on several advisory commissions including the National Commission for Employment Policy, the National Academy of Sciences, and the National Science Foundation. He has also advised private and government agencies as an economist consultant. These agencies include: the Bell Telephone Laboratories; the Rockefeller Foundation; and the Federal Trade Commission.

DR. CHARLES D. MOODY, SR.: Professor of Education and Director of the Program for Educational Opportunity, and the Center for Sex Equity in Schools at the University of Michigan. Dr. Moody received his Ph.D. from Northwestern University. He is a former superintendent of schools in Illinois. He is founder of the National Alliance of Black School Superintendents, now the National Alliance of Black School Educators. His dissertation, Black Superintendents in Public School Districts: Trends and Conditions is the first study and publication on the black superintendent ever done in this country. Dr. Moody has been on the faculty at The University of Michigan since 1970. He has served as a consultant to several hundred school districts and agencies including NAACP Education Committee, Community Service Society of New York City, Michigan State Superintendent of Public Instruction, and several federal courts. Dr. Moody has published numerous articles, newsletters, and research reports. He is in the process of completing the writing on a national survey of superintendents responsible for more than 50% of all black students in this country on what they are doing and saying about equity and excellence in their districts. Dr. Moody received an honorary doctorate from his alma mater, Central State University in 1981.

DR. DIANNE M. PINDERHUGHES: Assistant Professor, Afro-American Studies and Research Programs and Department of Political Science, University of Illinois at Urbana-Champaign. Dr. Pinderhughes earned her undergraduate degree at Albertus Magnus College, and her M.A. and Ph.D. at the University of Chicago--all in political science. Her academic appointments include Lecturer, Chicago State University; Instructor and Assistant Professor, Dartmouth College; Visiting Assistant Professor, Howard University; Guest Scholar, Brookings Institution; Adjunct Fellow, Joint Center for Political Studies; Postdoctoral Fellow, University of California. Dr. Pinderhughes has received a number of academic honors and has published extensively with her major fields being American Politics, Urban Politics, Racial and Ethnic Politics and Public Policy.

DR. DAVID H. SWINTON: Director, Southern Center for Studies in Public Policy, Clark College. An economist, Dr. Swinton earned his undergraduate degree from the New York University and his M.A. and Ph.D. from Harvard University. He served as a Teaching Fellow at Harvard and later as a Lecturer at City College of New York. He has also held positions as Assistant Director for Research, Black Economic Research Center; Assistant Professor of Urban and Policy Science, State University of New York; Senior Research Associate at The Urban Institute, and Director, Minorities and Social Policy Program, The Urban Institute. Dr. Swinton's writings on economic issues have been widely published in a variety of publications.

TABLE OF CONTENTS

: : :

AN OVERVIEW OF BLACK AMERICA IN 1985

By

John E. Jacob

As the economic recovery continued during 1985, black Americans slipped further and further to the rear of the parade. One of the tragic facts often overlooked in the euphoria attending the onset and continuation of a recovery following a recession is that the former always leaves blacks worse off than they were before. So precarious is the state of their economic health they never quite make up lost ground.

After two years of recovery, blacks in 1985 did not reach the same level of income they had attained prior to the recession of 1980, and if present trends and national policies continue, and history repeats itself, they will not. Indeed, racial economic inequity as measured by the ratio of black to white per capita income is increasing and is greater now than it has been at any time since 1970. In 1984, the last year for which official figures are available, the median black family had about 56 cents to spend for every one dollar white families had to spend, which was two cents less than they had in 1980, and almost six cents less than they had in 1970.

The hardest hit in all of this have been poor black families. The poorest 20% of black families had 22% less purchasing power in 1984 than in 1980, the second poorest quintile had 15% less income, while the third poorest quintile had 4% less. The income of the top 20% was virtually unchanged while the income of the top 5% increased by about 9%.

White America is getting back on its feet while much of Black America is still struggling just to start rising off the floor. Unemployment at the end of 1985 was down to 5.9% in White America, while in Black America it was 14.9%. Similar figures from 1984 had white unemployment at 6.5% and black unemployment at 16%.

The signs of a nation moving toward a state of being permanently divided between the haves and the have-nots were plain to see over the past months, but all too few took the time or the trouble to look at them and comprehend their implications for the future. When it comes to the reality of how quickly much of Black America is losing ground in comparison to others, it would seem that much of America has put on blinkers.

Within Black America, however, the pain is showing. It shows in the increasing groups of idle men who spend most of their days just "hanging out." If there was work they would take it, but they have tried so often and failed so many times that they have given up hope and resigned themselves to a lifetime of "getting by" through whatever means are required.

It shows in the rejection by a frightening number of black teenagers of the American dream of getting ahead by securing an education and working hard. They see the dream did not work for their kin and have no reason to believe that it will work for them. They could believe little else faced with an unemployment rate of 41.6%. They express their manhood or womanhood in other ways, many of them anti-social and self-destructive. It is shocking but true that the major cause of death among young black males is homicide.

These things represent tremendous losses to Black America and the nation as a whole. From a monetary view alone, the lower earnings of black males cost Black America $63 billion a year and accounts for over 84% of the black-white labor market earnings gap and for over 51% of the overall black and white income gap.

There is also the incalculable cost of the psychic damage sustained in Black America where job and income deprivation create an unhealthy atmosphere in which it is difficult to sustain the moral and social stability of individuals, the family and the community.

The employment predicament of Black America is due in large measure to the fact that the face of the American economy is changing and the most drastic changes have and are continuing to occur in those sectors of the economy upon which blacks have depended heavily as a source of jobs.

Since 1980, America has lost two-and-a-half million factory jobs. Another 200,000 jobs in the auto industry have disappeared, and still an additional 200,000 in textiles and 200,000 more in electronics have gone forever. A disproportionate number of those jobs, particularly in the unskilled and semi-skilled categories, were held by black males who without retraining—and there are precious few efforts taking place—have become superfluous in the labor market.

Further, economist Dr. David Swinton tells us that if the overall and relatively high unemployment rate of 5.6% which existed in 1972 was to have been maintained—and black unemployment was at 10.4% that year—some 28 million new jobs would have had to have been generated between 1972 and 1984 to provide for the 7.9 million white women and the some 500,000 black women who entered the labor market. However, the economy only generated an additional 23 million jobs with the difference being made up by higher unemployment rates and decreased labor participation among men of working age.

What the growing ranks of the black unemployed mean to the future of this nation was forecast by Ebony Magazine in August 1985, in an editorial included in a special issue on "Blacks and the Future; Where Will We Be in the Year 2000." It said in part:

"Because of the failures of the past, we approach the new century divided by irrational and costly racial fears and weakened by a growing army of unemployed and alienated citizens. There are also structural problems and the spectre of increasing pressure from foreign competition. But history tells us that an America which transformed large stretches of the earth and invaded space can solve these and other problems in a decade if America decides that it wants to solve them. And here, as elsewhere, the problem is the will. For where there is a will to national wholeness, there is a way to national wholeness.

"It is in the interest of all Americans to join in the effort to create this will. For America cannot reach its full potential if millions of blacks are condemned to wasted potential."

For those of us who have tried for so long to get this message across, we wonder what it will take to arouse America from its lethargy. Back in 1976, the National Urban League called for a National Youth Employment Program, that included education, training and work components. Some critics called it visionary and complained of the price tag, but if it had been adopted many of the unemployed young men and women who now spin out their days in idleness and hopelessness would be productive members of society.

Those disadvantaged youngsters we were concerned with in 1976 are the young black men and women of today. They grew up in poverty without the education and the training they needed to make it in this world. Some of them have joined the recent American phenomena of the homeless, eating in soup kitchens and sleeping in shelters or on outdoor grates warmed by whiffs of steam.

But it does not have to be like this. Despite the assertions of some that the programs of the Great Society and the War on Poverty were failures and wasters of the tax-payers dollars, we have never accepted this view and there is a substantial body of evidence to support our position. The only trouble with those programs is that they were never funded adequately and were abandoned when they did not produce the immediate results for which Americans seem to clamor.

We know that programs to take people out of poverty can work if they are constructed carefully, managed properly, and adequately funded.

One example is provided by the 27 Skills Training Centers the League operates in concert with IBM and other business firms to train the unemployed and underemployed in computer programming, clerical/secretarial skills, computer operations and word processing. A number of the enrollees are single female heads of households, others are former school dropouts, and still others possess limited skills that are no longer in demand in the job market. After training, which costs a little over $3,000 for each participant, some 85% of the graduates are placed in jobs at an average annual salary of some $12,600.

The fact that this program works so well--and there are other programs operated by other community based organizations that are also successful--makes it clear that the situation is not hopeless and what is required, in the words of Ebony, is "the will."

That "will" has to begin with the national government which sets the mood for the rest of the country. The task of preparing so many young people for the job market is much too great for the private sector alone. Delaying addressing this problem will only make it worse, as the experiences of the past year have shown.

A proper place to begin is by the adoption of a Voluntary National Service Program that will give disadvantaged young people skills training, educational experiences and jobs. There should also be a start made toward the establishment of a National Full Employment Program that would create training and work opportunities for unemployed young adults.

Of special importance is what is to be done about black male unemployment. This is not to ignore the importance of the employment of black females but without jobs, men don't get married, they avoid responsibility, they do not participate in the raising of families. True, there are many families, both black and white, that are functioning very well without a male figure, but the cruel reality is that the odds are stacked against such successes.

There are some words to describe the status of all too many black men in today's society. They are taken from a publication the National Urban League issued in 1984, "Running the Gauntlet: Black Men in America."

"The gauntlet that black men run takes its toll at every age, but at nearly every stage of life the toll is very high and the effect is cumulative. The attrition of black males from various causes from conception through adulthood finally results in an insufficient number of men who are willing and able to provide support for women and children in a family setting. Even though black men run the gauntlet all their lives, the wonder is not that so many are wounded and crippled during their passage, but that so many survive with their minds healthy and their souls intact. However, many do fall or are wounded and crippled and for each one who falls there is one less man to be a husband to his wife, a father to his children and a provider for his family."

The absence of black males as heads of households has had a devastating effect on Black America. Over 40% of black families are now headed by single females and while there is no denying the love and care they give their children, the bottom line is that they are the poorest of the poor with all the negatives this entails for the futures of their children.

Unless we deal directly with black male unemployment, we can only treat the symptoms of family disintegration. Black America cannot provide the needed jobs by itself, but in 1985 it devoted increased attention and resources to the things it could do best--providing support mechanisms for black families in trouble and seeking to strengthen black communities.

Efforts were mounted to deal with a number of problems including crime, education, and single female heads of households. Many of these were focused on teen pregnancy with has become a priority project of a number of national organizations including the National Urban League, the National Council of Negro Women and Delta Sigma Theta Sorority. Other organizations have also demonstrated a concern for this problem including the Sisterhood of Black Single Mothers, the Coalition of 100 Black Women, the Alpha Phi Alpha Fraternity, the Concerned Black Men of Washington, D.C, the NAACP and the Southern Christian Leadership Conference.

A most encouraging development in 1985 was the launching by the Children's Defense Fund, the nation's leading child advocacy organization, of a broad-based adolescent Pregnancy Prevention Project that is national in scope. The project was undertaken in collaboration with the National

Council of Negro Women and the Coalition of 100 Black Women.

The depth of the problem of black teen pregnancy is demonstrated in the statistics which show that 24.6% of all black births are to teens, that 87% of these are out of wedlock, and 90% to 94% of the mothers keep the children and do not place them for adoption. These teen mothers are rarely in a secure enough financial position or possessed of enough emotional maturity to rear their children properly thereby materially reducing their chances for growing into productive adulthood.

The black community is increasingly accepting more and more responsibility for dealing with this problem but, as Dr. Joyce Ladner, one of the nation's leading experts in the field of teen pregnancy, reminds us: "While the initiatives undertaken by black organizations are important, the size and seriousness of the problem makes it impossible for blacks alone to solve it...

"Ultimately, the society as a whole will continue to pay the cost, as the toll increases rapidly. Thus it is in the interest of public policy makers, child welfare advocates, parents, educators, the religious sector, taxpayers, employers, and every other special interest group to work collaboratively to find solutions to this problem."

The outlook, however, for increased assistance from the federal government for teen pregnancy or for that matter for any social service program remained bleak. As the Urban Institute reported in 1985, the retrenchment in spending for social services that has been going on since the start of the Reagan Administration, has seriously hurt programs for children, young adults and the long-term unemployed. From 1981 to 1984 the government cut its spending for 25 programs that focus on children and young adults by 11% over all, after accounting for inflation.

This included a 53% decline in job training for young people and cuts of 26% in mental health services, 18% in Aid to Families With Dependent Children and 12% in programs to prevent child abuse.

Lester M. Salamon, who directed the study for the Urban Institute, provided this analysis of what has taken place during the Reagan years.

"What we learned was the cuts translated at local levels into losses in a number of fields, principally employment and training, housing and community development, health care outside of Medicare, and social services. Especially hard hit were programs targeted on the unemployed, on families and on children."

The Administration's cuts and policies vis-a-vis social service programs have had a measurable impact on the poor. When the Census Bureau released official poverty statistics last year for 1984, Administration spokesmen pointed to the decline in the poverty rate from the 1983 figures and said it proved Washington's policies were working. But they are not. Cetainly, there was a decline in the overall poverty rate, down to 14.4% in 1984 as compared to 15.3% in 1983—but what the Administration ignored was that the 1984 poverty rate was the highest poverty level for a non-recession year since 1966.

The most tragic aspect of all is that there has actually been an increase in poverty among black children. A majority, (51.1%) of all black children are poor and that is the highest figure since the government started recording such statistics back in 1970.

Other data in the Census report disclosed:

- The overall black poverty rate in 1984 was 33.8% down from 35.7% in 1983, but higher than the black poverty rate for any non-recession year since 1968.

- Most of the decline in black poverty occurred among the elderly. The black elderly poverty rate fell for 36.2% to 31.7%. This drop was due in part to increases in Social Security and Supplemental Security Income benefits.

- Among black families headed by a female, 54.6% were poor in 1984. For black families with two parents, the poverty rate was 17.4%.

- 66.2% of all black children living in a household headed by a female were poor in 1984.

In an analysis of the poverty figures, the Center on Budget and Policy Priorities has warned that "since unemployment has stopped dropping in 1985 and since wages are lower than in 1984, no further significant drop in poverty is expected in 1985." Center Director Robert Greenstein went on to say:

"The modest drop in poverty in 1984 seems to be all the reduction we're going to get for some time. This means that poverty may be stuck at a new plateau where 8-9 million more Americans are in poverty than in the mid 1970's."

Directly related to the poverty figures is the fact that the domestic social service programs that have been cut most sharply since 1980 have been those aimed at low and moderate income individuals. Blacks are three times as likely to participate in these programs as other Americans so that budget cuts have hit them with a particularly heavy blow. The Center on Budget and Policy Priorities has concluded "that the average black family has lost three times as much from the cuts as the average white family."

In addition to its efforts to cut social service programs even further, the Administration continued its unrelenting assault throughout 1985 on civil rights laws and their enforcement.

It was a strange performance with the Administration on one hand declaring that it was an ardent and effective supporter of civil rights, while on the other it took a number of actions to reverse past civil rights gains. In effect, what the Administration was practicing can justifiably be described as "voodoo civil rights," since it is reasonable to ask how can an Administration in its rhetoric be for civil rights, when in its deeds it is so firmly against them? The answer is clear--it can't have things both ways and so the term "voodoo civil right" applies.

President Reagan remained more or less on the sidelines of the attacks on civil rights with Attorney General Edwin Meese taking the lead position. An example of Mr. Meese's convoluted thinking on the issue of civil rights took place last September at Dickinson College when he compared supporters of affirmative action to apologists for slavery, once again demonstrating that he lacks the sensitivity and capacity to make the moral and legal distinctions required by his role as the nation's chief law enforcement officer.

That Mr. Meese should take such a position was not really surprising. In January of 1985 the Department of Justice sent letters to 51 jurisdictions notifying them that existing consent decrees in employment discrimination cases required modification to comply with the Supreme Court decision in the Memphis firefighters' case Firefighters Local Union No. 1784 v. Stotts.

Not only was the Meese interpretation of the Stotts decision faulty since the Supreme Count only addressed the issue of seniority in layoffs and not whether race consciousness is permissible in hiring and promotions, but it produced cries of outrage from a number of the localities which had been successful with their affirmative action plans and wanted to retain them.

Mayor Richard Hudnut of Indianapolis said it best when he commented that the Department's "decision to turn back the clock on affirmative action and equality of opportunity is wrong constitutionally, it's wrong morally, and it's wrong politically."

Undaunted, Meese next took aim at Executive Order 11246 in an effort to modify it into impotence. In existence for more than 20 years under Democratic and Republican Administrations alike, the order obligates government contractors to refrain from employment discrimination on the basis of race, color, religion, sex or national origin, and to take "affirmative action" to assure that employees are treated without regard to these factors.

Meese would do away with the goals and timetables required by the order, thereby guaranteeing that the order would be turned into a worthless piece of paper. On pragmatic grounds, Meese does not have a leg to stand on. Affirmative action, which is the litmus test of civil rights, works and works very well. That is the problem--it works too well.

It works for states and cities that complied with court orders to hire minorities and women for jobs in city services, in police stations, in fire houses. It works for companies that hired blacks to have respectable numbers to show, and then concluded that affirmative action is just good business. In a recent survey of 142 chief executive officers, 122 or 85.9%, said they intended to use numerical programs to track equal opportunity programs in their corporations regardless of government requirements.

Testifying before the House Subcommittee on Civil and Constitutional Rights and Employment Opportunities, William E. McEwen of theNational Association of Manufacturers said that "affirmative action has been, and is, an effective way of ensuring equal opportunity for all people in the workplace."

He further stated, "business...sets goals and timetables for every aspect of its operations...setting goals and timetables for minority and female participation is a way of measuring progress and focusing on potential discrimination."

Meese cloaked his attacks on civil rights and affirmative action under the cover of seeking "a color-blind society," but the reality is that race conscious remedies are still needed to correct the evils of a race-conscious past. Meese's effort to apply the axe to Executive Order 11246, however, met strong opposition within the Cabinet, particularly from Secretary of Labor William Brock and Secretary of HUD Samuel Pierce, and at year's end the President had not made up his mind what action, if any, to take.

In the application of the Voting Rights Act, the Justice Department has also had a deplorable record. Since the Reagan Administration took office in 1981, the number of electoral changes submitted by various localities to the Justice Department for preclearance before their implementation has risen dramatically. From 1965-1980, the Department received 33,798 requests for election changes. Between 1981-1985 36,968 requests were received, representing 52.2% of all submissions since enactment of the Voting Rights Act. Despite the heavy increase in submissions since Reagan took office, the Department has objected to less than one percent (.63%) of the requests, as compared to 2.4% under other adminstrations.

The overall performance of the Administration in the area of civil rights has quite properly earned from the Leadership Conference on Civil Rights the judgment that it (the Administration) "has used busing and quotas as a smokescreen to mask the worst civil rights record of any administration in more than half a century."

On the Congressional front, there were voices raised on both sides of the aisle against attempts to choke off federal affirmative action orders and in support of the Civil Rights Restoration Act of 1985. This bill would have repaired the damage done by a Supreme Court ruling in Grove City v. Bell that gave institutional recipients of federal aid a huge loophole allowing them to escape from compliance with federal anti-discrimination laws. Despite bi-partisan support, the bill did not make it through the legislative process leaving an unfinished piece of business that Congress should make a top priority in this session. Congress should also press to correct the massive federal failure to enforce other civil rights measures ranging from housing discrimination to voting rights.

1985 also saw an increase in the tempo of assaults on black leadership coming from the White House and some parts of the conservative establishment. The intent was obviously to discredit black leadership which has been highly critical of a number of the Administration's programs and policies by making it appear that this leadership did not represent the thinking of the majority of blacks.

Any familiar with the history of Black America would have predicted that these efforts would fall flat on their faces--just as they did. Blacks are accustomed to having their leaders brought under attack by outsiders who are made uncomfortable by what the leaders have to say. Such attacks, however, have a way of backfiring since blacks see through them very easily and are rarely deluded as to who has their best interests at heart.

When the frontal attack failed, a flanking movement was developed under the mask of scholarly research. A public opinion poll was undertaken that measured the views of 105 black leaders and 600 randomly selected blacks in a national survey. It concluded that there is a wide opinion gap between black leaders and their constituents with the former being far out in front of the latter.

These findings were published in "Public Opinion," the magazine of the conservative think tank, the American Enterprise Institute, and widely reported in the media. However, the poll was fatally flawed and these flaws have been exposed by a number of sources, especially by Eddie Williams of the Joint Center for Political Studies who pointed out its bias and faulty methodology. Just one example of its unreliability will be reported here.

The poll reported a divergence of views regarding black progress with more leaders than followers saying that blacks are moving backward. Five years ago the National Urban League conducted the largest study of the black experience in history. A national sample of 3,000 black heads of households were interviewed face-to-face, and not over the telephone as with this new survey. Four-fifths of middle income blacks (83%) felt that the push for racial equality was moving "too slow," compared to three-fourths (73%) of poor blacks. Similarly, 70% of middle income blacks felt that there was "a great deal" of racial discrimination against blacks in this country, compared to 61% of poor blacks.

More recently, polls taken by the Gallup Organization for the Joint Center for Political Studies, and by Data Black, a private research firm, confirm that the views of black leaders conform to those of their constituents. This makes sense, for if the leaders were too out of step with their constituents, they would not remain leaders for long. Writing in the New Republic, (Nov. 14, 1985) Jefferson Morley said:

"Those who attack black leaders for being 'out of touch' with the black community are often the first to complain when any black leader begins to attract a large following within the black community...It seems that the more black leaders prove how 'in touch' they are with the black community, either by winning votes or drawing large audiences, the more 'out of touch' they are said to be...The black rank and file continue to support the black leaders from whom they are supposedly alienated."

This, however, does not mean that Black America is monolithic in thought and everyone marches to the same beat and follows the same leaders. No, Black America is more complex than that. It encompasses a wide variety of views ranging from one end of the spectrum—whether it be economics, politics or race relations—to the other end.

Therefore, it is not surprising nor unwelcome that new voices are being heard from Black America, new voices that are raising questions about policies and approaches toward solving problems that afflict this community. Harvard political scientist Martin Kilson calls them "neoconservative black intellectuals," but we are of the opinion that such a designation is too constrictive since they comprise such a diverse group that they cannot be so neatly categorized.

So that there will be no question of where we stand, we make it clear now that we are in disagreement with a number of their basic tenents, particularly those that oppose affirmative action in employment and other areas, and government sponsored programs that serve the needy. We also differ with them on their proposals to lower the minimum wage for youth, their minimizing of the importance of race in our society, and on other issues.

These reservations notwithstanding, we believe that encouraging dialogue on opposing ideas is a healthy process out of which positive things can come. It is that belief that has led us to include in this edition of "The State of Black America" two differing views on social policy and the role of government in helping to balance the scales of racial equity.

In summing up what 1985 was like in Black America, there were certainly trouble spots, but there were bright spots as well. Certainly the support from the corporate community for affirmative action was most encouraging. Most of the nation's large companies are saying that affirmative action works, that it is in their interest to implement it, and they'll continue to do so.

The political picture was also brightened by the election of L. Douglas Wilder, a black as the Lt. Governor of Virginia. It wasn't all that long ago when that state headed the South's resistance to desegregation so that the election of Wilder signaled that things can change. And the enthusiasm generated by Jesse Jackson's run at the Presidency did not fade as more and more new faces entered the political arena for the first time.

The nationwide movement of opposition to South Africa's apartheid was another bright spot. A grass roots revulsion to apartheid has mushroomed to include all shades of political opinion and may yet force the Administration to become more supportive of the black drive to freedom in South Africa.

Another positive is the likelihood that whatever tax legislation passes in 1986 will substantially relieve the tax burden on the poor, whose taxes have risen sharply even as taxes for the affluent have gone down.

Still, the most significant development in Black America in 1985—and we mentioned this earlier—was the growing activism within the black community to deal with problems like teenage pregnancy, education, crime and the plight of female-headed households. The black community knows that its problems will not be changed without significant changes in public policies, but there is also a conviction that they won't be changed without community participation either.

Within the following pages, we present major papers on a variety of subjects from eight outstanding scholars. The specific subject areas were selected because of the important role they played in Black America during 1985. We asked the authors to provide the readers of "The State of Black America--1986" with their own objective and independent evaluations. Their views, therefore, do not necessarily reflect the official position or policies of the National Urban League. Our own summation and recommendations appear at the end of this report.

It is our hope that this publication will help increase an awareness of the reality of life within Black America and influence the decision-making process in 1986. We express our gratitude to the authors.

: : :

ECONOMIC STATUS OF BLACKS 1985

By

David Swinton

I. INTRODUCTION

During 1985 the U.S. economy continued to experience what many economic commentators regard as a satisfactory recovery. Yet, despite the continuation of this so called recovery for 36 months, the black population continues to be caught in the grips of its most severely depressed economic conditions of the post war period. To be sure, the conditions in the black community have improved marginally since the depths of the last recession in 1982 and 1983. However, the small rebound that has occurred in the economic position of blacks still leaves the group at the most depressed level experienced in the last 20 years (excepting the depths of the Reagan Recession).

Indeed, the satisfaction that many economic observers have expressed with respect to the recent performance of the U.S. economy is quite puzzling since unemployment levels, income growth, poverty rates and other such indicators are all at relatively sub-par levels by recent historical standards. Moreover, many observers do not expect even the current mild recovery to continue and many predict an upcoming setback. Indeed, the improvement in overall economic conditions during the past two years as measured by income, poverty, and unemployment was marginal at best. The economic performance of the past two or three years only looks good in comparison with the depths of the Reagan depression. Such a conclusion is particularly appropriate when one takes into account that even the current weak economic performance is being propped up by historically high budget deficits.

The statistics that will be cited in Section II of this paper will make it clear that for the black population the low income levels, and high poverty rates that are currently occurring can hardly constitute a satisfactory recovery. Poverty and unemployment rates for blacks are at their highest levels of the post 1964 period. Real income has been declining and is also at its lowest point in the past 15 years. Moreover, racial inequality is increasing in most of its dimensions. Many of the gains of the past two decades in reducing racial inequality have now been eroded. Compared to the overall level of economic well being attained in earlier periods of prosperity, the Reagan recovery has indeed been anemic at best.

The severe economic recession that continues to grip the black population is a reflection of increasing difficulties in the labor market. Section III of this report will explore this issue using data on employment and unemployment rates. Section III reaches two major conclusions. First, blacks wage rates continue to be low absolutely and relative to white wage rates and the gap has been widening. Second, blacks have been losing ground in gaining employment for the last decade. These two facts together have resulted in the observed increased economic difficulties in the black community.

-1-

There has been increased speculation lately concerning the causes of the persisting economic difficulties of blacks. Blame has been placed on everything from the lack of preparedness for a high tech society, to the failure of social programs and welfare policy over the last few years. In section IV, however, we will link the increasing economic difficulties of blacks to the general failure of the economy to perform well for American workers in general over the last decade. This poor performance of the American economy has persisted through the last five years. In general American workers are worse off to day than they were 15 to 20 years ago.

In the concluding section of the paper we will argue that the prospects for sustained improvement in the economic conditions of blacks depends primarily on improving the overall performance of the economy. The argument will suggest that this will depend primarily on adopting more effective public policies than have been pursued over the last few years.

II. THE ECONOMIC HEALTH OF THE BLACK COMMUNITY*

A. Total Income

In 1984 the aggregate income of the black population was about $172 billion. Given the black population of about 27.9 million this resulted in an income per person of $6152. In constant purchasing power terms the per capita income of blacks was about 3.3% larger than it was at the beginning of the Reagan Administration in 1980. However, the per capita income was still slightly less than it had been before the onset of the recession in 1980. Thus, despite two years of recovery, blacks had not attained the same level of income that had been attained prior to the recession of 1980. Measured from the recession year of 1980, per person income over the first four Reagan years for blacks grew by only 3.3% or less than .825% per year. Measured from the high activity year of 1970 to the recession year of 1980 per person income in the post-Reagan era averaged better than 2.5% annual growth.

Moreover, racial inequality as measured by the ratio of black to white per capita income increased between 1980 and 1984 as white per capita income grew at a faster rate than black per capita income during the recovery and declined at a lower rate during the recession. The racial inequality between blacks and whites by this measure in 1984 was greater than it had been in any year since 1970. To get a clearer picture of the implications of the sluggish economic performance for blacks, we will examine the economic status of black families more closely.

---

*Statistics cited in this report are all drawn from data obtained from the U.S. Census Bureau or the Bureau of Labor Statistics. The references at the end of the paper contain a list of publications from which most of this information has been obtained. All dollar comparisons are made in constant purchasing power terms.

B. Black Family Income

As suggested in the introduction, the economic recession in the black community has continued. In 1984, the last year for which income information is available, black family income continued to stagnate and racial inequality worsened. Poverty rates also remained at very high levels both absolutely and in comparison to whites. Although the data is not yet available, it is likely that there will be little improvement in these indicators for 1985 in light of the persisting employment difficulties experienced by blacks during 1985.

Median family income in 1984 was $15,432 for blacks. While this figure was up $800 from the levels it had reached at the depths of the recession in 1982, it was up only another $250 from the 1983 level. Moreover, median family income in constant dollars was $540 lower than it had been at the beginning of the Reagan Administration in the recession year of 1980. Compared to the real puchasing power available to the black community in 1978, the peak year for black family income, the purchasing power attained after two years of the Reagan recovery was almost $2000 less. Indeed black family income in 1984 in constant dollars was almost $1500 less than it had been 15 years earlier in 1970.

Racial inequality in this measure of black economic status also has been at record high levels during the Reagan Administration. Indeed the ratio of black to white family income declined slightly in 1984 in comparison to the 1983 level. The measured impacts of the recovery have been larger for the white population. It is likely that this trend will continue into 1985.

The net impact of this racial inequality is revealed by the fact that although blacks were 12.4% of the families in 1984, they received only 7.6% of family income. In 1984, the median black family had about 56 cents to spend for every one dollar white families had to spend. This was two cents less per dollar than blacks had in 1980 and almost six cents less than blacks had in 1970 in comparison to whites.

Despite the alleged recovery, black income measured in constant dollars lagged behind its level of 1980 in all regions of the country except the South. The economic status of blacks as measured by family income were lowest in the Mid-West region at $14,367. This continues a trend which first emerged in 1982 when the Mid-West replaced the South as the region in which blacks were worse off. This development is particularly distressing since the Mid-West has historically been a region in which blacks have fared relatively well. Black family income was highest in the West ($19,209), followed by the East ($16,326) and then the South ($14,863).

Racial inequality was also highest in the Mid-West as measured by the ratio of black to white median family income (.518). The Mid-Western region has fallen below the South in terms of racial inequality. Moreover, the East also had more inequality than the South by this measure continuing the long-term trend of increasing racial inequality in that region. In both the Mid-West and the East there has been a significant increase in racial inequality since 1980. Racial inequality by this measure increased by 17% in the Mid-West and 13% in the East between 1980 and 1984. Racial inequality by this measure has also increased in the West by about 12%. However, the West is still the most equal region for black families with a black to white income ratio of .673 in 1984. The degree of inequaltity in the South in 1984 with a ratio of .57 is practically unchanged since 1980 when the ratio was .56.

Black family income also varies with the number of earners in the family. In general, black family income has stagnated across all families irrespective of the number of earners in the family except for families with three earners whose incomes increased by about 12%. The median income actually was lower in 1984 than in 1980 for families with no earners, one earner, and four or more earners.

In general the degree of decline in family income decreases as the number of earners increase. Families with no earners had median incomes of only $5277 in 1984 which represents about an 8.4% decrease in constant dollar income since 1980. The constant dollar income for families with one earner decreased by about 11%. The earnings of those families with two earners and four or more earners were about equal to their 1980 earnings.

Racial inequality increased in every category except the three earner category which registered a moderate decline in inequality between 1980 and 1984. Inequality increased most for those families with the least number of earners. Since these families already had the most unequal conditions this trend further increased the disparities. Families with no earners and families with one earner saw the ratio of their income to white income decline from .485 to .404 and from .575 to .535 respectively. The decline for families with two earners was only from .811 to .785 and for families with four or more earners the decline was from .767 to .743.

The disadvantages which blacks derive from their less favorable relative earnings within each number of earners category is increased by the fact that blacks have fewer earners overall. Blacks had larger proportions in the no earner and the one earner category and fewer families in the multiple earners category. Moreover, the proportion of black families with no earners increased between 1980 and 1984 and the proportion in every other earners category decreased except for the three earner category. The net result of the changes in number of earners per family in the black and white communities was to increase the relative disadvantages of black families.

Black families of each type of family status have experienced income stagnation. Married couple black families had median incomes that were barely higher overall in 1984 than in 1980. However, the income of married couple families with no wife working actually declined between 1980 and 1984 by about $900 while the median income of those with a wife working increased by about $500. The incomes of single male headed families also inched up slightly in comparison to 1980 while the incomes of female headed families fell by about 6%.

Overall, between 1980 and 1984, the proportion of married couple among all black families declined from .545 to .520. However, within the married group more wives worked in 1984 than in 1980--64.1% v. 59.1%. The proportion of single male headed families increased slightly to 5.2% from 4.7%, while the proportion of single female headed families increased from 42.3 to 44.4%.

Racial inequality in family income also persisted for each family type and in fact increased for each type between 1980 and 1984. The ratio of black to white median income was highest for married couples whose wives worked (81.1%) and lowest among female headed households (58.5%). Black married couples without a working wife had about 62 cents for each dollar available to white married couples without working wives while black single male households commanded about 67 cents income for each dollar available to white single male household.

The differences between black and white family structures also intensified during the past few years. In 1984 there was almost 33 percentage points fewer black married couple families than white--52% of black families were married couples versus 84.9% of white. The absolute gap between the proportion of black and white married couple families increased from 31.5 percentage points in 1980 to 32.9 percentage points in 1984. Blacks had almost three and one half times as large a percentage of female headed families in 1984 than did whites (44.4% v. 12.9%) and about one and a half times as large a proportion of male headed families-- 5.2% v. 3.4%. Thus the relatively disadvantageous family status distribution of black families has intensified in the last few years.

The income depression in the black community has been most severe for those with the lowest incomes. Compared to the situation in 1980, the poorest 20% of black families had 22% less purchasing power in 1984 than in 1980. The second poorest quintile had 15% less income while the third poorest quintile had 4% less income. The income of the top 20% was practically unchanged while the income of the top 5% increased by about 9%. Thus, within group inequality intensified during the past four years as it has been doing since at least the early 1970s. The black community is increasingly becoming a community of two classes--those who have and those who have-not. The have-nots are by far the largest group and their size has been rapidly increasing. Moreover, the have-nots are actually becoming poorer while the haves are experiencing modest income gains.

In constant purchasing power dollars, 34% of the black population had incomes below $10,000 in 1984. This percentage had increased from 28.8% in 1978 and 28.4% in 1970. On the other hand the proportion of black families who had incomes greater than $25,000 had fallen from 33.7% in 1978 to 29.4% in 1984. The proportion with incomes greater than $25,000 was actually slightly lower in 1984 than it had been in 1970 when it was 29.6%. However, the proportion of blacks with incomes over $35,000 and $50,000 actually increased in comparison to both 1978 and 1970. Thus, while income stagnated or declined for 85% of the black population, income increased for the top 15%.

Racial inequality persisted throughout the income distribution in 1984. Both the black poor and the black wealthy have lower incomes than whites at similar positions in income distribution. However, racial inequality is greatest among the lower income groups. Blacks at the top of the lowest quintile for example had about 44 cents for every dollar that whites in the lowest quintile had. Blacks at the bottom of the top 5% commanded 70 cents for every dollar that whites in the top 5% commanded. In between these extremes, at the top of the second lowest quintile blacks had 51 cents per dollar, at the top of the third quintile they had 58 cents per dollar, and at the top of the fourth quintile they had 67 cents per dollar in comparison to whites at similar positions in the income distribution. Thus, the black poor are considerably poorer than the white poor and the white rich are considerably richer than the black rich.

Moreover, larger proportions of blacks have low incomes than whites. In 1984, while 34% of black families had incomes less than $10,000 only about 12% of white families had such low incomes. At the other end of the scale, 29% of blacks had income over $25,000 and 56% of white families had such high incomes. Sixteen percent of black families had income over $35,000 compared to 36% of white families.

Racial inequality was greater in 1984 than in 1980 at all positions of the family income distribution. However, the sharpest increases in racial inequality were registered among the poorest segments of the population. Income has declined by less than about one percent since 1980 in each of the two lowest income white quintiles in contrast to 11 and 4% declines registered in the two lowest income brackets for black families. The ratio of the black to white quintile limit fell from .49 to .44 for the lowest quintile and from .54 to .51 for the second lowest quintile. The increase in inequality by this measure at the top of the fourth quintile was only about 3 percentage points as the black to white income ratio declined from .70 to .67 percent. The decline for the top 5% was very slight from .71 to .70 percent. Inequality clearly increased most for the lowest income blacks.

C. Trends in Black Poverty

The trends in income discussed above have resulted in a worsening in black poverty over the past few years. In 1984 about 34 out of every 100 black persons was in poverty according to Census Bureau statistics. Black poverty in 1984, although down a couple of percentage points from the highs of the preceding two years, was higher than it had been in any of the ten years preceding the Reagan Administration. Thus the recovery has not made much of a dent in black poverty rates. Black poverty rates have also gone up to their highest points of the last 15 years under Reagan when measured by the proportion of families in poverty and the proportion of individuals living in families who are in poverty. It seems unlikely that official poverty by any of these measures will decline to the levels which existed prior to the recession of 1980 during 1985.

Black poverty rates were high in every region of the country in 1984. Moreover, except for the South, black poverty has gone up relative to its 1980 level in all regions of the country. The highest poverty rates for blacks were registered in the Mid-West were 38 out of every 100 blacks were in poverty in 1984. Poverty for blacks in the Mid-West has increased more than in any other region since 1970. In the last few years the deteriorating situation of blacks in that region has been so marked that for the first time since such statistics have been kept, a non-southern region has higher black poverty rates than the South. The percentage of blacks in poverty in the Mid-West has almost doubled since 1970. In the last five years another 4.5 percentage points have been added to black poverty rates in the Mid-West.

Poverty for blacks has also increased in the Northeast and the West. The increase in the Northeast has been almost as dramatic as it has been in the Mid-West although black poverty in the Northeast, at about 32 out of every 100 persons, is still slightly less than it is in the South. Black poverty is lowest in the West where about 27 persons per hundred were below poverty in 1984. To understand the dramatic reversal of black fortunes in the Northeast and West note that these regions had a combined poverty rate of 19 per hundred population in 1970 and the current rate is about 33 per hundred population. In fact black poverty in the Northeast and West is greater than it was in 1959.

Black poverty in the South is the second highest of the four census regions. In this region about 34 out of every 100 black persons are poor. However, the recovery has reduced black poverty in the South to its lowest point ever in 1984. Thus with respect to poverty in the South the recovery appears to have had a positive benefit on blacks although as noted the overall poverty level in the South is still very high. The South is in fact the only region in which there has been improvement in the poverty rates of blacks relative to the 1970 level. Moreover, the 1984 rate is significantly less than the 1970 rate and the one year measured drop in black poverty in the South between 1983 and 1984 was very high by historical norms. The drop in the poverty rate is particularly surprising in light of the fact that the improvement in black income in the South overall was not nearly so pronounced. Thus, if this trend should prove to be more than a statistical fluke and should be maintained in the future, this would represent one of the few bright spots for the black economic situation.

Racial differences in poverty rates are still dramatic overall and in each region of the country. Nationally, while about 34 black per hundred are below the poverty level about 12 whites out of every hundred are below poverty. Thus blacks are almost three times as likely to be in poverty as whites. Racial inequality in poverty levels are greatest in the Mid-West and Northeast. In both of these regions blacks are over three time as likely to be poor than are whites. Moreover, in both of these regions the degree of racial inequality in poverty is dramatically worse than it was in 1970.

Compared to the 1980 situation, however, the degree of racial inequality has not intensified. In fact as measured by the ratio of black to white poverty rates there was slight improvement in both the Northeast and the Mid-West. However, there was no significant change in the absolute gap between the black and white poverty rates. This suggests that although blacks in the Northeast and Mid-West were effected more overall by the poor economic performance of the last few years, poor whites were hit about as hard as poor blacks by these events.

Racial inequality in poverty rates was lowest in the West in both absolute and relative terms in 1984. The ratio of black to white poverty rates was about 2.25 to 1 in the West in 1984. The absolute gap between the proportion of blacks in poverty and the proportion of whites in poverty was about 15 percentage points v. over 21 percentage points in each of the other three regions. Just like in the Northeast and the Mid-West, the degree of racial inequality increased between 1970 and 1984 by both the absolute and the relative measure. However, unlike the case in the other two non-Southern regions the events of the last four years had a greater impact on black poverty than they did on white poverty rates. As a consequence the intensity of racial inequality in the West has also increased significantly since 1980.

Racial inequality in poverty rates was lower in the South than it was in the Mid-West by both the absolute and the relative measure in 1984. In comparison to the Northeast, racial inequality in poverty rates was slightly less as measured by the relative measure and barely more as measured by the absolute gap.

The South is the only region in which the relative degree of racial inequality improved in both absolute and relative terms in comparison to 1970. The degree of racial inequality in poverty rates was significantly higher in the South in 1970 than in any other region. However, black poverty rates in the South were nine percentage points lower in 1984 while white poverty rates were only .2 of a percentage point lower. Moreover, as was the case in the Northeast and the Mid-West, racial inequality in poverty rates declined in the South between 1980 and 1984. While the recession had a relatively even impact on black and white poverty in the South, the recovery clearly had a more beneficial impact on the black poor in the South than on the white poor. While this progress is welcome, one should temper one's enthusiasm in view of the fact that black poverty rates in the South are still very high at 34% and still exceed white poverty rates by about 22 percentage points.

In 1984, the black poor on average were poorer than the white poor. The average income deficit for black poor families in 1984 was $4,547 which was about 15.5% larger than the average deficit of $3,934 for white families. Overall, it would have taken over 9.5 billion dollars to eliminate black poverty in 1984. Relative to 1980, the black poor had become about 8.8% poorer as the mean income deficit had gone up. Moreover, the disparity between the income deficit of poor black and white families had increased by about 1.3 percentage points since 1980. In constant dollar terms, the aggregate income required to eliminate black poverty increased by about 1.9 billion dollars or 25%. Poverty among blacks in 1984 was clearly more pronounced than it had been in 1980.

D. Characteristics of Poor Black Families

In general, the rate of poverty of black families varies by the age of the head, family size, number of children, education of head, and family type. However, black families in all categories have higher poverty rates both absolutely and relative to the poverty rates of white families. Moreover, poverty rates in most categories have increased since 1980 in absolute terms. In comparison to whites the absolute gaps have increased in most categories while the relative gaps have declined in most categories.

The rate of poverty among black families declines rather dramatically as the age of the family increases up to the 35 to 45 age group and only modestly after that point. Almost 61 out of 100 black families with heads under 25 were in poverty in 1984. For families headed by individuals over 25, about 29 families out of every hundred were in poverty. Still, over 39% of those with heads between 25 and 35 were in poverty. The poverty rates for all older groups were between 21 and 26%. Moreover poverty rates increased between 1980 and 1970 for all age groups except the 35 to 44 age group and the 65 and over age group. The absolute increases were largest for the youngest age categories. Poverty rates among the 25 and under group were 25% higher in 1984 than in 1980. They were 19% higher for those families with heads between 25 and 35. The poverty rates for all other groups increased by less than 10%.

White poverty rates were substantially lower for all age groups. The absolute differences in black and white poverty rates, however, were largest by far for the younger age groups. White families headed by persons under 25 had a poverty rate that was 37 percentage points lower than that of black families under age 25. White families whose heads were aged 25 to 35 had poverty rates that were 27 percentage points lower than similarly headed black families. In all other categories the gaps between black and white poverty rates ranged from 14 to 18 percentage points. For all families with heads over age 25 the absolute gap was 20 percentage points. White poverty rates at all age groups were about three to four times larger than black poverty rates.

Between 1980 and 1985 white poverty increased for all age categories under age 65. The absolute increases in poverty rates were greater for black families with heads under 35 and with heads between 45 and 60 years old. Poverty rates increased more in absolute terms for whites aged 35 to 44 and 60 or over. In relative terms the ratio of black to white poverty rates declined for every group except those aged 25 to 34 and over 65. So by the absolute measure, racial inequality increased for most age groups while by the ratio measure, racial inequality decreased for most age groups.

Black poverty rates were also high for all family sizes ranging from 26% for two person families to 55% for seven or more person families. Family size does not have a dramatic effect on black poverty rates except for those families with six or more members. Between 1980 and 1984 poverty rates went up for all black families except those with five members where there was a less than one percentage point decline. The observed increases in poverty rates were greatest for the two largest family size categories.

In comparison to whites, blacks poverty rates are much larger at all family sizes. The absolute differences in black poverty rates range from 18 to 28 percentage points and generally increase with family size. The ratio of black to white poverty rates ranges from 2 to 3.5 and generally declines with family size. Between 1980 and 1970 the absolute gap between black and white family poverty rates increased for all family sizes except the five person family. The ratio of black to white poverty rates declined for all except the two person family size.

Poverty rates also vary by numbers of children. In 1984 family poverty rates ranged from about 15% for black families with no children to about 75% for black families with five or more children. The poverty rates for families with one child (28.5%) were double those of families with no children. Families with two, three, four, and five or more children had poverty rates that were about two and one half, three, four, and five times respectively the poverty rates of black families with no children.

Between 1980 and 1984 black poverty rates increased for every family size category. The absolute increase were all under three percentage points for families with fewer than four children and were about 9 and 11 percentage points respectively for families with four and five or more children.

Black family poverty rates are about 34 percentage points higher than white family poverty rates for all numbers of children categories greater than two. For families with none, one, and two children, black families poverty rates are higher by 10, 18, 20 percentage points respectively. In ratio terms, black family poverty rates vary from 3.2 to 1.8 times white family poverty rates as the number of children varies from none to five or more. Between 1980 and 1984 the absolute gap between black and white family poverty rates increased for all families except families with five or more children. The ratio of black to white poverty rates increased for families with no children and families with five children and declined for all other categories.

Black poverty also varies by the educational attainment of the household head. However, for increases in education under high school graduate, black poverty rates increase with education. Thus, the poverty rates of blacks with less than elementary school education (36.4%) is slightly lower than the rate among those families with an eighth grade education (39%) which is lower than for those with one to three years of high school (41%). For families with the high school diploma the black poverty rate falls to about 26%. Blacks with some college had poverty rates of about 16% in 1984.

Between 1980 and 1984 black family poverty rates went up for every educational category. The increases were from less than one to about four percentage points. The highest increases were for those with high school diplomas and for those with some college. The lowest increase was for those with less than eight years of schooling.

In comparison to white families, blacks have higher poverty rates at all educational levels. In fact black families headed by individuals with some college have higher poverty rates than whites with eight or more years of schooling. The absolute difference between the poverty rates of black and white families is about 14 percentage points for those whose heads have fewer than eight years of schooling. The difference is about 25 to 26 percentage points for those families whose heads have eight or more years but less than a high school diploma. Families who have high school diplomas have poverty rates that are 18 percentage points higher than white families headed by high school graduates. Finally, blacks with some college have a poverty rate that is 11 percentage points higher.

Education clearly has a more powerful impact on white poverty rates than on black poverty rates. The ratio of black to white poverty rates generally increases with the education of the black family head. In 1984, black families whose heads had some college were four times more likely to be poor than white families whose heads had gone to college. Black families headed by high school graduates were almost three and one half times more likely to be poor. On the other hand black elementary school dropouts were less than two times more likely to be poor than white elementary school dropouts.

White family poverty rates also went up for every educational category between 1980 and 1984. Racial inequality measured by the absolute differences in black and white poverty rates actually declined for families whose heads did not attend high school. In these categories the absolute increases in white poverty rates were higher than the increases in black poverty rates. For high school dropouts the absolute racial gaps remained the same, since the poverty rates of white high school dropouts increased by about the same amount as the poverty rates for black high school dropouts. For families headed by those with a high school education or better the absolute difference in black and white poverty rates increased. In relative terms, the black to white poverty rate ratio decreased for all educational categories except the college educated category in which it increased. Thus, in the last few years racial disparities in poverty incidence increased most for those families whose heads had the most education.

III. THE LABOR MARKET STATUS OF THE BLACK POPULATION

The single most important cause of the depressed income, high poverty rates and persisting racial inequality which we discussed in the foregoing section is a general worsening of the labor market position of blacks during the past ten years are so. During this period of time, black employment and constant purchasing power earnings have declined both absolutely and relative to whites. The labor market position of blacks has been helped less during recent recoveries and hurt more during recent recessions as compared to the experiences of blacks during the earlier post World War II period. The deteriorating trend has continued and perhaps even intensified during the last few years. The general worsening of the black labor market position has been more pronounced for black males but has also affected the relative position of black females.

When examining recent trends in the labor market position of blacks one must keep in mind that the labor market position of blacks was already less than satisfactory in 1980. For example, in 1980 black males were only able to contribute about 47 cents to the per person income of blacks for every one dollar white males contributed to the per person income of whites. Moreover, erosion in the black labor market position was already evident in 1980. Blacks like other Americans in 1980 were hoping and seeking relief from the trying times of the previous few years. Moreover, since the black situation was so much more desperate, blacks were in greater need for a reversal of the trends that had been evident since the early 1970s.

During the last four years, there has been a slight increase in the proportion of the black population of working age. This proportion, however, has declined a little for the white population. Thus, all other things being equal, blacks should have gained both absolutely and relative to whites in terms of the contribution which work makes to income. However, this has not been the case. In fact, between 1980 and 1984 both the absolute per capita earnings in constant dollars and the ratio of black to white per capita earnings actually went down. Overall, the contribution of earnings to per capita income dropped by about $40 and the ratio of black to white per capita earnings decreased by two-tenths of a percentage point.

The erosion in the contribution of work to per capita income has been caused entirely by an erosion in the contribution that males make to income. The constant dollar contribution of black males fell by about $138 between 1980 and 1984. This was partially offset by a $98 increase in the contribution of black females to per capita income.

Racial inequality increased slightly for both sexes. The income contributed by black males declined proportionately more than the income contributions of white males—6% vs. 3.9%. The ratio of black to white male contributions to per capita income fell by one percentage point from 47.3% to 46.3%. Although the black female contribution to income has grown during the past few years, it has grown at a slightly slower rate than the white female contribution—6.3% vs. 7.7%. Thus, inequality between females also inched up slightly one percentage point as the ratio of black to white female contributions to per capita income decreased from 8.6 to 87.4%.

To place these numbers in perspective, rough calculations suggest that the lower earnings of black males cost the black population about $63 billion or $2288 per person in 1984. The labor market difficulties of black males are thus the major reason why blacks have such an unequal economic position. This factor accounts for over 84% of the black-white labor market earnings gap and over 51% of the overall black income gap. Moreover, this rough calculation does not even take into account the fact that black males have a smaller proportion of their population of working age. Racial inequality for black females cost the black population much less. In 1984 black female labor market inequality cost the black population only $62 million or about 1000 times less than black male inequality cost the black population.

Although the erosion of the position of blacks in the labor market may appear to be small, it is none the less costly. The erosion of the position of black males between 1980 and 1984 cost the black community $4.7 billion in 1984 dollars. This was partially offset by a gain of $3.4 billion registered for black females. However, the net lost was still $1.3 billion. Moreover, the increase in inequality for black males since 1980 cost blacks $1.6 billion while the increase in inequality for black females cost blacks about $800 million.

The persisting economic problems of blacks can be traced specifically to a decline in real wage rates for blacks who are employed and to a decline in the relative proportion of blacks who are working. The median weekly earnings for full-time black workers in 1984 dollars fell from $284 in 1979 to $267 in the first three quarters of 1985. Black male earnings have declined most falling from $321 in 1979 to $294 in 1985. Black female earnings were $244 in 1985 which was up slightly from $236 in 1979. Wage stagnation has been a consistent characteristic of the past five years. Both black male and female usual weekly earnings declined during the recent recession and rebounded since. However, black male earnings rates peaked in 1983 and have declined since. The 1985 level is in fact below the 1982 low point. Black females did not lose the gains made in the first year of the recovery but the rate of wage growth has slowed down to near zero in the last two years.

The wages of blacks which were already lower than white wages at the onset of the last recession were affected more than the wages of whites by the last recession. Overall, while the constant dollar usual earnings of full-time black workers was $17 lower in 1985 than in 1979, the wages of full-time white workers were only $10 lower. Full-time black male workers lost $27 compared with a lost of $24 for full-time white male workers. Black female wages were $8 higher in 1985 than in 1979 as compared to a white female gain of $15. Thus, inequality as measured by the ratio of black to white wage rates has increased since the onset of the last recession by about 2.6 percentage points overall, 2.3 percentage points for black males and 2.1 percentage points for black females.

The wage stagnation has had an important impact on the economic position of blacks. However, another significant factor has been the absolute and relative decline in black employment rates. The last recession had a devastating impact on black employment and while the recovery has resulted in some improvement all of the lost ground had not been regained through the third quarter of 1985.

Black participation rates have held up reasonably well despite the increased employment difficulties of the last recession. Taken as a whole, black participation rates did not decline very much during the recession and since the start of the recovery have moved to the highest levels of the past 15 years. The participation of black males over 20 has fallen slightly since the onset of the recession. This has been offset in the overall average by a significant increase in the participation of black females. Even the participation rates of black teenagers have rebounded from their recession lows. In comparison to the early seventies, however, black male adult participation rates are still depressed averaging 75% in the third quarter of 1985 vs. 78.5% in 1972. Black teenage participation rates are slightly higher in 1985 than in 1972 (40.3 vs. 39.1%). Black female participation rates are up sharply from 51.2% in 1972 to 58.6% in the third quarter of 1985.

Black participation in the labor market started the 1970s equal to the participation rates of whites, and overall participation increased for the last 15 years as increases in black female participation more than offset the small declines in black male participation. However, in comparison to whites, black participation has declined from the early 1970 period. Although, during the past five years the relative black to white participation rate has improved slightly.

Since the early 1970s, the black male adult participation rate has ranged from 95 to 98% of the white male adult participation rate. The participation gap has been more marked for black teenagers with their labor market participation ranging from 63 to 72% of white teenage participation. However, relative to whites, both black male adult and black teenage participation rates have improved from what they were at the onset of the recent recession. Black female participation rates have always been higher than white female rates. At the start of the seventies 20 to 30% more black females participated in the labor force. However, the black female advantage narrowed steadily from the early 1970s to the depths of the last recession. Black female participation rates have grown slightly faster than white female participation rates since the last recession. During 1985 about 7% more black female adults participated in the labor market.

Black unemployment reached record levels for the post WW II period during the recent recession. Thus, this latest recession continues the trend of each recession having a more devastating effect on the black population. Moreover, black unemployment rates were already high at the onset of the recession at 12.3% in 1979. The recession pushed the average black unemployment to 19.5% in 1983 even though the recovery phase had already begun. Since 1975, the annual average black unemployment rate has been 15.2%. There has been no year during this period in which black unemployment was less than 12%. Since 1981 the black unemployment rates have averaged 17% and there hasn't been a single year in the last five when black unemployment was less than 15%. Even for the first three quarters of 1985, the third year of the recovery, black unemployment averaged 15.1%.

The devastating unemployment experience of the last 11 years has effected all black demographic groups, adult males, adult females, and teenagers. Black men over 20 have averaged 12.9% unemployment since 1975 and 15.4% unemployment during the last five years. In the first three quarters of 1985 their unemployment rate was 13.1%. The unemployment rates of black females over 20 have also been high. They also have averaged 12.9% since 1975. For the past five years their unemployment rate has averaged 14.4% and during 1985 they have averaged 13.3% unemployment. Black teenagers have had unemployment rates that have averaged 41.3% since 1975, 44.1% for the last five years and 40.1% during 1985. Thus even after three years of a recovery, black unemployment remains at record high levels for the post war period excepting the depths of the recent recession.

The unemployment rates of the last five years was particularly severe for black male and female adults age 20 to 24 and 25 to 35. Unemployment rates for the 20 to 24 year old group were pushed to over the 30% level for both sexes, while 25 to 35 year old black males had unemployment rates that reached 20% and the rate for females 25 to 35 exceeded 18%. Even in 1984 after two years of recovery, 20 to 24 year-olds had over 26% unemployment.

The devastating unemployment experiences of blacks have not been as severe for whites. As a result the racial gap which was already high at the beginning of the seventies has since increased. The unemployment rate for whites averaged only 6.7% over the last 11 years versus the 15.2% rate for blacks. In the last five years when black unemployment averaged 17%, white unemployment averaged 7.3%. The increase in disparities affected all demographic groups. Over the last five years, adult black male unemployment rates averaged 8.9 percentage points more than whites, black women averaged 8.1 percentage points more unemployment, and black teenage unemployment rates were 26.4 percentage points higher than white teenage unemployment rates. Moreover, the devastating impact of the last recession on blacks under 35 were not nearly so severe for whites under 35. White males and females 20 to 24 had unemployment rates about 17 percentage points lower than blacks of this age group during 1984. Blacks of both sexes aged 25 to 35 had unemployment rates that were 11 percentage points higher than the rates for whites.

The effect of the increasing racial inequality in unemployment rates is revealed by the fact that the ratio of black adult to white unemployment rates which was around 2 to 1 for males and less than 2 to 1 for females during the first half of the 1970s has increased significantly. For adult males, the ratio of the average unemployment rates for the last five years was 2.37 and for adult females the ratio was 2.29. The increase in this measure of inequality has been especially pronounced for black men and women under 35. In 1984 for example the ratios for both black males and females aged 20 to 24 were over 2.7, whereas these ratios had been under 2 to 1 during the early 70s.

The net result of the participation and unemployment experiences are reflected in employment proportions. The overall share of the working age black population employed was already lower than the white proportion at the beginning of the 1970s. In 1972 for example 53.7% of the black population of working age was employed versus 57.4% of the working age white population. The 3.7 percentage point difference which existed in 1972 became a 7.6 percentage point difference by 1985 when the employment population ratios were 53.3% for blacks and 60.9% for whites.

The decline in black employment rates between the early 1970s and the present time was caused by a 8.5 percentage point decline in the employment rates of adult black males and a moderate 4.3 percentage point increase in the employment rates for black females. The racial gap has widened because the white male employment rate fell less (5.7 percentage points) and the adult white female rate increased more (10.2 percentage points).

All black groups had their employment rates affected more seriously by the last recession than did white groups. The employment of black males over 20 dropped 7.5 percentage points versus 4.7 for whites. Adult black female employment rate declined by 1.9 percentage points versus a 1.6 percentage point increase for white females. In absolute terms white teenagers who had over twice as large an employment proportion in 1979 dropped from 52.6 to 45.9% employed in 1983 while the black teenage employment proportion fell from 25.4% to 18.7%.

The employment ratios have improved for all black groups since 1983.

However, adult black males still have significantly lower employment rates in 1985 than they did at the start of the recession--64.6 versus 69.5%. Black teenage employment proportions have recovered most of the ground lost during the recent recession and adult black females are currently employed at slightly higher rates than they were in 1979. Most of the recent gains were made in 1984. Black employment during 1985 has been stagnate and at the end of the period employment may even be deteriorating.

IV. RECENT ECONOMIC PERFORMANCE AND BLACK ECONOMIC STATUS

There has been much recent speculation about the causes of the persisting economic difficulties of the black population. Much of the recent popular discussion has allocated blame to deficiencies within that population in education, motivation, attitudes and values. The speculation suggests that these problems have been intensified by the social welfare policies of the past two decades which have promoted family breakups and an attitude of dependency.

In our view these conclusions are seriously defective. The economic difficulties of blacks have been caused primarily by the general economic problems of the economy at large, the persistence of labor market discrimination, and the impact of the disadvantages inherited from the past. The observed increase in social pathological outcomes are primarily symptoms rather than basic causes of the persisting economic difficulties of blacks.

A number of aspects of the performance of the economy over the last 15 years have increased the economic difficulties of blacks. First, the share of the population seeking jobs has increased dramatically during this period. Since 1972 the proportion of the population participating in the civilian labor force has increased by four percentage points from 60.4 to 64.4%. Thus, in addition to having to provide jobs to take care of a growing population, the economy also had to provide jobs to take care of the increasing number of people desiring to work. The increased labor force participation necessitated the addition of about seven million more jobs than would have been required if the participation rate had remained constant.

This rapid expansion in the labor force was caused entirely by increasing participation among women. The biggest part of the increase is attributable to the huge increases among white women as their participation rate increased from 43.2% in 1972 to 53.3 percentage points in 1984. Thus over 7.9 million additional jobs were required just to absorb the additional participation of white women. Black female participation rates also increased over this period from 48.7% to 55.2%. Thus, an additional 530 thousand jobs would have been required to absorb the increased black female labor force participation.

If male participation rates had remained constant the economy would have had to generate an additional 28 million jobs between 1972 and 1984 just to maintain unemployment at the relatively high 5.6 percent rate which existed in 1972 and absorb all of the additional female workers. In fact the economy only generated an additional 23 million jobs. The difference was made up by higher unemployment rates and decreased labor force participation among men of working age.

The implications of these facts are obvious. There has been a major job shortage over the last few years. This has had the impact of increasing the difficulties that blacks have finding jobs. The impacts have been particularly severe for black males. We might note that the overall job creation of the economy has not been that low over the period taken as a whole. However, in view of the changing labor force participation of females an extraordinary performance would have been required to prevent a job shortage and this was not forthcoming.

During the past few years overall labor force participation rate growth has slowed down considerably although there was a little rebound in upward labor force growth in the last year. Despite these favorable circumstances, however, job growth since 1979 has not been high enough to lower the unemployment rate or permit a rebound in black male participation rates or black teenage participation rates. In fact, average annual job growth since 1979 has been about half the rate of the 1970 to 1979 period.

In addition to the relatively low job growth another feature of recent economic performance has resulted in disadvantages for the black population. Job growth has shifted away from the high paying goods producing industries to the lower paying service, finance and trade sectors. Between 1981 and 1985, for example, total private employment increased by about 8.1%. However, employment in the goods producing sector declined by 2%. In fact employment in the goods producing sectors is about 1.4 million jobs less in 1985 than it was in 1979. The manufacturing sector by itself has more than 1.6 million fewer jobs in 1985 than in 1979. In fact, manufacturing employment in 1985 was barely even with its 1970 level. All of the job growth in manufacturing which occurred during the 1970s has been lost in the first half of the eighties.

In contrast, between 1970 and 1979 over 16 million private sector jobs were added in the non-goods producing sector. Moreover, between 1981 and 1985 more than 6.8 million private sector jobs were added in the non-goods producing sectors. Most of these job were added to the service and the retail trade sector whose combined increase was almost 5.5 million jobs. Thus, the structure of employment has been changing dramatically from the goods producing to the service providing sectors.

To illustrate the dramatic nature of the shift in the job structure we note that in 1970 maunfacturing accounted for 33% of all private jobs. By 1985 the manufacturing share had dropped to 23.8% of private sector jobs. In contrast the retail trade and service sectors combined accounted for about 38.7% of all jobs in 1970. However, by 1985 their share of private sector jobs had increased to 48.2%.

There are several characteristics of this structural shift that are relevant to understanding the economic problems of blacks. First, the sectors that have been growing most rapidly have traditionally employed more women than men. For example, in 1984 only 32.2% of those employed in manufacturing were women and fewer than 20% of those employed in any of the other goods producing sectors were women. In contrast, the share of women employed in the retail trade sector was 52.2%, in finance insurance and real estate 57.7%, and in services 60.7%. Given the growth patterns, these developments put great pressure on male employment in general and exceptional pressure on black male employment.

The other fact about the job growth of the last few years that is important for understanding the economic problems of blacks is the fact that the sectors in which most of the job growth is occurring are also the lowest wage sectors. For example, in 1984 the usual weekly earnings of full-time workers was $373 in manufacturing compared to $176 for retail trade and $249 for services. Thus the average employed worker, especially the new workers, are finding relatively fewer high wage jobs available and relatively more low wage jobs available. Even the relatively fast growing finance sector pays relatively low wages.

A third factor that is relevant to understanding the economic difficulties of the black population is the recent slowdown in real wage growth for non-supervisory workers. In addition to the fact that employment has been shifting to lower wage sectors, real wage growth in most sectors has actually been negative since the early 1970s. This pattern reverses the trend of the 1960s when positive real wage growth was recorded in most sectors.

From 1964 to 1972 there was positive real wage growth in every major sector. Overall real wages increased in the private sector by 11.2%. Each major sector recorded positive constant dollar wage growth of from 5.2 to 24.2%. In general the fastest real wage growth occurred in the goods producing sectors. Although there was higher than average real wage growth in the service sector and the transportation and utilities sector as well. Slowest wage growth during this period took place in the finance and trade sectors.

In contrast to the positive wage growth observed from 1964 to 1972, overall constant dollar wages declined by 13% between 1972 and 1980. Constant dollar wages fell in every major sector except mining between 1972 and 1980. The declines ranged from 5.5% to 19%. The steepest declines took place in the retail trade sector. In the private sector overall, the trade sector, the finance sector, and the service sector, the very sectors where most of the job growth was occurring, constant dollar wages were lower in 1980 than in 1964.

Between 1980 and 1984 wage stagnation continued. Overall constant dollar wages grew by about four-tenths of one percent. However, there was modest growth in constant dollar real wages in every sector except construction and retail trade. Positive growth ranged from .6% in transportation and public utilities to 6.7% in the finance sector. In 1984, the overall average private sector wage was still below the 1964 level as were wages in the retail trade and the finance sectors. Real wages in all sectors except mining were below the levels obtained in the late 1960s. Once again the slowest wage growth was recorded by the fast growing retail trade sector. This sector which had the lowest wages in 1964 has been falling further and further behind.

We should also note that the minimum wage has also been falling since 1964 both in comparison to the falling average wage and in constant dollar terms. Moreover, the decline in the minimum wage has accelerated during the last four years. For example, the minimum wage averaged about 52% of the average private sector wage from 1964 to 1970. However, during the past five years the minimum wage has averaged only about 43% of the average private sector wage. In 1985, the minimum wage was only 38.5% of average private sector wage. In constant dollars, the minimum wage is worth less than it has been at any time in the last 20 years. Moreover, during the four years between the ends of 1980 and 1984, the minimum wage lost 25 cents in 1977 dollars.

This slow up in real wage growth and the decline in the share of jobs which pay decent wages has undoubtedly contributed to the growth in female employment. In today's labor market it has become increasingly difficult for young men to find jobs that will enable them to support a family. Thus more wives and teenage children have to work to make ends meet. Even with the great expansion in female participation income has declined in real terms for the typical family. The difficulties of black males supporting families are obviously much greater than it is for white males in light of their greater unemployment and generally lower wages.

V. CONCLUSIONS

In the analysis of the preceding sections we have presented evidence in some detail which shows that the black community is currently experiencing very serious economic problems. As we have seen, income is low both in real terms and in comparison to whites. The degree of poverty and low income recipiency is too high and has been increasing. Moreover, an unacceptable level of racial inequality is persisting and in many respects is increasing. Moreover, it was also made clear that the current so called economic recovery is not resolving the economic problems of blacks at a satisfactory pace.

We also suggested that much of the persisting economic difficulties of blacks is traceable to poor labor market outcomes. We examined the employment and earnings experiences of blacks in some detail. We found unacceptably high unemployment rates, low employment rates, and unacceptably low earnings. The analysis suggested that a large part of black economic difficulties are attributable to the labor market problems of black males.

In the last section we suggested that the labor market difficulties of blacks were due primarily to the fact that the overall economy has performed poorly during the past decade. This poor performance resulted in inadequate overall job growth and poor wage growth. As a result the economy has experienced a shortage of jobs in general and a shortage of good jobs in particular. It has thus become difficult for the average worker to keep from falling further and further behind. In the struggle to keep up, the degree of competition in the labor market has intensified. Of necessity some workers had to experience increased labor market problems. Racial discrimination and historical disadvantages in the possession of credentials in conjunction with the increasing competition for the shrinking supply of good jobs has caused the increasing black labor market difficulties.

It seems to us that an overall improvement in the economic state of Black America will require an improvement in the overall performance of the economy. In particular jobs must be created at a higher rate than they have in the past few years. Equally as important the decline in high wage jobs must be arrested and a larger share of high wage jobs must be created. The erosion of the real wages of workers also needs to be reversed and real wages need to be increased. More jobs in sectors that employ men must be created. Without changes such as these it is unlikely that there will be any short term improvement in the economic position of blacks. In addition to the direct contributions of such policies, they would also improve prospects for pursuing meaningful equal opportunity policies and dealing with the residual historical disadvantages of blacks.

However, current economic policies with their heavy reliance on laissez faire and free trade are unlikely to lead to anything but further economic difficulties. This is especially likely to occur if the artificial prop of the highest budget deficits in history is removed. The present malaise of the American economy in our view can not be solved by laissez faire policies. At least not in a fashion that would result in significant economic improvement for most blacks.

The continuation of current laissez faire policies will likely produce more of the same results that we have experienced for the last decade. We will continue to have a gradual erosion of the economic position of the working class, an increasingly large population of poor and near poor families, and increasing racial inequality in economic status. This is because left to themselves, economic incentives will continue to give signals that will lead to the decline of high wage sectors and the expansion of low wage sectors. They will also direct investment away from high value creating activities to financial and low value activities. They will also lead to a continued erosion of America's status in the international economic arena.

Black economic gains will require a dramatic reversal of current policies. Basic industries must be protected and expanded. Wage growth must be encouraged so that the typical worker can once again afford to raise a family in decent style without sending every household member into the labor market. Investment must be increased in goods producing sectors. All these results will require a more carefully managed economic system than we currently have.

In view of the disproportionately heavy impacts that poor policies have on the black community, black leaders must take the lead role in advocating a more effective national economic policy. In addition to a set of more rational and effective national policies, black leaders are justified in seeking policies to promote equal opportunities and to eliminate the historical disadvantages of blacks in wealth and human capital ownership. While we did not directly address this issue in this paper the persisting gaps in ownership of businesses and other productive assets is at the root of the black dependency that permits whites to concentrate the burdens of economic problems on blacks.

BIBLIOGRAPHY

Swinton, David H. "The Economic Status of the Black Population," in The Status of Black America 1983. Washington, D.C.: National Urban League, 1983.

Symposiun on Minority Youth Employment and Urban Disadvantaged Youth, sponsored by Institute for Economic Development and Shaw College at Detroit, 1980.

U.S. Department of Commerce, Bureau of the Census. Characteristics of the Population Below the Poverty Level, Current Population Reports (Series P-60), Washington, D.C.: U.S. Government Printing Office, various issues.

U.S. Department of Commerce, Bureau of the Census. Detailed Population Characteristics, United States Summary, Section A: United States. Washington, D.C.: U.S. Government Printing Office, 1984.

U.S. Department of Commerce, Bureau of the Census. Money Income and Poverty Status of Families and Persons in the United States, Current Population Reports, Advance Data, Current Population Survey, (Series P-60), Washington, D.C.: U.S. Government Printing Office, various issues.

U.S. Department of Commerce, Bureau of the Census. Statistical Abstract of the United States. Washington, D.C.: U.S. Government Printing Office, 1984 and 1985.

U.S. Department of Labor, Bureau of Labor Statistics. Employment Earnings, January, May, and October 1985.

U.S. Department of Labor, Bureau of Labor Statistics. Handbook of Labor Statistics. (Bulletin 2217) Washington, D.C.: U.S. Government Printing Office, 1985.

U.S. Department of Labor, Bureau of Labor Statistics. Geographic Profiles of Employment and Unemployment 1983 Washington, D.C.: U.S. Government Printing Office, 1984.

U.S. Department of Labor, Bureau of Labor Statistics. Statistics Derived From the Current Population Survey: A Databook, volume 1 (Bulletin 2096) Washington, D.C.: U.S. Government Printing Office, 1982.

U.S. Department of Labor, Bureau of Labor Statistics. Statistics Derived From the Current Population Survey: A Databook, volume 11 (Bulletin 2096-1) Washington, D.C.: U.S. Government Printing Office, 1984.

EQUITY AND EXCELLENCE: AN EDUCATIONAL IMPERATIVE

By

Charles D. Moody Sr.

"It is the business of the school to help the
child to acquire such an attitude toward the inequali-
ties of life, whether in accomplishment or in reward,
that he may adjust himself to its conditions with the
least possible friction."

Frank Freeman,
"Sorting the Students,"
Education Review, 1924

I. INTRODUCTION

The late Ronald Edmonds stated in 1979 that "we know all we need to
know to educate all children whose education is of importance to us."[1]
Yet, consciously or unconsciously, the American public school system has
systematically educated students so that some would be equipped with appropriate skills and knowledge to assume higher status roles. Others would
assume lower status roles with fewer skills and limited knowledge. One
does not need to be an educator to know which role was assigned to black
students.

Ogbu in his book **Minority Education and Caste** suggests two possible
approaches to investigating the education of caste minorities. Ogbu
states, "One may begin with classroom observations of the behaviors,
motivations, and achievement of children. Such observations will reveal
differences not only among individual pupils but also between minority
and non-minority children. If an age cohort is observed longitudinally
from elementary school through high school and college into occupational
and social roles of the adult world, the study will undoubtedly show that
fewer minority pupils complete high school or go to college and that very
few achieve high social and occupational roles. If the investigation as-
sumes, as is often the case with such studies, that the major function of
the school is that of manpower allocation, i.e., that the school selects
and trains pupils for various roles in adult life, two hypotheses usually
follow concerning differences in adult roles; (a) that people (minority
and non-minority alike) occupy different social and occupational roles as
adults because of differences in educational attainment; and (b) that they
differ in educational attainment because they also differ in family backgrounds, individual abilities, genetic makeup, and the like. The sources
of minority educational problems are therefore likely to be seen as located in the individual and his or her family."[2]

The other approach one may take according to Ogbu is to begin by
studying the motives of minority education, i.e., the way in which formal
education is related to the social and occupational status of adult members of the minority group. The real motives for minority-group education
are not to be discovered in the rhetoric of school people, be they practitioners or philosophers of education or educational psychologists. Such

motives are better discovered by studying the positions of adult members of the minority group and comparing their positions with those of the majority group.

Such a study seeks to answer the following questions: (a) to what extent is the present allocation of roles (social, economic, etc.) among adult members of the minority group based on formal education? (b) is the relationship between formal education and role allocation in the minority group the same as it is in the majority groups? In other words, are the motives of formal education the same for the minority and majority groups?

Since formal education is viewed as preparation for the future, it is imperative that we know the goals of education for both minority and majority students. Such knowledge has implication for the total society since demographic projections show that by 1995 40 to 60% of the school population graduating into the work force will be black, Hispanic or other minorities.[3] Knowing the goals of education, we can better understand the behavior of parents and pupils, teachers, counselors, school administrators, and other school personnel, as well as the behavior of local school boards and other political groups that influence formal education.

This second approach of Ogbu's suggests additional and more pervasive sources of educational problems among caste minorities, namely, that they do not share the same motives for formal education with the majority and consequently the two groups are not necessarily participating in the same education system, even when they attend the same schools. This approach further suggests that the educational problems of caste minorities cannot be adequately understood except when analyzed in the context of a caste or racial stratification system which defines the status of the minority groups.[4]

Ogbu echoes Ann Stein. She discusses how education in the United States has a dual nature, aiming toward producing different kinds of people. The education for the majority group is designed to equip them with the skills, knowledge, values, attitudes, and attributes that will enable them to perform the high status roles which have been ascribed to them, while at the same time equipping the minority groups with those skills, knowledge, attitudes, attributes, and values needed to perform the low status roles which have been ascribed to them.[5] Schools not only educate youngsters--they sort them out according to levels of ability.[6] When the need for talent is great, the sifting tends to become rigorous.[7]

Many reasons have been given for the poorer performance of black students. Dr. Linda Darling-Hammond in the Equality and Excellence Report states, "Overall, the evidence suggests that black students are exposed to less challenging educational program offerings that are less likely to enhance the development of higher-order cognitive skills and abilities than are white students." In the same report, we are told that black students are disproportionately placed in vocational courses or in low-track classes in which they are not intellectually challenged, in which teachers often lack enthusiasm, in which expectations normally are low, and in which children get the message that they cannot succeed.[8]

Educational and cultural deprivations caused by racism and cultural bias of tests are generally offered as explanations for the achievement gap. While agreeing that those factors have not disappeared, Jeff Howard contends that the "difference in scores have little to do with ability and a lot to do with what may be the biggest barrier to black education: a subtle, often subconscious cycle of self-doubt and an avoidance of intellectual competition."9/

For example, according to figures from the U.S. Department of Education National Center for Education Statistics, only 22.9% of black high school graduates in 1982 took three years of science.10/ For Asian-Americans and white students the figures were 45.2% and 33.7% respectively. In math the figures were:

Asian-American students	68.1%
White students	49.5%
Black students	38.5%

This cycle, Howard says, can be directly traced to one of the major legacies of American racism--"the myth that blacks are genetically intellectually inferior."11/ While this myth has been discredited and refuted by scientists and scholars, "rumors of inferiority continue to have a strong, largely subliminal effect on black academic achievement."12/

To help break the cycle and increase students' self-esteem, several approaches have been initiated. In one, social psychologists Jeff and Anita Howard, and physicians Ray and Gloria Hammond have developed a program, "Efficacy Detroit," that sends black professionals into classrooms to try and change the way students view their intellects, their futures, and their schooling. Howard stresses that "INFERIOR PERFORMANCE AND INFERIOR ABILITY ARE NOT THE SAME THING." The program was developed while he and his wife were at Harvard and participants showed a "significant increase" in grades and involvement in school activities.13/ Detroit school officials say that it is too early to accurately assess the program but that early statistics point to modest increases in attendance and grades.14/

A program that addresses the achievement gap as well as self-esteem is the School Development Program instituted by Dr. James Comer, a professor at Yale University, in the New Haven Schools. This program addresses the overall school climate as a way to increase both academic achievement and social adjustment skills. The SDP includes four basic components: the school governance and management team, mental health team, parents program, and curriculum/staff development program.15/

Another approach is represented by a private school in Detroit where the norm is African. It was founded by Carmen N'Namdi who says that you "simply take a traditional education and turn it upside down."16/ At the school, housing 55 students, pupils study the usual subjects. Instead of the terms black and white, they use the terms Africans and Europeans. But the reference point is African. The goal, she states "is to have children who love, respect, and are comfortable with themselves." The students score above average on tests and most, after leaving her school, go on to the city's two public high schools for high achievers.17/

Dale Mann states that "American public schools are at a fragile historical moment. Unless their role with the children of the poor can be strengthened, their social and political contributions may be lost to a publicly funded, private school sytem that would accelerate the inequities of the present system."[18] Mann further states that there is a set of known features that provide useful, operational guidance to educators and policymakers. He sees, "the key dimension of more schools becoming more instructionally effective has to do with attitudes and beliefs about what is possible given the state of the art and science of teaching and learning for poor children."[19]

The following passage taken from the **Economics of Racism U.S.A.: Roots of Black Inequality** summarizes the economic/educational discrepancies between blacks and whites:

> A common apologetic argument is that all that black people need to overcome their disadvantage is more education. Firstly, this overlooks or minimizes the serious handicap imposed on blacks by their access to equal educational opportunities--beginning with the inferior, and often crudely racist teaching practices in largely segregated schools to which most black youth are limited, and ending with the financial stresses which make it more difficult for blacks than whites to obtain a higher education.
>
> Secondly, a high school diploma or a college degree, are less advantageous for a black than for a white. Economic discrimination, relative to education, is the same at all levels of education, and seemingly increases with the amount of education. Roughly speaking, a black man has to obtain three to four more years education than a white man to rate the same income. Or, put it another way, a black man with more than an elementary school education will have an income about 30% less than that of a white man with the same amount of education.[20]

The educational system has been and continues to be used as a means to legitimize economic inequality by providing an open, objective, and ostensibly meritocratic mechanism for assigning individuals to unequal economic positions. The educational system fosters and reinforces the belief that economic success depends essentially on the possession of technical and cognitive skills--skills which it is organized to provide in an efficient, equitable, and unbiased manner on the basis of meritocratic principle. Of course the use of the educational system to legitimize inequality is not without its own problems. Ideologies and structures which serve to hide and preserve one form of injustice often provide the basis of an assault on another. The ideology of equal educational opportunity and meritocracy is precisely such a contradictory mechanism.[21]

Whether or not one accepts the premise advanced by Ogbu and others, an analysis of what is happening in this country relative to the education of black students suggests that there are perhaps different goals and objectives for black and nonblack students.

For example, the Detroit Free Press reports that on the College Board's 1984 Scholastic Aptitude Test (SAT) the difference between the combined median test scores of blacks and whites was 217 points. Even at incomes over $50,000 there was a 149 point difference between black and white students.[22]

According to the Equality and Excellence Report on the Educational Status of Black Americans published by The College Board, blacks have lost ground relative to non-blacks at each stage of the educational pipeline. For example, in 1980 only 19% of the total 18 to 24 year-old black population were enrolled in college, as compared to 27% of their white counterparts. The difference is, essentially, the high school dropout rate. While the national drop-out rate for black students declined between 1971 and 1981 from 26 to 18%, the rate for 14 and 15 year-olds actually increased from 1.6 to 2.9%. The steepest increase in this age category was for black females.[23]

The report also states that the educational performance of black students in elementary and secondary school, as measured by standardized achievement test scores, rose in many areas over the decade of the 1970s, although it remained lower than that of other racial and ethnic groups. For example, black 9 year-olds increased their percentage of correct responses in reading by nearly ten points from 49.7% correct to 59.5% correct. White 9 year-olds students for the decade of the '70s increased from 66.4% correct to 69.3% correct. While the gain for black students is greater, the academic gap still exists. The same pattern can be found with other age groups and in math. But black 17 year-olds made little headway in moving out of the lowest achievement group. In reading, 62% still scored in he lowest quartile.[24]

This educational gap is also important when blacks seek further education. As Dorothy Gilliam reported in the Washington Post, Cornell University discovered that it would not have a single black student among the hundreds admitted to the graduate physical science program for Fall 1985. Black enrollment in the graduate programs at the University of Illinois dropped almost 40% between 1974 and 1985. Although blacks are 12.1% of the population, they earned only 4% of the doctoral degrees awarded in 1983. Even though money is a big reason that fewer blacks are entering college, Ms. Gilliam states that "students, educators, and parents must get on the case themselves--for themselves. Too many minority students arrive at college poorly prepared."[25]

II. EQUITY AND EXCELLENCE SURVEY

The next sections will focus not so much on the problems facing urban education as it will on possible solutions to problems that have been identified by a number of researchers and practitioners in urban education.

Part of the data will be from my 1984 Equity and Excellence study that examined the perceptions of superintendents who are responsible for educating more than 50% of all black students enrolled in public schools in the U.S.

After completing the study it was possible to get a more accurate view of where black students were concentrated and how the superintendents viewed the districts in terms of several relevant criteria.[26]

To begin with "equity" as defined by Ron Edmonds is a public agenda that will benefit the least advantaged members of society. Equity asks the same thing of schools serving children from poor families that any parent might ask.[27] "Excellence" can be defined as the achieving of high standards of performance.[28] A conception of excellence can be applied to every degree of ability and to every socially acceptable activity.[29]

Education may be conceptualized as four-dimensional. The four dimensions of an equity-based education model are:

1. Access - as it relates to schools, programs, and classes;

2. Process - as it relates to the fair, humane, and dignified treatment of students, parents, teachers, and administrators;

3. Achievement - as it relates to test scores, grades, graduation rates, dropout rates, awards, rewards, and recognition;

4. Transfer - as it relates to additional opportunities for post-secondary education, vocational and job training, and improved life chances in the form of jobs that will provide equal pay, power, privilege, and prestige.

A. Access

One can get a pretty accurate view of the access black students have to the educational resources by examining the concentration of black students in a relatively few of the 15,538 districts across the nation. The breakdown of black student enrollment by geographic regions in the Equity and Excellence Superintendent study was:

Northeast Region: Northeast Regional data revealed that at the time of the survey (1984), there were approximately 7,828,198 students including 1,061,310 black students enrolled in the 2,980 districts dispersed throughout the following states: Massachusetts, Rhode Island, New Hampshire, Vermont, Maine, New York, Pennsylvania, and New Jersey. Twenty-three (23) districts participated in the survey representing .77% of districts in the Northeast Region but accounting for 63% of all of its black students.

North Central Region: North Central Regional data findings suggested that at the time of the survey there were approximately 10,407,345 students enrolled of which 1,304,585 were black. There were 6,135 school districts in the states of North Dakota, South Dakota, Minnesota, Missouri, Kansas, Nebraska, Iowa, Wisconsin, Illinois, Indiana, Michigan, and Ohio. The 48 districts participating in the survey represented .78% of districts in the region, however, they enrolled 66% of the region's black public school students.

Western Region: The Western Region data disclosed that at the time of the survey there were approximately 7,670,423 students including 511,182 black students enrolled in 2,966 districts throughout the following states: Montana, Idaho, Wyoming, Colorado, New Mexico, Arizona, Utah, Nevada, Washington, Oregon, California, Alaska, and Hawaii. Twenty-eight (28) districts from the Western Region participated in the study. These twenty-eight districts constituted .94% of the region's 2,966 districts but enrolled 49% of its black student enrollment.

Southern Region: At the time of the survey there were approximately 13,926,516 students including 3,541,117 black students enrolled in the 3,457 districts throughout the following states in the Southern Region: Delaware, Maryland, Washington, D.C., Virginia, West Virginia, North Carolina, South Carolina, Georgia, Florida, Kentucky, Tennesse, Alabama, Mississippi, Louisiana, Oklahoma, and Texas. The fifty-three (53) participating districts made up 1.53% of the region's districts and enrolled 28.7% of its black students.

Further demonstration of the lack of access is the fact that the 202 superintendents drawn for the initial sample, 120 blacks and 82 whites, constituted only 1.3% of all superintendents in the 50 states, D.C., and the Virgin Islands. They, however, enrolled 67.3% of all black students enrolled in public schools.

The 50 largest school districts in the nation account for approximately 37.9% of all of the black students enrolled in public schools. If we examined the enrollment of the 100 largest school districts, we would have well over 50% of the nation's black public school students. These data should point out the critical nature of our need to have effective schools and excellence in education in our urban schools. For, if we were to reach a state of excellence in these schools, we would be reaching virtually all of our black public school students.

Profile of the 32 Largest Participating School Districts

	Minimum	Maximum	Mean
Total Enrollment	53,777	980,000	146,810
Number of Enrolled Black Students	2,429	352,800	63,967
Number of Administrators	200	1,241	516
Number of Teachers	2,663	58,000	8,104
Average Years Teaching Experience	6	17	12.8
Average Teacher's Salary	18,000	33,000	23,793
Minutes in School Day	330	450	384
Days in School Year	174	190	180.6

96% of the districts have a K-12 grade structure.
71% of the superintendents are over 46 years of age.
77.4% of the superintendents have doctorates.

B. Findings

Although there are numerous variables that might contribute to student preparation and outcomes, only a few illustrative perceptions of the urban superintendents participating in the study will be used.

Sixty-two percent of the superintendents responded that _most_ of their graduates that go to college are academically prepared for college level study. To the question "How many graduates are able to reason well, that is formulate problems and determine ways of logically resolving those problems?" 50% answered _some_ of their students, while 43.8% answered most of their students.

Ninety percent of the superintendents believe that some of their students have a basic understanding of computers.

As far as their graduates having the personal discipline necessary to establish long-term goals, set priorities, and achieve desired results, the responses were evenly split 50/50 between some and most of their students.

The superintendents participating in the survey did not view the educational dimensions as dismally as the authors of A Nation At Risk. For example, while 56% of the superintendents in the survey thought that most of today's graduates are as well educated as the average graduate of their parents' generation, A Nation At Risk reports that the average achievement of high school students on most standardized tests is now lower than 26 years ago when Sputnik was launched. There was also disagreement with lengthening the school year as recommended by A Nation At Risk.[30/] 83.9% of the superintendents thought that the school year was long enough.[31/]

Agreement with A Nation At Risk was evident in some areas, such as the need for providing more higher-order thinking skills in the curriculum and higher expectations for students.[32/]

Over one-half (53.1%) of the superintendents responded Somewhat to the statement that staff are held accountable for their efforts. For the most part, they received periodic feedback about individual effectiveness.

Only 30% of the superintendents responded Very to the statement that staff have high expectations for student achievement. It has been shown through years of research that teacher expectations have great influence on student achievement. It has also been shown that teacher expectations influence how they interact with students. Many school districts are conducting in-service sessions for teachers so they can improve the quality and quantity of interactions with students for whom they have low expectations.

Only 22.6% of the superintendents responded that principals provide sufficient instructional leadership.

Forty percent of the superintendents said there were very

sufficient opportunities for teachers to keep up-to-date and improve their knowledge and 21.9% said there was little opportunity afforded teachers. With the new research emerging on learning styles, cultural congruence in instruction, and instructional skills for effective teaching, all teachers, especially those in urban centers should have the opportunity to keep up-to-date and to increase their knowledge about teaching and learning if we are to close the achievement gap.

Twenty-nine percent of the superintendents responded that their curriculum stressed higher-order thinking skills. These skills are needed in the business and corporate communities.

Fifty percent of the superintendents responded that graduation requirements are appropriate and challenging.

C. Influence of the National Reports

The final questions concerned the impact that a number of widely circulated reports on the public schools such as A Nation at Risk, Making the Grade, Action for Excellence, and the NAACP Report on Quality Education Update have had on the districts. Only 18.8% of the superintendents indicated that these reports had had no influence on their districts. The 81.3% of the superintendents that said the reports had some or little influence on their districts said that the influence was in the form of legitimizing things that they were already trying to do, and making the community aware of educational issues.

Eighty-seven percent of the superintendents said that equity and excellence were compatible.

These findings indicate that urban school districts need to forge ahead with an agenda for the education of black students which advances the motive of maximizing the potential of these students. This motive should not only increase the academic achievement of black students but should enhance the life chances for them.

III. THE EFFECTIVE SCHOOLS MOVEMENT

It is heartwarming to note that in the decades of the seventies and eighties there has been a renewed effort to not only identify schools that were effective in educating urban poor and black students but to categorize and label the correlates that are found in schools that are effective.

Clearly, effective black schools are not a new phenomenon in American education. Faustine Childress Jones, in her book **A Traditional Model of Educational Excellence: Dunbar High School of Little Rock, Arkansas,** discusses the adult roles and status of graduates of this all black high school.[33/] A quote from Edgar Epps in Jones' book may provide a glimpse of why these schools were effective and viewed as exemplifying excellence:

> [These] big city black schools generally had vi-
> able programs, the most highly qualified and best paid
> teachers, better facilities, higher ratings than they
> are now accorded...Dunbar of Greater Little Rock and
> many others in cities of the North and South produced
> hundreds of leaders of contemporary black society.
> Teachers and students in the community were mutually
> and emotionally involved in the community development.
> Extra effort was expended to make all proud of the
> school. The school was inseparable from the community
> and they proceeded together.[34]

A means of implementing a new urban education agenda to achieve effective black schools could be the translation of Ronald Edmond's Effective
Schools Correlates to classroom practice. He found successful teachers
for the urban poor were more task-oriented, provided more evidence of
student monitoring, and consistently expected the children to learn. Those
professional personnel that were less effective attributed children's
reading problems to non-school factors and were pessimistic about their
ability to have an impact. They created an environment in which children
knew that they were not expected to succeed. The children, in these less
effective schools, responded by being, predictably, apathetic, disruptive,
or absent.[35]

Edmonds identified schools that were effectively teaching children.
In those schools these characteristics prevailed: (1) strong administrative leadership; (2) a climate of expectation where no children are per-
mitted to fall below minimum levels of achievement; (3) an orderly but not
rigid atmosphere conducive to instruction; (4) a philosophy which makes
it clear that pupil acquisition of basic academic skills is the first
order of business, taking precedence over all other school activities;
(5) the flexibility to allow school energy and resources to be diverted
from other business in furtherance of the fundamental objectives; (6)
some means by which pupil progress can be monitored frequently and
evaluated.[36]

In 1971 George Weber examined four inner-city elementary schools
which housed poor, minority children with high achievement. Common
characteristics evident in these four schools were: (1) strong leadership; (2) high teacher expectations; (3) good atmosphere; (4) strong
emphasis on reading, additional reading personnel, use of phonics, indivi-
dualization; (5) careful evaluation of pupil progress.[37]

Barbara Sizemore in the early 1980's studied three black elementary
schools in Pittsburgh to see what routines had been modified to make them
effective. Sizemore also found those correlates of effective schools
present. She also did an in-depth study of the characteristics of the
principals in those schools and found that they exerted strong leadership
although their styles of leadership differed greatly.[38]

Sizemore found that parents and others in the beginning did not identify these effective schools as being effective. We must recognize and
reward those effective urban black public schools.

In his book "Making Schools Work", Robert Benjamin examined a number of urban schools and found the schools that were effective had the effective school correlates present. The data are there that clearly indicate that urban, poor, and black schools can effectively educate its students. The issue is not whether they can, but do we want to?[39]

Rep. Augustus F. Hawkins felt so strongly about the research done by Edmond and others on effective schools that he introduced H.R. 4731, the Effective Schools Development in Education Act in 1984 as an opportunity for the federal government to encourage the adoption of effective schools programs throughout the nation. While he notes that there is insufficient specificity concerning the exact number of school districts with effective schools programs, he feels it is reasonable to assume that some 15-25 states have implemented effective schools programs.

These programs typically are aimed at improving teaching practices, student achievement, and student behavior. Leadership teams, including teachers and administrators share decision-making. They are trained in how to guide the process, collect data, and review district policies. The data are analyzed in light of the effective school correlates. (Leadership, climate, teaching, expectations, and pupil monitoring.)

A plan is developed in each of the five areas and implemented with careful monitoring of progress. Dr. Matthew Miles found that most of the schools in Effective Schools Projects that he studied said "that the experience had a clear impact on their defined goals, student achievement and improved student behavior (attendance, vandalism reduction, improved discipline)."[40]

As a result of recent educational research, urban public elementary schools are now, in the judgment of Gary Ratner, legally obligated for the first time to effectively educate substantially all of their students, regardless of the percentage who are poor or members of racial minorities.[41]

Ratner found that in some of our urban schools as many as 65 to 70% of the students in one or more of the grades from 2nd to 6th were one year or more below grade level in reading and/or math, while 40 to 45% were two years or more below. Yet, he found in these same systems effective schools that served 10 to 100 % minority children. In these schools he found no more than 10% of the students more than two or more years below grade level. He states "the widespread assumption that the failure of public schools is inevitable must be overcome." Later, in the same article, he states "Any school in which more than 20% of the students in any grade are one year or more below grade level and/or in which more than 10% are two years or more below grade level must rigorously assess whether it has fully adopted the five characteristics (Edmond's correlates) and must be opened for public observers to do likewise."[42]

Ratner goes on to state,

> Previously, no such liability could be imposed because it could not be shown that it was possible to effectively educate the vast majority of students in

such schools, let alone that effective schools serving such populations had any characteristics in common that ineffective schools could be required to adopt. But research has now shown that effective urban public schools <u>do</u> exist across the whole range of poor and minority-student concentrations, and that effective urban public schools do have important characteristics in common. Moreover, these characteristics are within the schools' power to create.[43/]

Given the demonstrated capacity of schools to succeed, public policy no longer provides any valid justification for their failure. The interests of society in their success are too great to allow schools to perpetuate demonstrably ineffective approaches while refusing to institute the characteristics of success. The new legal duty effectuates this societal interest: it requires that every urban public elementary school, regardless of its percentage of poor and/or minority children, must educate its students to the national standards already achieved by many schools, or, at the least, adopt the characteristics of success.[44/]

However, we must make sure that our definition of basics includes, in addition to the 3Rs, critical thinking skills, problem solving, test-wiseness, and computer literacy.

Washington states that urban principals and their staffs often allow themselves to get caught in a web of negative thinking.[45/] This tendency to become bogged down in a quagmire of negativism points up a major leadership dysfunction--the unwitting communication of attitudes and feelings that translates into "The standards are lower in this school," or "I don't expect much from you or the children," or "We are fighting a losing battle," or "Don't be creative; just maintain order."[46/] It should come as no surprise that the performance of teachers who work in such organizational climates, more often than not mirrors the expectation of their principals.[47/] The seriousness of this situation is underscored by the research of Keeler and Andrews (1963), which suggests that it is the leadership behavior of principals which has the most influence on school productivity (as measured by pupil performance).[48/]

One of the greatest challenges facing urban school systems, as identified by superintendents in the Equity and Excellence Survey, is the selection, training, and retaining of competent staff committed to equity and excellence. Principals in urban school systems must be able to recognize and reward good instruction, see where it is lacking, and know what to do to bring it about.

Hollins urges that the cultural heritage and experience of black students become part of the everyday curriculum.[49/]

The new direction in initial reading instruction for black pupils is encompassed in the theory of cultural congruence in instruction, just as it has existed for the majority of Anglo pupils since the beginning of formal education in this country. Until recently,

attention was focused on analyzing black pupils' life
condition rather than analyzing classroom instruction
and its relationship to cultural values and practices.
Current research trends indicate that the inclusion of
black cultural values and practices hold great potential for reading instruction, as well as the improvement of black pupils' academic performance in general.

Recent research has led to the analysis of classroom instruction and
interactions. These analyses have led to a body of knowledge that clas-
sifies and labels instructional strategies, techniques, and theories.
Urban school systems should spend a greater portion of their resources,
energies, and efforts on staff development in the areas of effective instruction.[50] In addition, researchers have been investigating the impact of areas such as learning styles and hemisphericity. Urban schools
must continue the shift from an analysis of black pupils' life conditions
to analysis of the schooling process as it relates to black pupils. Researchers have begun to focus on the cultural bias in the schooling process and have discovered new factors that contribute to the disproportionately poor academic performance among black pupils. Hollins (1982)
pointed out that cultural bias can be found in many theories of learning
that could have yet undetermined implications.[51]

A cultural-linguistic approach that requires that educators recognize
and accept the ethnic heritage of their pupils and build the instructional
program around that cultural base has been developed by the faculty and
program staff at Northeastern Illinois University's Center for Inner-City
Studies. Directed by Dr. Judith A. Starks it is used in four Chicago
Public Schools and serves approximately 1,200 pupils per year. The program
addresses the unique language needs of its students through its highly
sophisticated language development curriculum, which builds on the language students have mastered. Yearly evaluations have demonstrated that
pupils score significantly higher on standardized tests than comparable
non-Follow Through pupils.[52]

Urban school systems must continue to develop effective preschool
programs. Enrollment in high-quality preschool daycare programs and added
academic help in the first three years of school significantly improve the
chances of disadvantaged children to achieve school success.[53] A study
by Frank Porter Graham shows that "We are now able to show that quality
preschool education has a significant impact on intelligence of high-risk
children, and that the impact is positive."[54] The next phase of his
study is to determine to what degree the gain continues. Graham will study
this group of students after they have completed the 6th grade. The High-
scope Study in Ypsilanti, Michigan's Perry School also demonstrated that
preschool has a positive impact on black students.

Urban schools must utilize and institutionalize those strategies,
programs, and plans that have been successful and modify, reform, and/or
discard those that are ineffective and unsuccessful.

Dr. Charles R. Thomas, superintendent of the North Chicago, Illinois
School District No. 64 and President of the National Alliance of Black

School Educators, has proposed a three-pronged strategic plan for black educators to assist in the improvement of the education for black students. His plan includes:

1. The establishment of an Institute for Research on Teaching and Learning;
2. The development and operation of a laboratory/demonstration school to pilot successful teaching and learning programs and strategies for black students; and
3. The establishment of a Development Foundation to fund and support the above two activities.

IV. CONCLUSIONS

As we move from an industrial society to an information society, blacks must demand and work for a new education with new motives. The following recommendations are made to help achieve that goal.

1. Urban schools must develop effective preschool programs based on successful models. Government and the private sector must ensure that poor and black students are not being locked out of the preschool experiences because of high cost;

2. Urban schools must teach, in addition to the 3Rs, higher-order thinking skills, problem solving, test-wiseness, and computer literacy to all of their students;

3. Urban schools, corporations, state agencies, and community groups must ensure that black students are a part of both the formal and informal training opportunities. It is also imperative that these students are able to transfer their new skills and knowledge to jobs that allow growth opportunities and equitable pay;

4. Urban schools must develop school-business partnerships. A significant part of the curriculum in these relationships should be apprenticeships, internships, mentorships, sponsorships, and networking. Schools should endeavor to help black students understand that the process of mentoring and sponsorship are legitimate and integral parts of the American way;

5. Urban schools, corporations, state agencies, and community groups must ensure that black students learn the fundamentals of entrepreneurship. These agencies must also ensure that adequate capital is made available to black entrepreneurs so they can transfer these new skills into a business;

6. Since the majority of black students are concentrated in less than 3% of the school districts in the nation,

-36-

it would be to our advantage to see that the necessary funds and other resources needed to ensure effective schools and excellence for black students be made available to those districts while the debate and litigation over desegregation is taking place;

7. Urban schools must develop sound and effective school/ community relations programs that ensure active and meaningful parent involvement. Schools that are effective have parental support for the instructional and educational goals of the school;

8. Urban schools must use technology to improve the quality of instruction and expand the number of students they reach; and

9. Both the private and public sector must have the expectation that black students not only can achieve academically, but can be contributing assets in the new information society.

The following recommendations to parents are offered as possible ways to correct some of the present inequities:

Access
1. Don't let anyone make you or your children feel that they are doing you a favor by letting you be a part of the schools. Education is a right.

2. Be active, vote on school issues, get group clout, learn about resource allocations, demand your fair share for your school and its programs.

3. Be sure to insist on your children getting the opportunity to participate in all classes and programs available in the district.

4. Don't let anyone make you feel badly by telling you that it wasn't like this before you came.

5. Remember that the historic Brown suit was brought about to insure access to the resources and their allocations, not just body mixing.

Process
1. Demand respect from school personnel for yourself, your children, and your school.

2. Make sure that discipline is administered fairly and equitably.

3. Read the policies and procedures of the district.

Achievement

1. Make sure that you, your children, and school personnel have high expectations for educational outcomes.

2. Make sure that tests and test results are not being used to stigmatize students.

3. Make sure that activities in the schools, home, and community are taking place that will help your child become test-wise.

4. Make sure that good instruction is going on in the school.

5. Make sure that your child goes to school ready and committted to learn.

6. Make sure that everyone understands that you will not accept the attitude that one or two or three years below grade level in academic achievement is acceptable.

7. Insist that all students graduate with academic competencies and that they get their due awards and recognition not just in athletics but in the academics and the arts.

8. Make sure that your district provides good staff development programs that will improve instructional skills of school personnel.

Transfer

1. Make sure that there is no bias taking place in career counseling.

2. Make sure that all students are afforded a fair chance at job opportunities and post-secondary educational opportunities.

3. Be sure to serve as a mentor, sponsor and/or advocate for some student.

4. Develop a program to provide training and skill development in networking and sponsorship to enhance career mobility.

All four of these dimensions are important, interrelated, and cyclic in nature. We must make sure that each dimension is strong as we help our children navigate this complex system called education to move on to improved life chances in the world of work.

The above recommendations are aimed toward parents but are applicable for use by non-parents, organizations, and agencies.[55]

Dr. J. Jerome Harris, superintendent of Community School District No. 13 in Brooklyn, New York, always challenges us with this statement, "If we don't make a difference in the educational achievement of black students in those districts where we are in charge as superintendents, principals, teachers, parents, and school board members, then people will be saying that it doesn't make a difference who is in charge."

We must make a difference this time around, for there may not be a third reconstruction.

: : :

FOOTNOTES

1. Edmonds, Ronald. "Effective Schools for the Urban Poor." _Educational Leadership_ 37 (October, 1979) pp. 15-24.

2. Ogbu, John U. Caste and Education and How They Function in the United States. Chapter I. _Minority Education and Caste: The American System in Cross-Cultural Perspective_. Academic Press. New York, 1978.

3. "Excellence in our Schools, Insights Into Tomorrow. A Television Production." The National Consortium for Graduate Degrees for Minorities in Engineering, Inc. and N.A.K. Production Associates. Notre Dame, Indiana 1985.

4. Ogbu, _op.cit._

5. Stein, Ann. "Strategies for Failure," _Harvard Education Review_ 41 (May 1971), pp. 158-204.

6. Gardner, John W. _Excellence: Can We Be Equal and Excellent Too?_ W.W. Norton and Company. New York 1984.

7. Ibid.

8. _Equality and Excellence: The Education Status of Black Americans._ The College Board. New York 1985.

9. "Race and How It Affects Our Everyday Life." _Detroit Free Press._ December 8, 1985, Section H, pp. 8 H and 14 H.

10. Ruffin, David. "Walking An Economic Tightrope," _Black Enterprise_, January 1986. Vol. 16, No. 6, p. 54.

11. _Detroit Free Press_, _op.cit._

12. Ibid.

13. Ibid.

14. Ibid.

15. _Resource Guide for Effective Education_, Current Direction, P.O. Box 8297, Ann Arbor, MI. To be published 1986.

16. _Detroit Free Press_, _op.cit._

17. Ibid.

18. Mann, Dale, "The National Council for Effective Schools." _Social Policy._ Fall 1984, Vol. 15, No. 2, p. 50.

19. Ibid.

20. Perlo, Victor. Economics of Racism U.S.A: Roots of Inequality. International Publishers, New York 1975.

21. Bowles, Samuel, and Gintis, Herbert. Schooling in Capitalist America. Chapter 4, Education, Inequality and the Meritocracy Basic Books, Inc. New York. 1977. p. 102.

22. Detroit Free Press, op.cit.

23. College Board, op.cit.

24. Ibid.

25. "A Minority Brain Drain," The Washington Post, December 9, 1985. p. B-3.

26. Moody, Charles D. "Equity and Excellence: A Superintendent Survey." PEO, The University of Michigan. Ann Arbor, 1984. Unpublished.

27. Mann, op.cit.

28. Gardner, op.cit.

29. Ibid.

30. The National Commission on Excellence in Education: A Nation at Risk. Washington, D.C. 1983.

31. Moody, op.cit.

32. Moody, and A Nation at Risk, op.cit.

33. Jones, Faustine C. A Traditional Model of Education Excellence: Dunbar High School of Little Rock, Arkansas. Published for ISEP by Howard University Press, Washington, D.C. 1981.

34. Ibid.

35. Edmonds, op.cit.

36. Ibid.

37. Ibid.

38. Sizemore, Barbara A., Carlos Brosard, and Berney Harrigan. An Abashing Anomaly: The High Achieving Predominantly Black Elementary School, A Final Report to the National Institute of Education Under Grant Application No. 9-0172. University of Pittsburgh.

39. Benjamin, Robert. Making Schools Work: A Reporter's Journey Through Some of America's Most Remarkable Classrooms. New York, Continuum Publications, 1981.

40. Hawkins, Augustus F. "The Effective Schools Development Act of 1984." Social Policy 15 (Fall 1984) p. 52-53.

41. Ratner, Gary. "A New Legal Duty for Urban Schools: Effective Education in Basic Skills," Education Week 5, October 30, 1985, p. 24.

42. Ibid.

43. Ibid.

44. Ibid.

45. Washington, Kenneth R. "The Urban Principal as a Positive Pygmalion: The Key to Enhancing Teacher Effectiveness," Urban Education, Vol. 15, No. 2, July 1980, pp. 183-188.

46. Ibid.

47. Ibid.

48. Ibid.

49. Hollins, Etta Ruth. "New Directions in Initial Reading Instruction for Black Pupils," Current Directions, Vol. 1, No. 3, Fall 1985.

50. Moody, Christella D. Handbook for Instructional Skills, Current Directions, Ann Arbor, Michigan. 1985.

51. Hollins, op.cit.

52. Current Directions, op.cit.

53. Bridgman, Anne. "A 14-Year Study of Pre-Schooler Finds Long-Term Gains for Disadvantaged," Education Week, October 23, 1985.

54. Ibid.

55. Moody, Charles D. "Equity and Excellence in Education for Blacks in Michigan: Where Are We?" in The State of Black Michigan 1985. Editor, Francis S. Thomas. Published by Urban Affairs Program, Michigan State University and The Council of Urban League Executives. East Lansing, Michigan, 1985.

THE BLACK MIDDLE CLASS:
PAST, PRESENT AND FUTURE

By

Robert B. Hill

I. INTRODUCTION

Over the past decade and a half, there has been continuing controversy about the nature and size of the black middle class.

According to Wattenberg and Scammon, over half (52%) of all black families were middle class by 1972.[1] Similarly, Freeman concluded that the "extraordinary" progress of blacks between 1948-72 reflected "a virtual collapse of traditional discriminatory patterns in the labor market."[2] And, Wilson contends that these gains have widened the gap between the black middle class and "underclass" to such an extent that class is a more important determinant of black life chances today than race.[3]

On the other hand, scholars such as Murray characterize recent gains of many middle class blacks as "illusive."[4] While Pinkney argues not only that the black middle class has not grown significantly during the 1970's, but has experienced some decline.[5]

What is, in fact, the current size and status of the black middle class? How has its ranks changed and grown over time? Have the living standards of middle class blacks converged markedly with those of middle class whites? Has the economic gap between the black middle class and poor widened? To what extent does the black middle class identify with the problems of the black masses?

We will attempt to address these issues and distill their implications for the future role and prospects of the black middle class.

II. HISTORICAL ORIGINS

As Frazier noted, the early precursors of contemporary middle class blacks can be found primarily among small elite subgroups of free blacks during the 18th and 19th centuries.[6] While many of these free blacks had been indentured servants, most were ex-slaves. Many of them had purchased their freedom, while many others had been manumitted because they were the offspring of slave women and plantation owners. Consequently, free blacks had an overrepresentation of mulattoes. In 1850, two of every five (37%) free blacks were mulattoes, compared to only one out of every twelve slaves.[7]

Between 1790 and 1860, the number of free blacks soared from 60,000 to 500,000, raising their proportion in the total black population from 8% to 11%. Most free blacks were concentrated in areas of the South and North where the plantation system was not a major factor in the economy.

Thus, the more prosperous free blacks in the South were situated along the port cities of Charleston, S.C., Mobile, Alabama, and New Orleans, Louisiana; the Tidewater region of Virginia and Maryland and the Piedmont region of North Carolina. In the North, they were concentrated in Boston, Philadelphia, Baltimore, Chicago, Cincinnati, New York and Washington, DC.[8]

Another important source of the early black elite were artisan slaves. Most accounts of the plantation system traditionally stratify slaves into two groups: house servants and field hands. It is then usually suggested that the bulk of the subsequent black middle class came from the house servants. But as many scholars, such as Billingsley have noted, artisans--a third group of slaves--were a more important source of the black elite than were house servants:

> In his still definitive study, The Philadelphia Negro, DuBois found that early in the history of the colony of Pennsylvania, "the custom of hiring out slaves, especially mechanics and skilled workmen" led to the early development of a skilled occupational class which laid the groundwork for the rise of the black middle class in colonial Philadelphia...Thus, DuBois tells us, "before and after the Revolution, there were mechanics as well as servants among the Negroes." In 1820, mechanics, coachmen, shopkeepers and barbers made up the small but growing basis for black leadership in the city. By 1848, men in these occupations represented about five percent of all black families in the city.[9]

The early black gentry comprised large landholders, businessmen, professionals and artisans. For example, 85% of the free black men in New Orleans in 1860 were proprietors, professionals or artisans. And many of the early black entrepreneurs (such as Fraunces Tavern in New York City and black caterers in Philadelphia) had predominantly wealthy white clientele. Moreover, some of the large black property owners also had slaves.[10] Yet, as DuBois observed, because of rampant racism, the economic condition of the early black middle class was precarious:

> Even more than the rest of their race, they feel the difficulty of getting on in the world by reason of their small opportunities for remunerative and respectable work. On the other hand their position as the richest of their race--though their riches are insignificant compared with their white neighbors--makes unusual social demands upon them.[11]

The economic status of the black elite was severely eroded after Emancipation, especially in the South. In order to eliminate the newly-freed four million slaves as major sources of competition for white workers, the Black Codes were instituted throughout the South. These Codes, which deprived free blacks of most of their civil liberties (such as owning property, the right to vote, the right to enter skilled occupations, etc.), severely undermined the existing black gentry. Thus, the number of black artisans declined sharply after the end of Reconstruction. By 1890, the skilled black worker had been eliminated as a competitor of the southern whites.[12]

On the other hand, the Jim Crow laws facilitated a growth in black business by restricting their clientele largely to the black community. Although free blacks in the North had always been subjected to discriminatory legislation, their black elite was not as severely affected as that in the South after emancipation, since there was no large-scale migration of blacks to the North until about 1915.[13]

The black middle class experienced its first major growth as a result of World War I. Because of the widespread labor shortage in vital industries--due to curtailment of European immigaration during that conflict--employers provided numerous inducements (such as paying their travel expenses) to rural blacks to come North for better employment opportunities.[14] This Great Northern Migration was also induced by a push--the mechanization of agriculture in the South which reduced sharply the number of farming occupations.

Thus, for the first time, black men and women were able to obtain unskilled and semi-skilled employment in public and private jobs that had been closed to them--prior to the World War. Except for setbacks due to the 1921 Depression, the 1920's was a prosperous decade for many blacks. Thus, black communities in the North experienced a "Negro Renaissance" by the "New Negro" in arts and letters and the expansion of an influential black press.[15]

The Great Depression of 1929-1933 sharply eroded the economic status of middle class blacks who had just obtained a foothold in American industry. Interestingly "lower class" blacks in agriculture and domestic jobs were not as severely affected by the Depression as were those in higher-level industrial occupations.

World War II facilitated a resurgence in the black middle class. Weaver observed that during that war blacks "secured more jobs at better wages and in a more diversified occupational and industrial pattern than ever before."[16] In addition to the wartime labor shortages, these occupational gains resulted from intensive pressures for equal employment opportunity from: (a) civil rights groups and the threatened March on Washington in 1941; (b) the establishment of a Federal Fair Employment Practice Committee (FEPC) by President Roosevelt that year; and (c) the labor unions, particularly the Congress of Industrial Organizations (CIO), which was founded in 1935.[17] Consequently, between 1940 and 1960, the proportion of blacks in professional, managerial and craft jobs doubled from 7% to 14%.

III. DEFINING THE MIDDLE CLASS

Who comprises the black middle class? How large is it? A major problem of most analyses of class in the black community is the failure to clearly specify the criteria for inclusion in the various class strata--

and to apply those criteria consistently! Terms such as "bourgeoisie" and "underclass" are used repeatedly without providing any operational definitions.[18] Some observers loosely use occupation while others use education or income, interchangeably, as criteria for class membership.[19]

In his pioneering work, The Philadelphia Negro (1899), DuBois used two different classifications of social stratification for the black community in Philadelphia's Seventh Ward. One measure consisted of four "grades" based solely on family income in 1896: "very poor (8.9%), "poor to fair" (57.4%), "comfortable" (25.5%) and "good circumstances" (8.2%). Families falling into the fourth grade were characterized as "middle class and above." While the second measure comprised four "grades" based primarily on "moral considerations" and style of life: (1) "well-to-do" (11.5%); (2) "respectable working class" (56%); (3) "the poor" (30.5%) and (4) the "criminals and prostitutes" (5.8%). DuBois characterized the 277 "well-to-do" families as "the aristocracy of the Negro population in education, wealth and general social efficiency."[20]

Frazier classified the "black bourgeoisie" primarily in terms of occupational strata. All workers in white-collar occupations (i.e., professional, technical, managerial, sales and clerical) are defined as "upper-middle class," while workers in crafts and skilled jobs are defined as "lower-middle class."[21] In many large cities, Frazier observed that successful black professionals (particularly doctors, dentists, lawyers, educators and ministers) are considered part of a small "upper class," particularly if they are light-complexioned.[22] Yet, as he notes upper class blacks are economically equivalent to middle class whites:

> The Negro upper class has its present status, primarily, because of its position in a segregated social world. If members of the Negro upper class were integrated into American society, their occupations and incomes would place them in the middle class.[23]

In a perceptive article, "Middle-Income Black Families: Are They Middle Class?" Newman observes important differences in the composition of the black middle class depending on whether the black or white median family income is used.[24] Middle-income black families were concentrated in the $6,000-$8,000 family income range in 1969, while middle-income white families were concentrated in the $10,000-$15,000 range. She proceeds to demonstrate that black families in the white middle-income category have much higher living standards than black families in the black middle-income category.

In fact, the analysis of the black middle class by Wattenberg and Scammon exemplifies the fallacy that Newman warned against. By using the black, rather than white, middle-income range, they were able to obtain a majority (52%) of black families in the middle-class. More specifically, they defined as "middle class," black families outside the South with incomes of $8,000 or more and black families in the South with incomes of $6,000 or more in 1971. In short, blacks were considered to be middle

-46-

class at annual incomes of $6,000 or $8,000, while whites were middle class at incomes of $12,000 or $15,000. In other words, Wattenberg and Scammon were determined that, if they could not get enough blacks up to the middle class, they would bring the middle class down to blacks![25]/

Most recent analyses of the black middle class, such as those by Landry and Wilson, tend to correspond to Frazier's occupational classifications.[26]/ However, while occupational criteria are very important for placing blacks in a class hierarchy within the black community, we think that income is a more reliable criterion for placing blacks in the class hierarchy within the larger white community.[27]/

A fundamental fallacy in most occupational classifications of class is the assumption that all white-collar workers have significantly higher incomes than all blue-collar or "manual" workers.[28]/ While it is true that black workers in professional, managerial and craft jobs tend to have higher earnings than all other workers--unlike whites, blacks in sales and clerical jobs often have earnings much lower than many blue-collar workers.[29]/

For example, among black male workers in 1978, semi-skilled operatives ($9,538) had higher median earnings than clerical ($8,735) or sales ($8,326). Moreover, almost half (45%) of all black male sales workers had earnings below poverty (i.e., under $7,000), compared to 39% of all clerical workers and 36% of all operatives. Similarly, among black female workers, two-thirds (65%) of the sales workers have poverty earnings, compared to two-thirds (66%) of the operatives and half (51%) of the clerical workers.[30]/ Thus, the fact that the majority of black sales and clerical workers do not have "middle-income" earnings severely undermines the reliability of any occupational classification that defines such workers as "middle class" in the class hierarchy of the larger white society.

Consequently, our analysis of the black middle class will conform to DuBois' use of income criteria. The ideal measures for such purposes are the various family budget levels developed by the U.S. Bureau of Labor Statistics. The BLS family budgets were updated annually to represent living standards of American families at various economic levels--upper, intermediate and lower.[31]/ In 1979, the upper standard was at $34,317, the intermediate at $20,517 and the lower (or "near poor") at $12,582. Families at the intermediate level are considered to represent typical "middle-income" Americans. Based on the BLS intermediate family budget in 1979, about one-fourth (24%) of black families were "middle class," compared to half (50%) of all white families. These proportions are not markedly different from those in 1970, when 23% of all black families were above the BLS intermediate level, compared to 47% of all white families. Consequently, one could conclude that, while the white middle class increased slightly during the 1970's, there was no significant change in the size of the black middle class.[32]/

Unfortunately, because of federal budget cuts, BLS has discontinued updating its family budget levels for the 1980's.[33]/ Consequently, we will operationally define all families with incomes above the U.S. median family income as "economically middle class." In 1983 (the latest year for which income data are available), the U.S. median family income was $24,580. In short, half of all American families had incomes below $25,000 in 1983, while the other half had incomes at or above that level. Accordingly, 27% of black families had incomes of $25,000 and over in 1983, compared to 52% of white families. Using income—adjusted for inflation— as our key criterion, we shall now examine the various social and economic characteristics of contemporary middle class black families.

IV. SOCIAL AND ECONOMIC PROFILE

Typically, middle class blacks are described as having: a college education, prestigious occupations, more than adequate earnings, regular full-time work, suburban residence, their own homes, their own businesses and stable family relations. We will now examine the extent to which contemporary middle-income black families, in fact, possesses these and related attributes.

A. College Education

Over the past two decades, blacks experienced a surge in persons with a college education. For example, between 1960 and 1980, the proportion of blacks aged 25 years and over with some college education tripled from 7% to 20%, while doubling among whites from 17% to 33%. Thus, the gap in median school years completed between blacks and whites narrowed from 2.7 years to 0.5 years between 1960 and 1980.

By 1983, one-fourth (24%) of all black family heads 25 years and older were college-educated, compared to two-fifths (38%) of similar-aged white family heads. Among middle-income families (i.e., these with incomes of $25,000 and over in 1983), however, two out of every five (42%) black households heads have some college education, while one-fourth (22%) have completed at least four years of college. Half of middle-income whites have gone to college, while one-third (33%) have completed four or more years of college. Although the majority of the heads of black middle class families today are not college-educated, a growing minority have obtained some undergraduate education.34/

B. High-Status Jobs

Over the past decade, the growth in workers in higher-paying occupations (i.e., professionals, managers and crafts) was much greater among blacks than whites. For example, while the number of professional and technical workers increased by 34% among whites between 1972 and 1980, it soared by 55% among blacks. Similarly, the number of managers and administrators rose twice as fast among blacks (69%) than whites (34%) over that period. And, the number of craft workers also increased twice as fast among blacks (32%) than whites (14%) between 1972 and 1980.35/

Consequently, the proportion of workers in professional occupations rose from 6% to 8% among black men; from 14% to 16% among white men; from 11% to 14% among black women; and 15% to 17% among white women between 1972 and 1980. In managerial and administrative jobs, the proportion rose from 4% to 6% among black men; from 14% to 15% among white men; from 2% to 3% among black women and from 5% to 7% among white women. In crafts and skilled jobs, the proportion of workers rose from 15% to 18% among black men; 21% to 22% among white men; from 0.9% to 1.4% among black women and from 1.3% to 1.9% among white women.

Despite these important advances by blacks into higher-level occupations, it is still the case that much smaller proportions of black workers are in those jobs relative to white workers. For example, over half (53%) of all white male workers were in professional, managerial or craft jobs in 1980, compared to less than one-third (31%) of black men, one-fourth (25%) of white women and one-fifth (19%) of black women.

Moreover, an insightful analysis by Westcott of detailed occupational patterns reveals that blacks are still concentrated in the lower-paying professional and managerial jobs:

> ...although a higher proportion of blacks could be found among the professional and technical occupations in 1980 than in 1972, they were concentrated in jobs at the lower end of the professional pay scale, such as nursing, technical trades and vocational and educational counseling. And even though their numbers have expanded in some of the more desirable and better paid jobs, there are few examples where black men and women have been able to significantly increase their representation in a particular job.[36/]

It is usually assumed that the overwhelming majority of middle-income blacks are in higher-level white-collar and craft occupations. But to what degree is this so? While the 1980 Census does not provide data relating family income to occupation by race and sex, it does provide data relating individual earnings to occupation. If workers with annual earnings of $15,000 or more in 1979 are operationally defined as "middle class," then 30% of black male workers and 12% of black female workers fall into that class.

Of the 1.5 million black male workers with annual earnings of $15,000 or more, 40% (or 604,000) held professional, managerial, technical and craft jobs in 1979. And, of the 554,000 black female workers with "middle class" earnings, 51% (or 284,000) held higher-level occupations. In other words, 60% of black male workers with "middle class" earnings are not in higher-status occupations, as is the case with half of black female workers with "middle class" earnings. In fact, a significant number of these other workers can be found in semi-skilled operatives or construction laborers occupations. In short, unlike whites, sizable proportions of middle-income black household heads are not in prestigious white-collar occupations.[37/]

On the other hand, it should not be assumed that all workers in high-status jobs have "middle class" salaries. For example, one-fifth of black males (17%) and females (21%) in professional jobs in 1979 had

-49-

poverty-level earnings (i.e., under $6,000), as did one-fifth (18%) of black female managers and 13% of black male managers.[38/]

C. Government Jobs

A significant source of the growth of the black middle class was the public sector. Between 1970 and 1980, the number of blacks in government jobs jumped from 1.6 million to 2.5 million, raising their proportion among all black workers from 21% to 27%. Among white workers, the proportion in government jobs edged up from 16% to 17% over that decade. Only about one-fourth of black public employees work for the federal government, half work for county and city governments, and the remaining one-fourth work for state government.[39/]

To what extent do black managers and professionals work in the public sector? While one-fourth (23%) of all black male workers are in government jobs, so are one-third (34%) of black male managers and half (51%) of black male professionals. Similarly, while about one-third (31%) of all black female workers are government employees, so are two-fifths (41%) of black female managers and two-thirds (69%) of black female professionals. Thus, unlike whites, the majority of black professionals and almost two-fifths of black managers are in government jobs.

In general, black government workers have higher earnings than private sector workers. In 1979, black male government workers had median earnings of $13,525, compared to $10,612 earnings among black male private workers. Similarly, among black female workers, government workers ($11,301) have higher earnings than private workers ($7,706). Consequently, government employment continues to be a major backbone of the black middle class.[40/]

D. Double Earners

Historically, the black middle class has had to rely on the earnings of at least two members of the family in order to attain and maintain an adequate standard of living. Thus, in 1969, there were more families with two or more earners among blacks (57%) than whites (54%). However, with the surge of white wives into the labor force, there were more double-earning families among whites (56%) than blacks (43%) by 1983.[41/]

Nevertheless, wives in black two-parent families today are still more likely to be in the labor force than wives in white two-parent families. According to the 1980 Census, three-fifths (61%) of wives among black couples were in the labor force (i.e., either working or looking for work), compared to only half (48%) of wives among white couples. This pattern held among young married couples between the ages of 25-34 as well--three-fourths (73%) of black wives are in the labor force, compared to three-fifths (57%) of white wives.

To what extent are wives working in middle-income black families? Two-fifths (43%) of all black couples had family incomes of $20,000 and over in 1979, compared to three-fifths (57%) of white couples. Of the 1.5 million middle class black couples, four out of five (78%) had wives in

-50-

the labor force, compared to three out of five (58%) middle class white couples. Thus, working wives characterize the overwhelming majority of black and white middle class families.

Working wives contribute more to the economic well-being of two-parent black than white families. One-earner black couples only have half ($11,662) the median income of two-earner black couples ($21,336), while one-earner white couples have three-fourths ($18,774) the income of two-earner white couples ($25,387). However, in the overwhelming majority of two-earner couples, the husband's earnings exceed the wife's. For example, in only 16% of two-earner black couples was the wife's earnings greater than the husband's in 1979, regardless of the educational level of the husband. Similarly, in only 8% of two-earner white couples did the wife's earnings exceed the husband--regardless of the husband's education.

In his "benign neglect" memorandum to Richard Nixon in 1969, presidential advisor Daniel Moynihan focused on the near "parity" of incomes between black and white couples under the age of 35 living outside the South as indicative of a sharp growth in the black middle class.[42/] However, that memo neglected to add that this "parity" was the result of more working wives in black couples than in white couples. Nevertheless, to what extent have black young couples achieved "parity" with white young couples over the past decade?

In the U.S. as a whole, black couples between the ages of 25-34 did make significant gains on comparable white couples. In 1969, the income of black young couples was 78% of white young couples. By 1979, the income of black young couples narrowed to 86% of the white young couples. However, since there are more working wives among black than white couples, it is necessary to examine these trends separate for couples with and without working wives.

The gap in incomes between two-earner black and white couples 25-34 years old narrowed from 82% to 88% between 1969 and 1979. However, the gap in incomes between one-earner black and white young couples widened slightly from 69% to 67% over that decade. In short, black young couples without working wives did not make any progress in closing the income gap with white young couples. (See Table 1)

Similar patterns result, when the incomes of black and white young couples are compared within regions. In every region, the incomes of two-earner young black couples gained on the incomes of two-earner young white couples to such an extent that black incomes are about 90% of white incomes. On the other hand, one-earner young black couples made no gains on one-earner young white couples--and, in some regions, actually lost ground. These findings reveal that having a two-parent structure does not insure economic adequacy among black couples--but having a working wife is a necessary requirement.[43/]

E. Single-Parent Families

Middle class black families consist predominantly of married couples. While three-fifths (57%) of all black families in 1979, comprised couples, eight out of ten (82%) middle-income black families consisted of two-parents. Consequently, while two-fifths (37%) of all black families are headed by women, only 13% (or 232,000) of middle-income black families are female-headed. Four out of five (78%) black women heading middle-income families (i.e., with incomes of $20,000 and over in 1979) are in the labor force. In contrast, only 4% of white middle-income families are headed by women. And only two-thirds of those middle class white women are in the labor force.

In most discussions of the recent growth in female-headed families, one fact is invariably omitted--that the largest increases occurred among "middle class" and not "underclass" families. Nine out of every ten (88%) black female-headed family formed between 1970 and 1981 were headed by women with at least a high school diploma, while one out of three were college-educated. Contrary to popular belief, only 12% of the increase in one-parent black families over this period was due to families headed by women who were high school dropouts. (See Table 2)

Similarly, 95% of the one-parent black families formed between 1970 and 1981 were headed by women who had been formerly married. Once again, contrary to conventional wisdom about the "predominant" contribution of teenage pregnancy to the formation of female-headed households, only five percent of the rise in black one-parent families during the 1970's occurred among women who had never married.[44/] Similar findings result for female-headed families among whites as well. In short, the largest increases in one-parent families during the 1970, occurred among the black and white middle class--primarily because of spiraling divorce rates over the past two decades. Thus, there is less and less empirical support for the popular view that female-headed families are an intrinsic characteristic of a "culture of poverty".

F. Residence

Home ownership has been a traditional indicator of middle class status for both blacks and whites. However, there was only a small rise in the proportion of home ownership among all blacks--from 42% to 44%-- between 1970 and 1980. Among all whites, the proportion of homeowners increased from 65% to 68% over that decade.

Yet, there were larger increases in home ownership among middle class black and white families. Between 1969 and 1979, the proportion of homeowners rose from 61% to 69% among middle-income black families, and from 76% to 82% among middle-income white families.

However, while middle class whites are concentrated in suburban areas, most middle class blacks still live in central cities. For example, over half (54%) of black families with incomes of $25,000 and over in 1983 reside in central cities, while only three out of ten (29%) live in the suburbs. Among middle-income white families, half (47%) of them live in the suburbs, while less than one-fourth (22%) live in central cities.

Middle-income black families are more highly represented in the Northeast and West than in the Midwest and South. About half (46%) of middle-income black families resided in the South in 1983, while one-fifth lived in the Northeast (22%) and Midwest (19%) and only (13%) in the West. Among all black families, 52% lived in the South, one-fifth in the Northeast (19%) and Midwest (19%) and only one-tenth (10%) in the West.[45]

G. Self-Employment

Another traditional characteristic of middle class status is self-employment and business ownership. However, the number of self-employed workers declined among blacks during the 1970's, but increased among whites. While the number of self-employed blacks--who are overwhelmingly men--fell from 267,000 to 224,000 between 1970 and 1980, it rose from 5.9 million to 6.7 million among whites. Nevertheless, the proportion of self-employed among all workers fell among whites (from 8% to 7%) and blacks (from 3% to 2%) over that decade.[46]

In general, the earnings of self-employed workers among blacks and whites are much lower than the earnings of private sector employees. For example, among black men, the self-employed ($7,061) had earnings in 1983 that were only two-thirds the earnings of private workers ($10,612). Similarly, among white men, self-employed workers ($11,311) had earnings two-thirds of those of private workers ($17,071).

But self-employed black men who work full-time have earnings almost equal to those of private full-time workers. Self-employed black men who worked year-round, full-time had median earnings of $15,346 in 1983, compared to $15,875 earnings among full-time private black male workers. However, among white men working full-time, the self-employed ($16,058) still had earnings that were about two-thirds of private workers ($23,128).

The number of black firms rose steadily during the 1970's, from 163,000 in 1969 and 175,000 in 1972 to 231,000 in 1977 and 339,000 in 1982. However, since the number of all U.S. businesses also increased just as fast, the proportion of black firms in the U.S. economy remained at about two percent from 1969 to 1982.[47]

Moreover, while 70% of the 15 million U.S. firms in 1982 were sole proprietorships, so were 95% of all black businesses. In fact, the proportion of black-owned firms with paid employees fell sharply from 23% in 1969 to 17% in 1977 and to 12% in 1982. The largest number of black-owned firms are in miscellaneous retail (54,000), personal services (40,000), health services (17,000) and trucking and warehousing (13,000). Automotive leaderships, one of the growth areas in black business, comprised 3,400 establishments in 1982. Yet, there have been significant advances for black businesses in many nontraditional areas (such as high-tech, marketing, advertising and manufacturing). Nevertheless, the combined sales of $1.2 billion of the 25 largest black businesses in 1982, according to Black Enterprise, equalled about five days of sales of Exxon.[48]

H. Children's Education

To what extent do young people from middle class black families attend college? In 1969, about one-fifth (22%) of youth 18-24 years old in all black families attended college full-time. By 1981, the proportion of black youth in college rose only slightly to 24%.

Young people from middle-income are about twice as likely to attend college as youth from low-income families. While only one-fifth (19%) of black youth from poor families were in college full-time in 1981, about twice as many (39%) black youth from middle-income families were in college. Similarly, among whites, youth from middle-income families are twice (45%) as likely to attend college as are youth from low-income (20%) families.[49]

However data from the NUL's Black Pulse Survey reveal that black youth from one-parent families are about as likely to attend college as are youth from two-parent families. While 13% of children in two-parent families were in college in 1979, so were 10% of the children in one-parent black families. Similarly, among black families with incomes of $20,000 and over, youth in two-parent families were about as likely to attend college (20%) as youth in one-parent black families (23%).[50]

I. Social Relations

The Black Pulse data also provide new insights about various social patterns among middle class blacks. Regarding religious affiliation, heads (60%) of low-income families (i.e., those with incomes under $6,000) are more likely to be Baptists than heads (50%) of middle-income families (i.e., those with incomes of $20,000 and over). On the other hand, middle-income blacks are more likely to be Methodists (14% vs 9%) and Catholics (8% vs 4%) than low-income blacks.[51]

Middle-income blacks (48%) are only slightly more likely to attend church each week than low-income blacks (44%). But middle-income blacks (72%) are much more likely to send their children to Sunday School than low-income blacks (63%). And, middle-income blacks (63%) are more than one and a half times as likely as low-income blacks (38%) to participate in regular family reunions.[52]

V. CONVERGENCE OR CLEAVAGE?

To what extent is the economic gap between middle class blacks and whites converging? A popular approach is to assess the degree to which the earnings of blacks in higher-level occupations approximate the earnings of whites in comparable jobs. Among year-round, full-time male workers, the ratio of black to white median earnings in professional occupations narrowed only slightly (from 73% to 75%) between 1969 and 1979. But, among year-round, full-time managerial male workers, the ratio of black to white median earnings narrowed sharply from 67% to 74%.

Among female workers, the earnings of blacks in higher-level occupations equalled or exceeded the earnings of whites in 1979 as well in 1969. The ratio of black to white earnings among women working year-round, full-time in professional jobs rose form 85% to 95% between 1969 and 1979. But the earnings of black female managers working full-time exceeded the earnings of white female managers working full-time in 1969 and 1979. However, one reason that black women have gained on white women is because the latter have not gained ground on white men.[53/]

A second popular approach to assessing changes in the economic gap between black and white families is to examine trends among all two-parent families. Between 1969 and 1979, the ratio of black to white median income among two-parent families rose from 70% to 79%.

However, when one separates couples with working wives from those without working wives, it is evident that all of the income gains occurred among couples with working wives. While the ratio of black to white income among two-earner couples increased from 75% to 84%, the ratio remained unchanged (at 62%) among couples without working wives. Thus, we obtain findings similar to those for young couples with and without working wives--regardless of region.

Yet, it should be clearly understood that convergence of incomes between black and white families does not necessarily mean convergence of economic conditions of blacks and whites. One needs to examine patterns of wealth (i.e., assets such as savings, stocks, bonds, land, home, businesses and other cashable properties).[54/] Unfortunately, census data do not provide detailed information relating to wealth patterns by race.

An analysis by O'Hare, however, revealed that the median wealth of black households in 1979 was $24,608, compared to $68,891 for white households. At the same time, the median income for black households was $10,133 and $17,259 for white households. Thus, he concludes:

> ...the income of whites was about 1.7 times that of blacks, but the wealth of whites was almost three times that of blacks. Looked at another way, white households had a total wealth that was four times their income, while blacks had a total wealth of about 2.5 times their income.[55/]

In 1979, blacks held approximately $211 billion in personal wealth, compared to $5 trillion in wealth held by whites. Thus, black households hold only four percent of the combined wealth of blacks and whites. In 1967, the average wealth of white families was $20,153 and that of blacks was $3,779. Thus, black wealth was only about one-fifth of that of white wealth in 1967. By, 1979, however, black wealth was about 36% of white wealth. Consequently, there is evidence of some improvement in black wealth relative to white wealth over that 12-year interval.[56/]

To what extent is the economic gap between middle-income and low-income blacks widening? Examination of income trends (in constant dollars) among black and white families between 1969 and 1983 reveals mixed results. On the one hand, the proportion of low-income families (i.e., those with incomes under $10,000 in 1983) among blacks steadily rose from 29% to 37%, while the proportion of middle-income black families remained at 27% in both 1969 and 1983. Thus, the proportion of middle class black families held at about one-fourth, while the proportion of poor families rose sharply. These data also reveal that 31% of black families were middle-income in 1978. Thus, there was a sharp decline in the proportion of middle class black families between 1978 and 1983.[57] (See Table 3)

Somewhat similar patterns occurred among white families. While the proportion of low-income white families rose from 11% to 13% between 1969 and 1983, the proportion of middle-income white families fell from 54% to 52%. But, 57% of white families were middle-income in 1978. Thus, there was a sharp drop in the proportion of middle class white families between 1978 and 1983.[58]

To what extent do middle class blacks identify with the problems of the black masses? Data from the Black Pulse Survey reveal that, contrary to conventional wisdom, middle class blacks are more militant regarding racial issues than are low-income blacks.[59]

Four-fifths (83%) of middle-income blacks felt that the push for racial equality in the U.S. in 1979 was moving "too slow," compared to three-fourths (73%) of poor blacks. Similarly, 70% of middle-income blacks felt that there was "a great deal" of racial discrimination against blacks in this country, compared to 61% of poor blacks.[60]

And, when black household heads were asked whether any member of their family had experienced racial discrimination over the past two years, middle-income blacks were about as likely as low-income blacks to report experiencing racial bias. For example, about the same proportion of middle-income (27%) and poor (30%) blacks said a member of their household recently experienced discrimination in trying to get a job. Similar patterns of bias among middle-income and low-income black families were prevalent regarding getting credit, applying for loans, property vandalism and contacts with the police.[61]

These and related findings reveal a high degree of convergence between middle-income and low-income blacks regarding racial attitudes and recent instances of racial discrimination. These data should help to explain why middle class blacks have traditionally been in the vanguard of the struggle for racial equality since slavery.[62]

VI. FUTURE PROSPECTS

The future prospects for the black middle class are difficult to gauge at this juncture. On the one hand, there are ominous trends that suggest that the proportion of middle class black families may decline during the rest of the 1980's. For example, between 1977 and 1983, the proportion of black high school graduates going to college plummetted from 50% to 39%, while rising from 51% to 55% among white high school graduates. Moreover, since the mid-1970's, the proportion of black undergraduates and graduate students in first-year professional schools (especially, law, medicine and dentistry) has steadily declined.[63/]

On the other hand, the steady increases in the numbers of blacks in major policy-making positions in law, business and government suggests that the growth in the black middle class may be slowed, but not reversed. Thus, for blacks, it may just be the "best of all times, and the worst of all times."[64/]

But more middle class blacks must commit themselves to improving the conditions of poor black families.[65/] They must indeed heed Dr. Martin Luther King, Jr.'s plea:

> It is time for the Negro middle class to rise up
> from its stool of indifference, to retreat from its
> flight into unreality and to bring its full resources--
> its heart, its mind and its checkbook to the aid of the
> less fortunate brother.[66/]

FOOTNOTES

1. Wattenberg, Ben J. and Scammon, Richard M. "Black Progress and Liberal Rhetoric," Commentary (April, 1973), pp. 35-44.,

2. Freeman, Richard B., Black Elite New York: McGraw-Hill, 1976.

3. Wilson, William J., The Declining Significance of Race, Chicago, Ill.: University of Chicago Press, 1978.

4. Murray, Albert, The Omni-Americans, New York: Vintage Books, 1983.

5. Pinkney, Alphonso, The Myth of Black Progress New York: Cambridge University Press, 1984; Denys Vaughn-Cooke, "No Recovery in the Economic Status of Black America," The Black Scholar (September/ October 1985) pp. 2-13.

6. Frazier, E. Franklin Black Bourgeoisie, New York: Collier Books, 1962.

7. Frazier, E. Franklin The Negro in the United States, New York: MacMillan Company, 1966.

8. Ibid., Horton, James O. and Horton, Lois E. Black Bostonians New York: Holmes and Meier, 1979.

9. Billingsley, Andrew "The Evolution of the Black Family," Black Perspectives on the Bicentennial. New York: National Urban League, 1976, p. 20.

10. Billingsley, Andrew and Greene, Marilyn C., "Family Life Among the Free Black Population in the 18th Century," Journal of Social and Behavioral Sciences Vol. 20, No. 2 (Spring, 1974), pp. 1-18.

11. DuBois, W.E.B. The Philadelphia Negro, University of Pennsylvania Press, 1899; New York: Schocken Reprint, 1967, p. 178.

12. Frazier, The Negro in the United States.

13. Berry, Mary F. and Blassingame, John W. Long Memory New York: Oxford University Press, 1982.

14. Puckrein, Gary "Moving Up: Blacks in America," Wilson Quarterly (Spring, 1984) pp. 74-87.

15. Berry and Blassingame, op. cit; Alain Locke (ed.) The New Negro New York: Charles and Albert Boni, 1925.

16. Weaver, Robert Negro Labor New York: Harcourt, Brace and Co., 1946, p. 306.

17. Newman, Dorothy K. et. al. Protest, Politics and Prosperity New York: Pantheon, 1978.

18. Auletta, Ken _The Underclass_ New York: Random House; Martin Kilson, "Black Social Classes and Intergenerational Poverty," _The Public Interest_, No. 64 (Summer, 1981), pp. 58-78.

19. Wilson, _op.cit._

20. DuBois, _op.cit._, p. 171, 309-321. Drake and Cayton classified class strata on the basis of life-style, see St. Clair Drake and Horace R. Cayton, _Black Metropolis_ New York: Harper & Row, 1962, Vol. 2.

21. Frazier, _Black Bourgeoisie_, p. 47.

22. _Ibid_; G. Franklin Edwards, _The Negro Professional Class_, Glencoe, Ill.: Free Press, 1959.

23. Frazier, _Negro in the U.S._, p. 291.

24. Newman, Dorothy K. "Middle-Income Black Families: Are They Middle Class?" _Tuesday at Home_, Sunday Newspaper Supplement, (October, 1971), pp. 8-10, 23.

25. Wattenberg and Scammon, _op.cit_; Hill, Robert B. _The Illusion of Black Progress_ Washington, DC: NUL Research Department, 1978.

26. Landry, Bart "Growth of the Black Middle Class in the 1960's" _Urban League Review_, Vol. 3, No. 2 (Winter, 1978), pp. 68-82; Wilson, _op. cit_, p. 127.

27. For insightful assessments of the unreliability of traditional "objective" measures for determining class strata in the black community, see Sampson, William A., "New Insights on Black Middle-Class Mobility," _Urban League Review_, Vol. 5, No. 1 (Summer 1980), pp. 21-41 and Billingsley, Andrew _Black Families in White America_ Englewood Cliffs, NJ: Prentice Hall, 1968, pp. 122-124.

28. Wilson, _op.cit_; Landry, _op.cit._

29. Hill, Robert B. _Economic Policies and Black Progress_ Washington, DC: NUL Research Department, 1981, Table 5.6.

30. _Ibid_, Table 5.5

31. For a detailed description of the BLS family budgets, see U.S. Bureau of Labor Statistics, "Three Standards of Living for a Urban Family of Four Persons," _BLS Bulletin No. 1570-5_ (Spring, 1967).

32. Hill, _Economic Policies and Black Progress_, Table 5.3: Faustine C. Jones, "External Crosscurrents and Internal Diversity: An Assessment of Black Progress, 1960-1980," _Daedalus_ (Spring, 1981), pp. 71-102.

33. The last BLS family budgets were prepared for Autumn 1981 and were released on April 16, 1982.

34. Reid, John "Black Americans in the 1980's," <u>Population Bulletin</u> Vol. 37, No. 4 (December, 1982).

35. Wescott, Diane N. "Blacks in the 1970's: Did They Scale The Job Ladder?" <u>Monthly Labor Review</u> (June, 1982), pp. 29-38.

36. <u>Ibid</u>, p. 31.

37. Levitan, Sar A. et. al, <u>Still A Dream</u> Cambridge, Mass.: Harvard University Press, 1975.

38. Hill, <u>Economic Policies and Black Progress</u>, Table 5.5.

39. For analyses of black growth in government jobs prior to 1970, see Newman, <u>op.cit</u> and Wilson, <u>op.cit</u>. Also see study of black mailmen in Noel A. Cazenave, "Middle-Income Black Fathers," <u>The Family Co-ordinator</u> (October, 1979), pp. 583-593.

40. Billingsley, <u>Black Families in White America</u>; Levitan, et. al., <u>op.cit</u>.

41. Farley, Reynolds, <u>Blacks and Whites: Narrowing the Gap?</u> Cambridge, Mass.: Harvard University Press, 1984.

42. Hill, Robert B., <u>Benign Neglect Revisited</u>, Washington, DC: NUL Research Department, 1973.

43. Rodgers-Rose, LaFrances (ed.) <u>The Black Woman</u>, Beverly Hills, Calif.: Sage, 1980; Henry E. Felder, <u>The Changing Patterns of Black Family Income: 1960-1982</u>, Washington, DC: Joint Center for Political Studies, 1984.

44. Hill, <u>Economic Policies and Black Progress</u>, Table 5.8.

45. Newman, et.al., <u>op.cit</u>.

46. Becker, Eugene, "Self-employed Workers: An Update to 1983." <u>Monthly Labor Review</u> (July 1984), pp. 14-18.

47. U.S. Bureau of the Census, "Black-Owned Businesses," <u>1982 Survey of Minority-Owned Business Enterprises</u> MB-82-1, August 1985.

48. Cross, Theodore <u>The Black Power Imperative</u> New York: Faulkner, 1984, p. 268.

49. U.S. Bureau of Census, "School Enrollment--Social and Economic Characteristics of Students: October 1981," <u>Current Population Reports</u>, Series P-20, No. 400, July 1985.

50. Hill, <u>Economic Policies and Black Progress</u>, Table 4.3.

51. Unpublished data from National Urban League's Black Pulse Survey of a nationally representative sample of 3,000 black households heads interviewed in their homes between October 1979 and January 1980.

52. Ibid. For an in-depth analysis of extended family patterns among middle-class blacks, see McAdoo, Harriette P. (ed.) Black Families Beverly Hills, Calif.: Sage, 1981.

53. Between 1969 and 1979, the ratio of female to male earnings among all white workers remained at 48%; Farley, op. cit.

54. Cross, op.cit; Landry, L. Bart "The Social and Economic Adequacy of the Black Middle Class," in Joseph R. Washington, Jr. (ed.) Dilemmas of The New Black Middle Class, University of Pennsylvania, 1980, pp. 1-13.

55. O'Hare, William P. "Wealth and Economic Status," The Crisis, Vol. 91, No. 10 (December 1984), pp. 6-7.

56. Ibid.

57. Palmer, John L. and Sawhill, Isabel V. (ed.) The Reagan Record Cambridge, Mass.: Ballinger, 1984; Center on Budget and Policy Priorities, "Falling Behind: A Report on How Blacks have fared under the Reagan Policies," Washington, DC, October, 1984.

58. Thurow, Lester C. "The Disappearance of the Middle Class," New York Times, February 5, 1984, Business Forum; Center on Budget and Policy Priorities, "End Results: The Impact of Federal Policies Since 1980 on Low Income Americans," Washington, DC: Interfaith Action for Economic Justice, September, 1984.

59. NUL Reasearch Department, "Initial Black Pulse Findings," Bulletin No. 1 (August 1980). For an in-depth study of militant attitudes of the black middle class, see Marx, Gary T. Protest and Prejudice New York: Harper & Row, 1967.

60. Hill, Economic Policies and Black Progress, Table 5.7.

61. Ibid.

62. Berry and Blassingame, op.cit.

63. Hill, Susan T. "Participation of Black Students in Higher Education: A Statistical Profile from 1970-71 to 1980-81," Special Report, National Center for Education Statistics, November 1983.

64. Jones, op.cit; Farley, op.cit.

65. Hare, Nathan The Black Anglo Saxons New York: Marzani and Mansell, 1965; Cole, Johnnetta B. "The Black Bourgeoisie," in Peter I. Rose, et. al. (ed.) Through Different Eyes, New York: Oxford University Press, 1973, pp. 25-43.

66. Martin Luther King, Jr., Where Do We Go From Here? New York: Harper & Row, 1967, p. 132.

TABLE 1

Ratio of Black To White Median Family Income
by Age, Region and Work Status of Wives, 1970–1980

Wives Work Status	All Couples		Couples, 25–34	
	1970	1980	1970	1980
Total U.S.[1]	61	60	65	60
Couples	70	79	78	86
Wives in Labor Force	75	84	82	88
Not in Labor Force	62	62	69	67
Northeast				
Couples	80	87	84	88
Wives in Labor Force	87	91	92	93
Not in Labor Force	72	68	65	67
North Central				
Couples	86	94	91	89
Wives in Labor Force	92	99	96	101
Not in Labor Force	79	77	82	81
West				
Couples	81	87	88	91
Wives in Labor Force	87	90	93	92
Not in Labor Force	74	69	78	69
South				
Couples	67	76	75	83
Wives in Labor Force	71	80	79	85
Not in Labor Force	58	60	95	66

[1]All families including single parents as well.

Source: U.S. Bureau of the Census, 1970 and 1980 Censuses.

TABLE 2

Change in Number of Families Headed
by Black Women by Education and Marital Status

(Numbers in Thousands)

| | Families Headed by Black Women | | | |
| | | | Change, 1970-81 | |
Education	1970	1981	Number	Percent
Total Families[1]	912	1,823	911	100
H.S. Grad. or more	310	1,113	803	88
College-educated	72	372	300	33
H.S. grad.	238	741	503	55
Less than H.S.	602	710	108	12
1-3 H.S.	344	533	189	21
0-8 Elem.	258	177	-81	-9

| | Families Headed by Black Women | | | |
| | | | Change, 1970-81 | |
Marital Status	1970	1981	Number	Percent
Total Families[2]	2,390	2,634	244	100
Never Married	705	716	11	5
Formerly Married	1,684	1,917	233	95
Husband absent	687	756	69	28
Divorced	474	614	140	57
Widowed	523	547	24	10

[1]Single parent families with children.

[2]Single parent families with and without children.

Source: U.S. Bureau of the Census, "Marital Status and Living Arrangements" and "Household and Family Characteristics" Current Population Reports Series P-20, 1970-1981.

TABLE 3

Income Distribution of Families

By Race, 1969–1983

Family Income[1]	Black Families			White Families		
	1969	1978	1983	1969	1978	1983
Total Families[2]	4,774	5,906	6,675	46,022	50,910	53,934
Percent	100	100	100	100	100	100
Under $10,000	29	30	37	11	11	13
Under $2,500	3	3	6	1	1	2
2,500–4,999	7	8	11	2	2	3
5,000–7,499	8	11	11	4	3	4
7,500–9,999	10	8	9	4	5	5
$10,000–24,999	45	39	36	35	33	35
10,000–12,499	9	8	8	5	5	6
12,500–14,999	8	7	7	5	5	5
15,000–19,999	18	12	12	15	11	12
20,000–24,999	10	11	10	10	11	12
$25,000 & over	36	42	37	64	68	64
25,000–34,999	18	15	14	29	21	20
35,000–49,999	6	11	9	14	21	18
$50,000 & over	3	5	4	11	15	14
Median Income[1]	$16,303	$16,614	$14,506	$26,617	$28,050	$25,757

[1]Income in constant (1983) dollars.

[2]Numbers in thousands.

Source: U.S. Bureau of the Census, "Money Income of Households, Families, and Persons in the United States: 1983," Consumer Income: Current Population Reports, Series P-60, No. 146, April, 1985.

TEENAGE PREGNANCY:
THE IMPLICATION FOR BLACK AMERICANS

By

Joyce A. Ladner

I. INTRODUCTION

In his powerful autobiography, "Manchild in the Promised Land," written twenty years ago, Claude Brown recalls a conversation he had with Reno, one of his childhood friends. Reno says to Claude (Sonny):

> Man, Sonny, they ain't got no kids in Harlem. I ain't never seen any. I've seen some really small people actin' like kids. They were too small to be grown, and they might've looked like kids, but they don't have any kids in Harlem, because nobody has time for a childhood. Man, do you ever remember bein' a kid, Sonny? Damn, you lucky. I ain't never been a kid, man. I don't ever remember bein' happy and not scared. I don't know what happened, Man, but I think I missed out on that childhood thing, because I don't ever recall bein' a kid (Brown, 1966).

There is no other problem in the black community today that is more threatening to future generations of families than teen pregnancy, a problem of monumental proportions that is producing the womanchild and manchild on unprecedented levels. It is a problem that will effect three generations -- the teen parents, their children, and the grandparents.

Teen parenthood enters the lives of young males and females when they are in the throes of their psychosocial development. It robs them of their unspent youth, and forces them into adult roles long before they have the capacity or the interest to become adults. It thrusts them into play-acting the roles of grown-ups with children to care for, pseudo-mates with whom to interact, and a society with which to contend, as they try in their young tender years to explain, interpret, and behave appropriately in an adult society that is at once tolerant but intolerant, punitive but encouraging, and hostile but willing to be the good provider. The adult-oriented society is so wed to a set of contradictory, confusing and some-times ambiguous standards of sexual conduct that it is both unwilling and unable to make clear cut choices. Youths are bombarded with sexually ex-plicit messages and innuendo from all quarters. The mass media's message has been pervasive through the sexually explicit lyrics in songs and videos, while television, movies and the print media encourage youth to develop self concepts of themselves as highly sexual individuals. Fashion designers such as Calvin Klein encourage young girls to adopt sensual be-havior ("Nothing comes between me and my Calvin's" is the theme of the commercial to sell jeans), while the church, school and family teach ab-stinence from pre-marital sexual relations. Since adults have inconsistent values and attitudes about human sexuality, it is no wonder that youth are confused. Therefore, teenagers are caught in a maze of confusion and conflict in values regarding sexuality in which early pregnancy and child-bearing are often the outcome.

Adolescent pregnancy disproportionately affects poor minority youths. The consequences of long-term poverty have a corrosive effect on many of these youths who have low self-esteem, are fatalistic, chronically de-pressed and needy. Many come from single parent families where their parents experience great amounts of stress. Lack of opportunity, and lack of training and education will often produce a person with no conceptuali-zation of the future. Consolation is found in immediate gratification. Babies become fantasized partners who will provide love and affection. Having children may be the only way of establishing "masculinity" and "femininity," or achieving an adult role (Silber, 1985; Ladner, 1984). Far too often the end result is that they become members of the underclass with little opportunity or hope of ever getting out of poverty.

Black teen pregnancy must also be placed within the context of other major social problems facing American youths of all racial, ethnic and social class groups. The rates of teen unemployment, drug and alcohol abuse, school drop-out, homicide and suicide are at record highs. Wide-spread poverty and alienation from and the declining role of traditional institutions such as family, church, school, community youth oriented organizations and civic and civil rights organizations serve to undermine the ability of many of today's youths to remain anchored to those agencies of socialization.

The high rate of teen pregnancy in the black community poses another serious risk. In combination with other socio-economic factors, it is robbing the family of its stability and strengths it has had to struggle to maintain over its entire history in America. They are strengths and stability that have been fought for and maintained through slavery, the era of Jim Crow, and the mass migrations of blacks from the agrarian South to the northern industrial areas where the slow but steady weakening of the extended family began to occur. In the good times and the harsh times, black families have had to contend with a variety of external and internal forces.

II. HISTORICAL BACKGROUND

One long-standing threat to black family and community stability was out-of-wedlock pregnancy. It was a problem which began in slavery when, in a legal or technical sense, all births were outside the boundaries of marriage since slaves could not legally marry. Still the illegality of marriage did not prevent slaves from placing a high value on the sanctity of the institution because they found ways to maneuver around these barriers. For example, one common practice among slaves wishing to marry was to "jump the broom," a ceremonial tradition undoubtedly imported from Africa. The couple held hands as they jumped over the handle of a broom while in the presence of others (Guttman, 1976). Immediately following Emancipation many slaves who had lived together or had become separated during slavery were reunited and were legally married. This was another indication of their strong affinity for having children in-wedlock.

A tradition developed whereby if a girl became pregnant she was always expected to marry. Therefore, the so-called "shot-gun" marriages were arranged and the young couple was given the assistance of their families and the community to build their family. Respectability was forthcoming to such persons who were willing to legitimate their child's birth. However, the black family has, due to its peculiar history of oppression, always been a fragile family in many respects at the same time that it has exhibited tremendous strengths. The cumulative effects of economic, racial, and political hardships over time did little to guarantee that all the children conceived would be born to married parents. Economic hardships have always had a disproportionately greater negative impact on black male household heads. Under more ideal circumstances legal marriage may have occurred in far greater numbers but the long-term effects of black men being unable to support families caused many children to be born to single mothers, and others to eventually grow up in homes where fathers were no longer present.

Blacks being no different than other races in America, have also had their given number of out-of-wedlock births due to the fact that the couples were involved in unstable relationships where marriage was neither expected nor desired by at least one partner. Teen childbearing in the white community and among the black middle class has usually been resolved by forced marriage or by placing the child for adoption, leaving relatively few children in out-of-wedlock status. However, a significant part of the black community has always considered it to be a gross violation of the subcultural norms to place the child for legal adoption. Adoption was always viewed as tantamount to "giving the child away to strangers," never to be seen again.

Moreover, it has only been within the past two decades that adoption agencies have made any significant attempts to serve a clientele that reaches beyond the middle class. Historically when black children became wards of the courts they were usually placed in foster care and institutions rather than in adoptive homes. The black community's perception of the adoption agency as a white, unsympathetic almost alien institution was not without foundation. Adoption agencies were, therefore, viewed with suspicion rather than a viable alternative to solving a family problem (Billingsley and Giovanonni, 1972).

The practices of adoption agencies also alienated many blacks who saw the practice of paying fees for a service as reminiscent of the buying and selling of slaves. Children, they reasoned, are in a category all to themselves and should not be bartered and bargained for lest it remind blacks of one of the darker sides of their history. Such an attitude still exists among some blacks.

There is a historical precedent for blacks adopting and caring for the homeless children within their midsts. During slavery, countless children were separated from their parents by slaveowners whose major concern was that of maximizing their profits instead of maintaining intact families. Writing in 1909, W.E.B. DuBois said: "Among the slaves the charitable work was chiefly in the line of adopting children and caring for the sick. The habit of adopting is still widespread and beneficient"

(DuBois, 1969). The tradition of informal adoption continued after slavery. Johnson noted that it was prevalent among poor blacks in the South in the early part of the twentieth century: "The breaking up of families, through desertion or migration, results in the turning over of children to relatives or friends, and since little distinction of treatment enters, they soon are indistinguishable from the natural children. ...children orphaned by any circumstances are spontaneously taken into childless families" (Johnson, 1934).

A strong value was placed on children. Oftentimes informally adopted children were granted a special place in their new families, perhaps as a way of compensating for their birth parents' absence. Such children were "pitied" in a manner that evoked tender feelings from others, since a prevailing religious value among these southern rural people was that orphaned children were to be regarded as "special," and adults were duty-bound to provide for them. Again, Johnson notes that "the sentiment is sometimes carried to the point of surrounding the child with an importance which many children in normal families lack" (Johnson, p. 71). Powdermaker makes a similar observation of black families' attitudes toward adoption in Mississippi in the 1930s: "Adoption is practically never made legal, and is referred to as 'giving' the children away... Because of the strong desire most people have for children, there is always someone ready to take them in" (Powdermaker, 1939).

Since these children were informally adopted within the communities in which they were born, they were expected and encouraged to grow up with the knowledge of their biological parentage. The prevailing attitude was that every individual has a right to know his/her roots. This practice was aided by the insular nature of the extended family into which many of the children were adopted. Members of the small communities of the South where informal adoption was and still is most prevalent, were expected to protect the child from the insults and assaults that the child's adoptive and out-of-wedlock status might occasionally evoke. Simply put, the child should not suffer the transgressions of his/her parents.

Frequently, it was regarded as shameful for parents to give a child to a complete stranger. Lewis suggests that regardless of how difficult the family conditions may have been, one was expected to "stick to your own, take care of your own, and never turn them away" (Lewis, 1965). This maxim applied equally to one's daughter becoming pregnant, one's son getting into trouble with the police, or whatever. Rarely did black families banish their children from their homes for some transgression.

It would be misleading to assume that all black children were informally adopted or taken care of by their extended families, or wider communities. Some children became wards of the court which entrusted them to the care of public welfare agencies. Other children were forced to fend for themselves at early ages. However, this practice of the black community using its scarce resources to take care of its own existed past the mid-twentieth century. Despite the hardships, in 1960 a majority of black families (79%) were husband-wife families. Hill documented the widespread practice of informal adoption in 1972. He found that 85% of all black children were adopted informally rather than legally, at a rate that far exceeded that of whites (Hill, 1971).

The widespread practice of black teen pregnancy is a relatively new phenomenon. Although the rates have steadily declined in recent years, they have been of a sufficient magnitude to cause great concern. Despite this, however, it was not until the mid-seventies that a small concerned group of blacks began to sound the alarm. The alarm was delayed in a deliberate sense because black civil rights leaders, policy analysts, and scholars, were still reeling from the controversy produced by the Moynihan Report which aroused national fervor in 1965 when it stated that "at the heart of the deterioration of the fabric of Negro society is the deterioration of the Negro family." The author, Daniel Patrick Moynihan, outraged blacks when he referred to the family as constituting a "tangle of pathology" (Moynihan, 1965; Rainwater and Yancey, 1967). Moynihan was then an Assistant Secretary of Labor under President Lyndon B. Johnson and was in an influential role as public policy adviser to the President. Alarmed over what was interpreted to be his "blame the victim" analysis, many blacks denounced the report as an inaccurate portrayal of the black family because he did not give sufficient attention to the historic role of racial discrimination, nor did he accurately assess the diversity or the multiple strengths the black family exhibited despite the handicaps of racial and economic discrimination.

The impact of the Moynihan Report was felt long after it was thrust into the national policy arena. A particularly important reaction to the report was a "closing of the ranks" behind black families among black leaders, policy analysts and scholars for several years following. There was little public discussion of the problems of black families including the growing problem of teen pregnancy, the increase in female headed households, and black on black crime lest they be guilty of exposing some of the "in-house" problems of blacks to a white society that had already proven to be hostile to the needs and aspirations of black people.

Blacks also reacted strongly to the "social pathology" label the Moynihan Report applied to the family. This reaction was so strong, it has been suggested, that it led to the creation of a so-called "strengths of black families" body of scholarship in an effort to counteract the impact of those studies which portrayed black families from a negative perspective (Johnson, 1981; Dodson, 1981). This school of thought developed empirically based alternative perspectives and interpretations of black family life which differed sharply from the prevailing social pathology school of thought.

The strong emphasis on "strengths" of black families as well as an attempt to minimize the escalation of such problems as teen pregnancy, female headed households and black on black crime, may have unwittingly led to an exacerbation of these problems. During this dormant period the problems worsened. In retrospect, the frontal assault of the Moynihan Report made it impossible for blacks to respond in any other way at the time. It came during the height of the civil rights movement when blacks were asserting a sense of pride, dignity and self-worth as they struggled for civil rights. The negative connotation of the report did nothing to promote this sense of urgency for positive social change.

Another equally compelling reason for teen pregnancy having reached its present state is that no one really knew what to do about it, or where to intervene. There was little agreement among social welfare or civil rights organizations as to what were the causative factors, or what should be common strategies for intervention, in order to lower the rate. By the late seventies, there existed a potpourri of programs on sex education, contraception, and counseling, but little emphasis was placed on economic deprivation and the lack of life options as sources of the escalating problem.

III. SCOPE OF THE PROBLEM

About one million teens become pregnant each year (Guttmacher, 1981). In 1982, there were 523,531 births to teens. The births to teens rose when the baby generation entered the teen years and has since fallen. Moreover, the number of births to married teens have also decreased (Moore, 1985). The major change has occurred in the increase in out-of-wedlock births to teens. Today, a majority of births to adolescents are out-of-wedlock. In 1982 whites accounted for 362,101 or 38% of the out-of-wedlock births while black teens had 145,929 or 87% of the births outside marriage (Moore, 1985). By their 18th birthday, 22% of black females and 8% of white females have given birth. By the time they turn 20, 41% of black females and 19% of white females have given birth (Moore, 1985). In 1982 teens accounted for 24.6% of all black births and 12.3% of all white births (Children's Defense Fund, 1985). Therefore, while the birth rate for white teens is increasing and the rate for black teens has shown a decline, the overall rate for black teens is still very high.

TABLE 1

Births to Females under 20	1960	1970	1982
Total Births	593,746	656,460	523,531
Rate (births/1000 aged 15-19)	89.1	68.3	52.9
Marital Births	502,046	456,560	254,185
Out-of-Wedlock Births	91,700	199,900	269,346
Percent Out-of-Wedlock	15%	30%	51%

Source: K.A. Moore, Fact Sheet, Child Trends, Inc., Washington, DC: January 1985.

Black adolescent out-of-wedlock pregnancy poses special problems since the magnitude is so great (87%), and because the vast majority of black teens (90 to 94%) keep their children and do not place them for adoption (Guttmacher, 1981). Moreover, the overall rate of out-of-wedlock births to teens has dramatically increased over the past twenty years, from 15% in 1960 to 30% in 1970 to 51% in 1982.

In 1978 1.3 million children were living with 1.1 million teenage mothers. An additional 1.6 million children under the age of five were living with mothers who were teenagers when they were born (Guttmacher, 1981).

The changing world view of today's youths, precipitated by the rapidity and scope of changes in the wider society, has brought about unprecedented shifts in attitudes, values and behavior. Teens are faced with the residual effects of a sexual revolution which brought about a decline in the double standard of sexual conduct, an increase in premarital sexual activity, a lessening of the stigma attached to having a child out-of-wedlock, the legalization of abortion, and the widespread availability of contraceptives. In fact, the availability of contraceptives and abortions made it possible for American females to separate sexual relations from procreation.

American teens today also entered adolescence at a time when they experienced widespread alienation from traditional norms. By the early 1970s premarital sex had become so widespread that an estimated five million teen females and seven million teen males were sexually active. Only about 8.5% were married. The number of sexually active teenagers increased by two-thirds during the 1970s (Guttmacher, 1981). However, the proportion of teen females having premarital sex seems to have leveled off. In 1982, 30% of females aged 15-17 and 57% of females aged 18-19 reported they had had sex (Moore, 1985).

Early pregnancy is often the end result of unprotected intercourse. Adolescents seeking information on contraception do so on an average of approximately 14 months after their initial sexual experience (Guttmacher, 1981). Half of all first pregnancies occur to young women who have first had intercourse within the previous six months (Moore, 1985). However, younger teens are especially ineffective contraceptors. Among teens younger than 15 at first intercourse, only three in ten used contraception, compared to five in ten at ages 15-17 and six in ten at ages 18 or older (Moore, 1985). Of today's teens, it is estimated that four out of ten 14 years old and younger will become pregnant; two out of ten will give birth and three out of 20 will have an abortion (Guttmacher, 1981).

IV. CONSEQUENCES OF TEEN PREGNANCY

One of the major problems associated with teen pregnancy is infant mortality in which a major cause is low birth weight. One in eight black newborns is underweight (less than 5.5 pounds), compared to one in 18 white newborns. Babies born to teenage mothers are 25% more likely to be underweight than those born to 20-29 year old mothers (Children's Defense Fund, 1985). While infant mortality rates have declined since 1940 for the nation as a whole, black rates have remained about twice those of whites and are about the same as they were for whites 20 years ago (Children's Defense Fund, 1985).

Teen parents are considered high risk in pregnancy outcome because of their immature body stature and gynecological development (Hollingsworth and Kotchen, 1970). The emotional immaturity of many prevents them from seeking early prenatal care and following medical advice, thus causing them to produce low-birth weight babies (Stickle, 1981). Low birth weight babies tend to die within the first year of life, and if they survive, they may suffer from a host of serious childhood illnesses, birth injuries and neurological defects, including mental retardation (Guttmacher, 1981).

Providing medical care for the low birth weight baby is also very expensive. It can cost as much as $1500 a day to maintain an infant in a neonatal unit. Black babies are twice as likely as white babies to be born to mothers who received late prenatal care or delivered their babies without having ever had a prenatal examination. Almost one black baby out of 10 is born to a mother who received late or no care. Among black teenage mothers under age 15, the proportion increases to two in ten (Children's Defense Fund, 1985).

In addition to the many health problems, the teen mother will also have to cope with the long-range consequences of being able to receive an education and compete for adequate employment since becoming a teen parent most often means that the young mother will be unable to complete her education. One study based on a national sample found that mothers who had given birth before they reached 18 were half as likely to have graduated from high school as those who postponed childbearing until after they turned 20 (Card and Wise, 1978). This same study found that adolescent males who became fathers before age 18 were two-fifths less likely to have graduated from high school than those who waited.

With little education most teenagers are unable to obtain jobs paying decent wages and their family incomes tend to be much lower than those earned by adult families. In October, 1985 the Bureau of Labor Statistics reported that the black teenage male unemployment rate was 41.4% and the female rate was 37.9%. The rates for white teenage males was considerably lower at 18.8% and the female rate was 15.5%. (U.S. Bureau of Labor Statistics, 1985). Increasingly many of these unemployed black youths who are frequently unskilled, are the parents of young children. Chronic unemployment for adolescent males and pregnancy for adolescent females are increasingly becoming the twin social problems that afflict black youths, each of which renders hundreds of thousands impotent to cope with the exigencies of day to day living and the future.

The consequences continue to follow teen mothers throughout their lives. At any given time, 60% of children born to teenagers outside marriage, who lived and were not adopted, receive welfare. Women who had their first baby as a teenager can expect to have lower status jobs, accumulate less work experience, receive lower hourly wages, and earn less per year (Moore and Burt, 1982). While many teen parents initially perceive welfare to be a short-term stop gap method of providing for their economic needs, the reality is that their inability to complete high school, find a decent paying job, and adequate child care encourage long-term welfare dependency. In 1975, about half of the $9.4 billion invested in the Aid to Families of Dependent Children Program (AFDC) went to families in which the woman had given birth as a teenager. Six out of ten women in families receiving AFDC payments had given birth as teenagers, compared to just about one-third of women in families not receiving such payments (Guttmacher, 1981). In 1985 60% of all teen mothers received AFDC.

As already stated, an estimated 3.3 million children now live with teenage mothers, and 1.6 million children under age five live with mothers who were teens when they gave birth (Guttmacher, 1981). It is this group, the "third generation," to which serious attention must be given because the social consequences of too-early childbearing pose a dangerous and insidious threat to their lives. Born into poverty as infants to parents who are little more than children themselves, they are at serious risk educationally. The data have shown that children of teen parents suffer educational and cognitive deficits. They tend to have lower IQ and achievement scores than the children of older parents. They are also more likely to repeat at least one grade in school (Baldwin and V. Cain, 1980). This problem is exacerbated by the fact that an increasing number of teen mothers are assuming a larger and major role in the day to day care of their children. With increasing numbers of grandmothers in the labor force, and with many refusing to accept what was once the traditional responsibility of providing child care for their grandchildren, a generation of infants and children are being reared by parents who have little preparation for that role. With little education herself, the teenage parent is unable to offer the intellectual nurturing and stimulation the child needs. The teen parent also has little capacity to tend to such routine matters as assisting the child with homework, meeting with teachers on a regular basis, and encouraging the child's progress if the young parent has been an educational failure. The adolescent parent has not had the experiences nor developed the emotional maturity to provide a child with a sense of identity, self worth and stability. In an even more direct way, the teen parent is unable to provide for the child's basic material needs. Lacking the proper perspective because the young mother's psychosocial development has been severely interrupted, she is simply unable to give to the child that which she does not know how to provide. If current trends continue, it is likely that child neglect and abuse will become more heavily correlated with being a teen parent. The stress of being unemployed, the inability to pursue educational opportunities, and to conceptualize the future with life options and goals combined with emotional immaturity encourage child abuse.

Since about 1970, more than two-thirds of the first-born children of teen mothers have been conceived outside of marriage. With the lessening of societal pressures to marry to legitimate a child's birth combined with the inability of most teen fathers to become economic providers, very few teen parents marry. In fact, the Children's Defense Fund reports that over a 20-year period, since the late 1950s, the marriage rate for young black women dropped 74.1% for 15 to 17 year olds and 61.6% for 18 and 19 year olds. White rates are down by about one-third (Children's Defense Fund, 1985). Among women aged 19, the proportion of singles has risen from 60% in 1960 to 69% in 1970 to 83% in 1983 (Moore, 1985).

Even if the pregnant teenager does marry, the prospects for developing and maintaining a stable marriage are fraught with problems, and marital disruption is a frequent outcome. Divorce and separation are three times more likely with teenagers than for couples who postpone having a child until their twenties. Today's teens find it extremely difficult to sustain a marriage without the traditional family support system which would enable them to continue their education, provide child care and economic support.

V. TEEN PREGNANCY IN A BROADER CONTEXT

A recent study conducted by the Joint Center for Political Studies found that between 1980 and 1984 the number of black families headed by a separated or divorced woman increased by an average 11,500 a year, and that increase was counterbalanced by an equivalent drop of about 11,500 a year in the number of families headed by a widow. But the number of black families headed by women who had never married increased by an average of about 167,000 each year... (T)he enormous increase in the number of black female-headed families in the early 1980s was almost entirely due to out-of-wedlock births (Joint Center for Political Studies, 1985).

The increase in the number of female headed households is closely linked to teen pregnancy. While roughly 85% of black teen mothers continue to live with their families, many of their parents are single household heads living at or below the poverty level. There is also mounting evidence that many teen mothers were born to adolescent mothers, a group that is now referred to as the YGM (young grandmother), who typically are in their late twenties or early thirties. Since they were unable to achieve upward mobility in their own lives, they have often moved into an adulthood of poverty and dependency. Moreover, a large percentage of these young grandmothers were never married, nor did they have the opportunity to acquire education, jobs, decent housing, and provide a quality life for their children. In effect, they have reared their children under precarious economic circumstances. Their daughters were high risk for repeating the familial patterns of their own mothers adolescence. The most significant consequence facing both generations of women is the increased incidence of poverty. As the society moves toward a highly trained work force, both generations of women are joining the burgeoning underclass whose economic futures are severely restricted by the lack of marketable skills.

A study conducted on two generations of black teenage mothers noted that the mothers and daughters appear to have adopted a quiet resignation to their limited opportunities, and they view the current living conditions and their futures as being harsher than a similar population the author studied 20 years ago (Ladner and Gordine, 1984; Ladner, 1971). For these poor families, resources appear to be scarcer, and there is less to share, even among extended kin. If the household heads are fully employed, it often requires that all of their income be used to support their own households, and they are unable to provide for less fortunate extended family members (Ladner and Gordine, 1984).

The weakening of the extended family is closely associated with teen pregnancy. The black family has always relied heavily on the extended family to meet its obligations, especially in the area of childrearing. Urbanization has been identified as a factor in the demise of the black extended family (Martin and Martin, 1978). For example, when black families migrate to an urban area, they are faced with two major problems - jobs and housing. Unemployment and inadequate housing for multigenerational households have contributed to the weakening of the black extended family structure (Martin and Martin, 1978).

Any analysis of teen pregnancy must view it within the context of a larger number of societal problems affecting American adolescents across ethnic, social class and racial boundaries. It is increasingly likely that today's teen mother will also have problems in school and employment. Alcohol and drug abuse contribute to low birth weight infants. The teen father may also face similar social problems and is unlikely to be able to offer the sustained economic and emotional support needed by the mother and infant.

A recent study conducted by the Education Commission for the States, notes that by conservative estimates the number of at-risk youths include 1,250,000 white, 750,000 black and 375,000 Hispanic 16 to 19 year olds. In some large cities, this constitutes half the high school population, including an "unconscionable number of blacks and Hispanics." The following represent further problems affecting American youths:

- Drug and alcohol abuse among young people is up 60-fold since 1960.

- Teen pregnancy is up 109% among whites and 10% among nonwhites since 1960.

- Teen homicide is up "an astounding 232% for whites" and 16% for nonwhites since 1950.

- Suicide is up more than 150% since 1950 with a teenager committing suicide every 90 minutes (Education Commission for the States, 1985).

These alienated and economically disadvantaged youths are "disconnected" from the mainstream of the society and unless major interventions occur, they will not be able to function adequately as adults. Thus teen pregnancy is but one of the many social problems with which American youths must contend. A conclusion to be drawn is that there has been a transformation of major institutions that traditionally anchored young people, including the family and schools. Many of the functions traditionally provided by the family have been supplanted by social service and other agencies. The interruption of traditional norms for socializing youths of all backgrounds has given rise to widespread alienation. The black church, which serves as a focal point for the community, has not assumed a leadership role on teen pregnancy prevention. Most black churches tend to be conservative on the issues of premarital sex, contraceptives and abortion, especially for teens. Therefore, only the most secular-oriented progressive churches can be expected to take a leadership position on this problem. The long-term prospects are dire unless massive efforts are undertaken by private and public groups (and individuals) to address the problems.

VI. COMBATING BLACK TEEN PREGNANCY

Teen pregnancy in the black community is no longer an issue that is discussed in hushed tones among blacks. Fortunately, it is now a problem that is widely discussed, debated and dealt with openly by blacks at all levels who understand the long-term consequences it has for the family and the society at large. Social policies are unfavorable to the young and the poor, the two populations that are relatively powerless to effect substantive change in their own behalf. For example, children do not vote and adults often see teenagers as reckless, unruly individuals who have little regard for authority. Teenagers are also viewed as bringing many of their problems on themselves. Children and youth are the victims of abuse, neglect and sexual exploitation. Millions of children live in dire poverty. As a result, many of these youths have lowered aspirations and fail to strive to overcome their social disadvantages and marginality. Moreover, the structural problems including major changes in the nation's market economy, have lessened the youth's ability to become upwardly mobile. Thus the problems go far beyond those over which the teenager has control.

In confronting teen pregnancy, there is now a realization among blacks that self sufficiency and self help must become integrated into prevention programs. The traditional approaches involving teaching sex education, counseling, and providing contraceptives must be combined with an equally important comprehensive approach to the development of the total individual. Central to such a focus is the assumption that effective intervention involves shifting the emphasis from treatment of the individual pregnant adolescent to the entire adolescent population (Baldwin, 1976 and Silber, 1982).

The response of the black community to the problem of teen pregnancy has been encouraging. It is now a priority project of the National Urban League, the National Council of Negro Women and Delta Sigma Theta Sorority. Other groups have targeted high-risk populations to work with on a range of issues including teen pregnancy prevention. The Sisterhood of Black Single Mothers, the Coalition of 100 Black Women, Alpha Phi Alpha Fraternity, the Concerned Black Men of Washington, DC, the National Association for the Advancement of Colored People and the Southern Christian Leadership Conference are examples of organizations which have demonstrated concern for the problem. The Sisterhood of Black Single Mothers also played a key role in the implementation of Project Redirection, an effective secondary prevention program organized in several major cities that linked a teen mother to a "surrogate-mother" in the community who could assist the teenager with meeting her parental, school, and employment obligations.

The Children's Defense Fund, the nation's leading child advocacy organization, has launched the most ambitious program to date. With the collaboration of the National Council of Negro Women and the Coalition of 100 Black Women, the Children's Defense Fund has a broad-based adolescent Pregnancy Prevention Project that is national in scope. Among the Children's Defense Fund's various approaches to the problem is the Child Survival Bill that was introduced in the U.S. House and Senate, again this session. Specific parts of the bill address teen pregnancy including job training, health care, family planning, and school drop-out prevention for at-risk students.

To reduce teen pregnancy, a variety of approaches are now being used by private and public organizations on the local, state and national levels. In a survey conducted by the United States Conference of Mayors in May, 1985, ten cities across the country had task forces to address teen pregnancy (U.S. Conference of Mayors, 1985). Several states including Maryland and New York have statewide task forces. The multifaceted approach is needed to address the multiple causes of too-early childbearing for which there are no simple solutions. The complexity of the problem notwithstanding, the state of Wisconsin recently adopted a law that holds parents financially responsible if their children under the age of 18 have babies. Under the law, a welfare agency may take either pair of grandparents to court to make them pay for the costs of rearing an out-of-wedlock child. While the wisdom of such a law may be questioned, provisions are also included to allocate $1 million for pregnancy counseling, hospitals and clinics are prohibited from notifying parents of a girl's intent to have an abortion unless she consents, and it repeals restrictions placed on the advertising and sale of contraceptives (New York Times, November 14, 1985).

There is an emerging consensus in the field of teen pregnancy prevention that while the problem is perhaps most rooted in poverty and its attendant consequences, there are additional influential factors related to changing societal norms. These include a high divorce rate, a weakening of kinship ties, greater sexual permissiveness and the demise of many traditional values. The influences of the mass media on early sexual development of children of all races cannot be ignored. The recent victory obtained by the Washington-based Parents Music Resource Center, to label records with sexually explicit lyrics should be encouraging to those who wish to have radio and television (especially the video industry), examine the impact the industry has on encouraging youths to engage in early sexual behavior often leading to pregnancy.

A multi-faceted, comprehensive approach to teen pregnancy prevention should involve every possible segment of the community in which a program is launched, including teen males and teen fathers, parents, schools, churches and other religious organizations, social welfare and health organizations, professional and social groups, the media and public information, advocacy and other groups. The magnitude and complexity of the problem certainly encourages the involvement of the broadest group of the public and private sectors working in a collaborative effort. While the initiatives undertaken by black organizations are important, the size and seriousness of the problem make it impossible for blacks alone to solve it. Nor should it be perceived as a problem confined to and affecting only blacks, but rather one which cuts across all boundaries. Ultimately, the society as a whole will continue to pay the cost, as the toll increases rapidly. Thus it is in the interest of public policy makers, child welfare advocates, parents, educators, the religious sector, taxpayers, employers, and every other special interest group to work collaboratively to find solutions to this problem. It will not be solved by governmental decree, nor by simply ignoring the problem or by using traditional formulas which have not proven successful over time.

VII. RECOMMENDATIONS

In accordance with the view that a comprehensive community-based and family-centered approach should be undertaken in those geographical areas in which there is a high teen pregnancy density, the focus should be on several high priority areas. This was highlighted by The Mayor's Blue Ribbon Panel on Teenage Pregnancy Prevention, a city sponsored initiative in the District of Columbia that was chaired by the author in 1984-85.

The Blue Ribbon Panel was appointed by Mayor Marion Barry to achieve the following goals: (1) develop a broader public understanding of the many factors relating to early parenthood among District of Columbia teenagers and; (2) develop a program of action to reduce teenage pregnancy in the District. Over a 12-month period this 90-member panel held public hearings in high schools, and conducted a media awareness campaign and parent town meetings. The panel concluded its fact finding investigation with a major report that included 25 recommendations, some of which are incorporated in this section.

A. Parental Involvement

It is exceedingly difficult to combat teen pregnancy without the active involvement of parents of the male and female. It is within the family where parents and significant others transmit values, attitudes, and teach children coping skills. A significant aspect of the socialization process is that of teaching normative sexual behavior. A major consequence of a society that still embraces the "double standard" of sexual conduct is that, despite the existence of advanced contraceptive technology, millions of American adults lack the proper sex education, and are ill-at-ease in discussing premarital sex, contraceptives and abortion with their children. The media and peers often provide the information that parents are unable to pass on, but in the most unsatisfactory manner. Some parents want the schools to deal with such topics but few do in the consistent, informed manner in which they should. Efforts must be undertaken to work with parents in these problem areas. They should be given adult-education mini-courses on "how to talk to my child about sex." Such courses and workshops should be taught by trained personnel and offered in churches, community centers and other accessible facilities. Parents should also be an integral component of any and all initiatives addressing teen pregnancy prevention.

B. Male Involvement and Responsibility

Pregnancy and childbearing have always been considered the woman's responsibility. Pregnancy prevention is also considered to be primarily the woman's responsibility. When a teenager becomes pregnant accidentally, it is considered to be her "fault," and males are treated as if they had only nominal, if any, involvement in the conception. This has encouraged many males of all ages to shun responsibility for fatherhood, while women have been forced to assume greater responsibility. Young men must become actively involved in every phase of pregnancy prevention. Not only do they need to be aware of their responsibilities, they also need to be aware of their rights: the right not to be sexually active; the right to be, or not to be a parent; and the right to determine when they choose to become parents. In effect, they must learn that manhood is defined in terms of the ability of the individual to achieve maturity and assume responsibility for one's actions. To "father" a child does not automatically bestow "manhood" onto an individual.

The current trend in pregnancy prevention programs is to involve males as integral components. Teen pregnancy prevention will not be successful until males assume responsibility. However, considerable efforts must be undertaken before this becomes reality. Programs must be developed at the local, state and national levels to work with young men. They should focus on such issues as redefinitions of "manhood," rights and responsibilities including child support, self esteem, education, job training and placement, family planning, sex education, parenting skills, and structured opportunities for young men to discuss their feelings about sex, pregnancy, abortion, and other sensitive topics men usually are not encouraged by the society to be introspective about. The National Urban League's Male Responsibility Campaign which includes posters ("Don't Make a Baby If You Can't Be a Father") and a record by James Ingram and Howard Hewitt using the same theme is an example of the type of community awareness and public information campaign that can be undertaken. The Alpha Phi Alpha Fraternity has a program geared toward male high school student leaders, while the Concerned Black Man in Washington, DC goes into the high schools to counsel teen males.

A critical issue that blacks must deal with is the fact that a significant number of teens are impregnated by adult males who engage in exploitative relationships with these adolescents. Many of these men do not acknowledge paternity publicly nor do they contribute to the maintenance of the children. This is an issue which must be addressed immediately. Males who engage in such behavior should be prosecuted in accordance with local statues. All males, teens and adults, must be forced to assume some financial responsibility for their children whether they are born in or out-of-wedlock.

C. Schools

The schools should take greater initiative in developing relevant curriculum for sex education. All school districts across the nation should have mandated sex education from kindergarten through the 12th grade, including a special emphasis on decision making. School districts in which teen pregnancy is a problem should design intervention programs to address the high drop-out rate among teen mothers and fathers. Most schools have not focused on pregnancy prevention but must find the proper and effective techniques to do so. This includes special training for teachers, counselors, and requiring more involvement of parents in this process.

Schools are also in a unique position to offer a service to high-risk youths, who are least likely to have parents who can provide for their emotional and material needs. Self-image and school success are critical factors for adolescents. Teens who see themselves as "winners" generally have high expectations for themselves. Students who are not making it in school, do not expect that life has much to offer them in the future, and are more likely to develop a fatalistic attitude about becoming a teen mother or father. A way to counter this problem is for schools to build in recognition and success for all students at every level, K-12. Award recognition assemblies sponsored by the schools, churches, business organizations, and social groups can recognize individual students for accomplishments such as near-perfect attendance, punctuality, citizenship, volunteerism, talent, cooperation, club involvement and personal achievement-as well as academic excellence. The important factor is that the high-risk student's strengths must be built on, including traditionally non-academic achievement criteria.

Moreover, the reality is that most teenagers live and think in the present, not in the future. They need help in thinking and planning ahead for adulthood and responsibility for their lives. Programs need to be developed in the schools to help students to think ahead, formulate goals and make informed decisions about the conduct of their lives-especially with regard to family planning and careers. Specific areas of content should include:

- Occupational knowledge, decision making, career selection, education requirements and training opportunities for specific jobs, job readiness and job search skills.

- Sex education, including birth control, male responsibility, paternity rights and responsibilities and child support laws.

D. Jobs Program for High-Risk Teens

Many teens engage in sexual behavior, often leading to parenthood, because of low self-esteem emanating from the lack of material resources (money, nice clothes, recreational outlets, etc.) as well as emotional neglect. Early sexual involvement often become a substitute for the lack of such resources. Girls with low self-esteem may feel that the only thing they have of worth to offer a boyfriend is sex. Teen males frequently engage in the same type of behavior because they, too, lack those resources required to affirm their sense of worth, identity and positive self-esteem. To become a mother or a father becomes a way of proclaiming to others that one has a sense of worth and value. Therefore, it is important to provide part and full-time job opportunities to high-risk youths so they may achieve self-sufficiency without having to resort to sex as a way of affirming womanhood and manhood. Economic independence can be the most important avenue for achieving viable pregnancy prevention programs.

E. School-based Health Clinics

Perhaps the most effective intervention method for teen pregnancy prevention is the school-based health clinic which offers general health screening and physical examinations, counseling, family planning services, etc. The school-based health clinic in St. Paul, Minnesota reports a 50% decline in teen pregnancy since it opened over a decade ago. The clinics in several cities either dispense contraceptives on site or the physician writes a prescription for contraceptives for the teenager. The close physical proximity of the services provided by professionals known to the students in a friendly atmosphere of trust encourage students to use the services. A recent controversy arose over a school-based clinic at DuSable High School in Chicago when clergy and other community residents protested its presence in the school. Blacks should become more familiar with the high rate of effectiveness of this method of intervention and lobby to have them organized in schools with high rates of teen pregnancies. They would be even more effective if they incorporate job training information and referral services, and if clinic operators work collaboratively with parents (and parents groups), clergy, community leaders et al.

F. Day Care

Unfortunately, many teen parents do not complete school because of an absence of child care. They lack the money to pay for this service, and they must compete with working adults for the scarce number of day care spaces available. Failure to find adequate day care often means the girl becomes a high school drop-out, which significantly increases her chances for having a repeat pregnancy. If prevention is defined solely as "primary prevention" (i.e., preventing first pregnancies), no attention will be given to the population most likely to perpetuate the phenomenon: those teens who have already given birth are at very high risk of having rapid, repeat pregnancies, and the children of teen mothers are more likely to become teen parents themselves.

Some schools have responded to this problem by providing on site day care for the children of teen mothers. It enables the mother to continue her education, and her child can receive quality care with her involvement. While this is an added expense for school systems, the long-term benefits can be enormous since the data indicate that postponing the second pregnancy until age 20 greatly enhances the girl's opportunities for achieving self-sufficiency (Guttmacher, 1981).

G. Adoption and Foster Care

As already noted, some blacks have traditionally held negative views toward legal adoption. However, as increasing numbers of teen parents surrender their children to the courts because of neglect, abuse, and their overall inability to provide for the child's welfare, teens should be counseled to consider adoption as a viable alternative. Long-term foster care, in the long run, places the child in the "hard to place" category because of his/her age and race. Vigorous efforts must be under-taken to work with teens (and to educate the black community) on the advantages of adoption.

VIII. CONCLUSIONS

While teen pregnancy is one of the most serious far-reaching problems the black community is facing, it is one which can be resolved if the appropriate methods and commitment are devoted to solving it. Multiple intervention strategies at all levels and involving the broadest sector of the community are necessary. Primary and secondary prevention geared toward teen males and females are equally important. Various support systems must also be provided to the non-sexually active teens in order to reinforce their abilities to avoid too-early sexual involvement. The family-centered approach should be undertaken whenever possible.

While this paper has focused on the social problems facing black adolescents, it is important to emphasize that most black youths are functioning in a capable manner. Their abilities to live normal lives would be greatly enhanced if this society were to provide the necessary opportunity structures for them and their parents.

: : :

REFERENCES

1. Baldwin, W.H., "Adolescent Pregnancy and Childbearing: Growing Concerns for Americans," Population Bulletin Vol. 31, No. 1, 1976.

2. Baldwin, W.H. and Cain, V.S., "The Children of Teenage Parents," Family Planning Perspectives, Vol. 12 p. 34, 1980.

3. Billingsley, A. and Giovanonni, J. Children of the Storm: Black Children and American Child Welfare. New York: Macmillan and Company. 1972

4. Brown, C. "Manchild in the Promised Land," New York: New American Library, pp. 54-55, 1966.

5. Card, J.J. and Wise, L.L., "Teeanage Mothers and Teenage Fathers: The Impact of Early Childbearing on the Parents' Personal and Professional Lives," Family Planning Perspectives, Vol. 10 p. 199, 1978.

6. Children's Defense Fund, "Black and White Children in America: Key Facts." Washington, DC. 1985.

7. Dodson, J. "Conceptualizations of Black Families," in McAdoo, H. Black Families, Beverly Hills: Publishers, 1981.

   DuBois, W.E.B., "Efforts for Social Betterment Among Negro Americans," Atlanta University Publications No. 14, (New York: Russell and Russell, 1969), p. 10, 1909.

8. Education Commission for the States, Reconnecting Youth, 1985.

9. Alan Guttmacher Institute, "Teenage Pregnancy: The Problem That Hasn't Gone Away," New York, 1981.

10. Guttman, H. "The Black Family in Slavery and Freedom," New York, Vintage Publishers, 1976.

11. Hill, R. "Informal Adoption Among Black Families," Washington, DC: National Urban League, 1971.

12. Hill, R. "Strengths of Black Families," Washington, DC: National Urban League, 1974.

13. Hollingsworth, D.R. and Kotchen, J.M., "Gynecological Age and its Relation to Neonatal Outcome," (McAmarney et al [editor]), in Pregnancy and Childbearing During Adolescence, New York: Allan P. Liess, Publisher, 1978.

14. Johnson, C.S., "Shadow of the Plantation," Chicago: University of Chicago Press, pp. 64-65, 1934.

15. Johnson, L., 1981, "Perspectives on Black Families," Empirical Research: In McAdoo op.cit, 1965-1978.

16. Ladner, J.A., "Tomorrow's Tomorrow: The Black Woman," New York: Doubleday and Company, 1971.

17. Ladner, J.A. and Gordine, R.M., "Intergenerational Teenage Motherhood: Some Preliminary Findings," SAGE: A Scholarly Journal on Black Women, Vol. 1, No. 2, Fall, 1984.

18. Ladner, J.A., "Teenage Pregnancy: A National Problem," Washington, DC: New Directions, 1985.

19. Lewis, H., Agenda Paper No. V: The Family-Resources for Change, Washington, DC: Government Printing Office, p. 15, 1965.

20. Martin, E. and Martin, J., "The Black Extended Family," Chicago: University of Chicago Press, 1978.

21. Moore, K.A. and Burt, M.R., "Private Crisis, Public Cost - Political Perspectives on Teenage Childbearing," Washington, DC: The Urban Institute, 1982.

22. Moore, K.A., "Fact Sheet" (on Teenage Pregnancy), Washington, DC: Child Trends, Inc, 1985.

23. Moynihan, D.P., "The Negro Family: The Case for National Action," Washington, DC: Government Printing Office, 1965.

24. New York Times, November 14, 1985.

25. O'Hara, William P., "Dramatic Increases in Single Black Mothers," Focus, Joint Center for Political Studies, Vol. 13, No. 9, p. 3, September, 1985.

26. Powdermaker, H., "After Freedom: A Cultural Study in the Deep South," New York: Viking Press, 1939.

27. Rainwater, L. and Yancey, W., "The Moynihan Report and the Politics of Controversy," Cambridge: M.I.T. Press, 1967.

28. Silber, T.J., "Adolescent Pregnancy Programs: A Perspective for the Future," Journal of Sex Education and Therapy, Vol. 8, p. 48-50, 1982.

29. Silber, T.J., "Notes on the Dynamic Causes of Adolescent Pregnancy," (incorporated into the Blue Ribbon Report) op.cit, 1985.

30. Preventing Children From Having Children: Final Report of the Mayor's Blue Ribbon Panel on Teenage Pregnancy Prevention, Washington, DC: Department of Human Services, 1985.

31. United States Conference of Mayors, "City Initiatives Addressing the Problem of Teen Pregnancy," Washington, DC, 1985.

32. United States Bureau of Labor Statistics, The Employment Situation - Current Population Survey, Oct., 1985, USDC 85-471.

POLITICAL CHOICES:
A REALIGNMENT IN PARTISANSHIP AMONG BLACK VOTERS?

By

Dianne M. Pinderhughes

I. INTRODUCTION

Black voters are Democrats, among the strongest partisan identifiers as a group in contemporary American politics.[1/] However, they have not always so identified. As recently as the 1930's, blacks voted very heavily for the Republican Party. Is there a possibility in the near future that they will shift allegiance again, and return to that party? Will they change not only their present partisan identification, but also their pattern of interaction in the party system: from alliances with one party for a period of time to a more complex relationship with both or with multiple parties?

In the wake of the Jesse Jackson campaign, some blacks have expressed considerable dissatisfaction with the Democratic Party and with the Walter Mondale campaign's treatment of the Jackson candidacy. In reaction to that experience, blacks are in the process of examining and reviewing not only the logic of their alliance with the Democratic Party, but also with the structure of their partisan identification. Black political activists, and organizational elites are asking themselves, is it appropriate to change party and/or to change the way in which black voters place themselves in American politics? Having been so strongly aligned with one or the other party in the past, they wonder whether it might be politically and substantively more productive to shift to a stance to encourage competition for their support from both the Democratic and Republican parties. They also want to avoid the present situation where one of the major parties is all-white in terms of voting support, and therefore able to ignore policy concerns of black voters.[2/]

Jesse Jackson posed the question of strategy during the Carter years when he discussed greater ties with the Republican Party. More recently John E. Jacob, President of the National Urban League stated in his suggestions to the author for this paper: "This wedding to a single party is understandable when one considers that voters make choices according to what they view as in their best interests. The danger, however, is that by being so firmly committed to one party, blacks exercise only minimal influence in the other party."[3/]

In this article therefore I discuss several issues: first, I examine some of the fundamental factors which shape how racial issues affect partisan politics; secondly, I look at the possible locations of partisan change among black voters and compare them with recent 1984 survey data from the University of Michigan National Black Election Study (hereafter NBES) and from the Joint center for Political Studies/Gallup Poll (hereafter JCPS/Gallup); I discuss the concepts of partisan identification and electoral alignments and black political alignments and spin off scenarios with likely results in public policy. I also discuss the Democratic and

Republican parties' incentives to attract black voters, the benefits for blacks of continued alliance with one party in a competitive two party system, the possibility of a shift in partisan identification among black voters, the rewards of some combination of a third party independent candidacy option, and the varying policy impacts for these partisan alternatives.

II. RACE AND PARTISAN POLITICS

Racial hierarchy and collectivism, the subordination of blacks as a group to whites politically, socially and economically was incorporated into the American constitution in 1789, and though addressed periodically in the last two centuries, remains unresolved today.[4/] Hierarchy and collectivism have clearly left their imprint on the American party system: the political parties have rarely if ever competed for black voters. The American party system functions around a number of factors which are linked to economic issues, but are strongly determined by and through the primacy of race in American politics. Most black voters are only one generation into full political participation though they have lived on American soil for many more. The range of policy options offered by the parties does not appeal directly or fully to this segment of the electorate.

To understand whether blacks are realigning, or whether they should be, requires discussion of several factors. What is the status of the national system of partisanship at the moment? How do blacks affect the national system; will changes strengthen or weaken their bargaining power in national politics, for that ultimately is what such a realignment means. The answer is directly related to the position of the rest of the American electorate.

If you locate the national electorate on a continuum with liberal on the left at 10 and conservative on the right at 0, the national population centers at 5, the Democrats and Republicans center at about 4, but blacks center at 8.5. Therefore, it is structurally impossible for blacks to swing left or right between the parties. Their location on the electoral continuum precludes that strategy unlike the Free Democratic Party in West Germany which is located between the Social Democratic Party on the left, and the Christian Democratic Party on the right, and consequently serves as the political balance between them.[5/] With blacks so centered, a small shift to the right, does not necessarily increase their bargaining power because as a group they are too far from the center to affect the overall balance of power. (See Chart 1)

A question arising from this national electorate's locus is why do blacks want to change? If their goal is primarily instrumental, to increase bargaining power and political status, then the shift in alignment is sensible; if it is to enhance the group's ability to win socioeconomic benefits at the national level, one has to ask what the group, or what individuals within the group would gain by a move toward the Republican Party. Some sectors in the black population would gain and some would lose by such a shift, but would the number of those who gained or the value won by them as individuals or as a group outweigh the losses by others?

Another question which derives from this is what do the respective parties offer to blacks; that is have they pursued or have they wanted black votes as evidenced by specific policy appeals? What have blacks won from their alliance with the Democratic Party during the most recent electoral era, and what have they won or are they likely to win with the Republicans in the future?

One of the issues which will shape my response to these questions is the structure of party competition. If blacks are to increase their power through a decline in allegiance to the Democratic Party, and an increase with the Republicans, does it make sense to do so? Is the national electorate (1) predominantly allied with one party, or the other, (2) divided evenly between the two parties, (3) divided among the parties with a strong segment of independents who swing freely to one or to the other, or (4) divided among the parties with independents who lean strongly one way or the other. If one of the parties strongly dominates the electorate, then blacks have less leverage: if the Republicans hold the balance of power, they don't need blacks, and/or don't want them because of ideological differences, and the Democrats can't win even with black support. If the Democrats hold the balance of power, they can win without blacks. Theoretically blacks' position is strongest if there is an equal division in the white electorate and between parties and if there is agreement on substantive issues between blacks and the rest of the electorate. If one of the parties dominates the electorate, and if there is agreement on the issues in opposition to the position of blacks, then maneuvering room is quite limited for blacks.6/

All these issues: the ideological location and partisan identification of the rest of the electorate, the amount of competition on the partisan issues of particular significance to black voters, and relations between the parties, form the context against which and within which black voters and political strategists have to make their decisions.

III. SOURCES OF REALIGNMENT AMONG BLACK VOTERS

There are several internal factors which might generate shifts in partisan alliances among blacks; whether they result in long term realignment will depend on the Democratic Party's (and also the Republican's) response to these conflicts, and how individual black voters react to the party's answers. I project several possible situations: (1) realignment growing out of ideological or pragmatic forces, (2) realignment toward some form of third party option, (3) dealignment or movement away from partisan identification, or (4) the status quo.

Blacks are among the strongest partisan identifiers in the American electoral universe, they are the strongest Democrats, and they are the largest group within the party, constituting a full 20% of Democratic voters. As data on partisan identification from the National Black Election Study shows, 52.6% of the sample of 1139 blacks surveyed by telephone reported themselves strong Democrats, 18.3% weak Democrats. (See Table 1). By contrast only 4.0% reported themselves Republicans (2.5% weak and 1.5% strong respectively). The independents, those who lean Democratic, those who lean Republican and the independent independents equal 20.9%, although

John Petrocik argues that independents are primarily Democratic. His research shows that only 6% of black independents voted for Reagan. The JCPS/Gallup Poll shows that though the differences are minor, 55% of blacks are strong Democrats, 21% weak Democrats, 17% independents, and 6% Republicans. Independents who leaned to the Republicans were classified as Republicans. To talk of realignment at all in light of these data is especially curious.7/

The possibility of ideological realignment is most likely not for the group as a whole but for specific segments of the black population; blacks with the highest socioeconomic status for example, might be more responsive to the substantive views expressed by the Republican Party. However, much research shows the opposite: blacks at the upper end of socioeconomic status rankings fall at the liberal and Democratic end of an electoral continuum. Data from the NBES show partisan identification varies inversely by income and education. Higher income blacks are somewhat more likely to identify themselves as strong or weak Democrats as is shown in Table 1. Party identification does not vary as clearly by education since 79.3% of those with some college were strong or weak Democrats while those with a high school education or less, and those with a university degree varied from 64.9% to 68.7% in no consistent pattern. While this is a portrait at only one point in time, these figures suggest enormous population shifts would have to occur for a black Republican alliance to develop. Lower income blacks are only somewhat less likely to be strong Democrats so that there is a difference in degree rather than direction. No more than 2.1% of any income group identified as strong Republicans (the highest support possible), and that was among blacks with incomes from 0 to $10,000. The highest proportion of blacks who identified with the Republican Party were young (18-29) and suburban (10%), followed by blacks with incomes between $12,000 and $24,999 (7%), with less than a high school education (9%) and blue collar workers (7%).8/

However as the economic demarcations within the black population grow more distinct, idiosyncratic possibilities of political expression of these views increase. The first honorary recognition by Republicans of former President Richard M. Nixon since his resignation was held in New York City this past October 1985 by the National Black Republican Council. The Nixon they honored was the President who had strengthened affirmative action and implemented a minority business enterprise program: that approach is quite distinct from the policies of the Reagan Administration which has sought to end affirmative action programs and programs taking 'minority' status into account.9/

A second set of issues which might contribute to this ideological realignment affects those with high socioeconomic status, but who are also political activists, elites in government, politics, business and the professions who were activated by or affected by the Jackson campaign for President in 1984. While Jackson's original goal specified an impact on the Democratic Party's nomination process, the campaign took on a life of its own and engaged this group so strongly that it began to contemplate an actual race by Jackson for the Presidency. (See Table 2) The NBES asked respondents to evaluate whether it was good or bad for Jackson to have run for the Democratic nomination for President. While 82.3% of blacks thought it was a good idea for him to have run, the positive evaluation increased for blacks of higher income and education. As Table 2 shows, 78% of blacks from $0 to $10,000 income thought it a good idea, but 90.4% of those with incomes above $30,000 thought so. Similarly 74.4% of those with a college degree thought it a good idea. It was less important that a victory was very unlikely, than was the effect participation in the campaign had upon this group of activists who for the most part had not been involved in party or national politics before.[10]

This group was quite dissatisfied with the outcome of the Democratic convention, with the fact that Jackson won very few white votes, and with the fact that his delegate vote count did not reflect his primary or convention votes because of the Democratic Party's rules requiring a candidate to win at least 20% of the vote in a primary before he/she qualified for any delegates. Blacks were also aroused by the question of black-Jewish relations which developed from the "Hymie" incident and from Jackson's support from Louis Farrakhan, and finally by the Ferraro vice-presidential nomination.[11] All of these issues resonated with questions about the status of blacks in the party. Calculating their considerable electoral significance to the Democratic Party, blacks felt their concerns ought to have priority, but in fact found themselves jostling with other segments of the Democratic coalition, losing leadership positions and substantive battles.

Louis Farrakhan speaks out of a black nationalist tradition, and his political expressions resound with great familiarity to blacks with any degree of racial self-consciousness. His ideology is especially attractive as blacks compete with whites for status and find themselves checkmated. In eras when the rest of the nation has reacted negatively to racial reforms, blacks express greater interest in racial identity and pride, as happened in the early 1920's, after World War I, with Marcus Garvey, and in the late 1960's and early 1970's with their interest in black power, the Nation of Islam, and Pan Africanism. Whites hear Farrakhan and conclude he hates whites; blacks hear him and respond favorably to his articulation of racial pride and self-consciousness. Yet they found that the Democratic Party required Jackson to disavow his relationship with Farrakhan, in fact to deny aggressive expressions of racial pride, because they were viewed as racist and anti-Semitic.[12]

Both blacks and women sought group recognition in the 1984 campaign and blacks were angered by Mondale's failure to consult with them on the Ferraro nomination, and with his failure to recognize their concerns in the construction of the platform. Since Ferraro was chair of the platform committee their alienation was redoubled by her vice-presidential nomination. Some of these sentiments probably reflect sexism, and a misunderstanding of the platform procedures, but Shirley Chisholm who is clearly no sexist nor unfamiliar with party procedures, was no less stinging in her criticism of Mondale for his selection of Ferraro. Nevertheless, this was one of the factors shaping the response of sectors of the black elite to the Mondale candidacy and to the party in the post-election period.

They reflected these concerns to a cetain extent when queried in the NBES on how hard the Democrats work on the issues. (See Table 3) Blacks of both sexes thought the Democrats worked very or fairly hard, 71.6% of men and 76.8% among women, though the largest numbers fell into the fairly hard category for both. Upper income men were more likely to think the Democrats worked not too hard, while upper income women were more likely to think the Democrats worked fairly hard. Only black women in the $10,001-$20,000 income category thought the Democrats didn't work hard at all. Thus 27.3% of black men and 23.3% of black women thought the Democrats work not too hard or not hard at all on the issues.

The Republicans work not too hard or not hard at all according to 74.8% of black males and 75.5% among black women. About a quarter of the male and female population think the Republicans work very hard or fairly hard. Black attitudes are therefore inversely related: a quarter of blacks in the telephone survey think the Democrats work not so hard, while only a quarter think the Republicans work very hard.

Blacks activated by the civil rights movement, by party politics, and by community action programs mobilized at some stage of the last 20 years into participation within the Democratic Party, now feel discontented with the present situation which requires them to continue to play a role subordinate to whites; they feel they ought no longer have to alter their political beliefs, or their drive for leadership to other groups in the society, nor especially should they have to within the Democratic Party. Some members of this group are in search of an alternative strategy, party, or system of party politics to resolve these issues. Further research will have to investigate the specific impact of the 1984 Democratic convention on black attitudes toward the party.

A second type of realignment might arise out of more pragmatic forces. If the parties are treated as two competitive arenas which compete with each other, but which also operate somewhat independently of each other, some interesting possibilities arise. The Democratic Party has attracted increasing numbers of blacks over the last 50 years. In the early years of blacks' affiliation with the party, northern blacks who benefitted from the Roosevelt welfare programs voted Democratic. Southern blacks who might have benefitted could not vote because of southern economic and political discrimination. Most of the black population living in the rural South, was excluded from the ballot altogether. As blacks moved into northern urban areas, and as the civil rights revolution and national legislative reforms facilitated by Democrat Lyndon B. Johnson, mobilized the majority of the black voting age population, blacks voted for the Democratic Party.[13]

In recent years, the pool of black voters, professionals and managers and political activists has increased dramatically. The total black voting age population has increased from 10.5 million in 1966 to 18.4 million in 1984. Black professionals and managers have also increased dramatically since 1960 as Table 4 shows. Not all these new voters are party activists nor are all members of these professions politically active, but activists are somewhat more likely to be drawn from these groups. The extent that other unionized workers, craft and service workers have also mobilized, only strengthens the argument. As a result of these demographic changes which have directly enhanced black political organizations, blacks have won control or influence in more cities and states. The Democratic Party has benefitted from virtually all of these new voters, activists and elected officials. It is a highly competitive, very crowded arena for blacks.[14]

Several generations of black activists compete for position and benefits: the war on poverty leaders of the 1960's and 1970's, black elites who became active in the late 1970's, and now younger black professionals, the awkwardly labelled BUPPIES of recent vintage. These three groups of blacks compete, not only with each other, but with other urban ethnics, with Mexican Americans and with women.

Albert O. Hirschmann has analyzed how people behave in situations of discontent, and concludes that they have several options: loyalty: silent agreement with the organizations' operation; voice: articulation of dissatisfaction in the expectation that change will occur if a credible threat of departure is offered; and exit: the conclusion that little or no change will occur and that the best choice is therefore exit. Hirschmann offers many possible variations of how people behave, when and why they remain loyal, when they voice and when they exit. Hirschmann's theoretical models fit very nicely with the contemporary Democratic-Republican Party arenas. This is an example in which discontented blacks may use the exit option if they are further back in the Democratic Party's benefits queue. The Republican Party offers a considerably less crowded arena within which to compete.[15/]

The national parties offer radically different competitive arenas. While they also differ on their direct substantive appeals to black voters, one is overcrowded and a highly complex environment while the other has few other blacks with which to compete. The combination of high dissatisfaction and high competition within the Democratic Party for what seem to be declining benefits may encourage blacks to make use of the exit option, despite ideological incompatibilities with the Republicans.

At the local level, St. Louis and Detroit fall into this category; each has lots of blacks interested in participation and leadership, but only a limited amount of political benefits and political positions open to some black participants. Reports from both cities indicate that political control by Democratic incumbents (Detroit's Mayor Coleman Young is black) and effective competition for access to the centers of power is very high. By contrast the Republican Party has some benefits and little competition. Wayne County, Michigan County Executive William Lucas' exit to the Republican Party in preparation for a run for Governor against Democratic Governor James Blanchard may reflect the dramatic imbalance in the two parties' arenas. It may also reflect the active attention paid to Lucas by the Republican Party which is reportedly in search of credible black elected officials who can make appeals to the black population. While no such shift in party identification by a black leader has occurred in St. Louis, some reports suggest the conditions are right.[16/]

The notion of exit, voice and loyalty provides a number of possible scenarios. First will any blacks exit? In one case, some will voice but not exit, while others will exit but won't voice their dissatisfaction. Which option they choose will depend on many things including the available electoral alternatives. When the group and voter has a strong concern for and interest in substantive issues within the Democratic Party, the greater the chance of voice to rearrange policy, but if exit is chosen the less the probability the movement will be toward the Republican Party. These voters would probably move toward a third party, whether black or coalition, or a black independent candidate because the Republicans do not have the appropriate policy range to attract strong Democrats.

However, for voters and elites not so ideologically motivated, the less the opportunity for voice, the greater the chance for exit and that they will exit toward the Republican Party because costs are lower for exiting from, than for staying within and attempting to effect change within the Democratic Party, lower than third party alternatives, and lower and benefits greater within the Republican Party. Thus the question is how do blacks view the present situation; what factors will shape their reaction to their present partisan identification?

One early measure of shifts in black partisan identification could be associated with black voting behavior. In their votes for President, blacks in the NBES reported they overwhelmingly supported Mondale, though 91.4% of black women and 87.2% of black men voted for him. By income categories, black males earning $10,001-$20,000 ranged from a high of 13.0% for Reagan to a low of 9.3% for those earning $0-$10,000. Among women the range was not as great, nor was the support as strong: 9% among $10,001-$20,000, and 6.4% for $30,001-$40,000 earners. The highest support for Reagan among black women in the survey was below the lowest for Reagan among black men. There are variations in support by income category, but they are quite small.

A second area is support for Democratic and Republican candidates in races below the Presidential or ticket splitting level. Seventy-seven percent of the NBES group reported voting in House and Senate, and 82% in state and local races. Individuals typically overreport their electoral participation; the census estimated 47% of the total U.S. population voted in elections for U.S. House of Representatives and 52.6% for President. Of the NBES group who reported voting, 66.7% said they voted a straight and 33.3% a split ticket. Of those who voted for a party ticket, the over-whelming majority 95.7%, went Democratic and only 3.7% Republican. Of those who split their vote, 63.5% supported mostly Democrats, and 34.2% reported they split their support equally between the Democrats and Republicans, and only 2.3% voted mostly Republican. On the whole the black electorate shows no immediate movement toward the Republican Party.17/

Ronald Brown of the Institute for Social Research at the University of Michigan, states that younger blacks who have "been socialized at a different time, do not share the same experiences of the civil rights movement...And...this is especially true for the young, educated blacks, who feel that they have a chance of getting a good job and succeeding in this society." 18/ I predict that younger blacks will be more likely to use the exit option, perhaps with very little voice since this group also gives a 33% approval rating to President Ronald Reagan. Although their approval rating was reported as a comment on Presidential popularity rather than on the party, some of these individuals will undoubtedly carry that positive impression of Reagan into their choice of party candidates and party in years to come. This will perhaps reshape their party identification toward the Republicans, quite distinctly from that of older cohorts of blacks.

So far this essay has presumed blacks' choice of exit necessarily

involves movement into the Republican Party, but there is a another alternative: dealignment, where exit does not mean shifting from one party to
another but a movement toward partisan independence. The NBES shows that
12.4% of blacks are Independent Democrats, 5.9% are Independent Independents, and 1.6% are Independent Republicans while the JCPS/Gallup Pol-
ling data shows about 17% of all black voters are independent. Given the
different ways in which the two surveys report independents, their figures
are approximately equal.[19]

There is also a fourth option: an independent party including coalitions with other groups, an extension of the Rainbow Coalition started by
the Jackson campaign for example, or an independent black political party
in which blacks form and organize a party.

Brown, Jackson, Hatchett and Shepherd of the NBES report that 24.9%
of their sample favored a black independent party. A black party was organized as recently as 1980. The Rainbow Coalition was attractive enough
that another group called the Rainbow Alliance was formed after the 1984
campaign, which evokes but is not actually the same organization as the
one founded by Jackson. Finally blacks could focus their energies on an
independent race for the presidency, a Jesse Jackson for President race
without the ideological limitations of a Democratic campaign, and without
the organizational or ideological demands required for organizing a party
and campaign simultaneously.[20]

The final possibility of course is the status quo.

IV. REVIEW OF THEORIES OF PARTISANSHIP AND REALIGNMENT

A. The National Electorate

The American electorate has ordered itself in consistent partisan
alignments for periods lasting from three to four decades through much of
American history. These alignments survive until an accumulation of political conflicts reaches a crisis. The earliest alignment of Federalists
and Republicans competed in the late eighteenth century, the era of Jack-
sonian Democracy created the Democratic Party and brought large numbers
of new voters into politics in the 1820's; the conflict between North and
South over economic dominance created the Republican Party and secured the
solid, white dominated Democratic South; the economic crisis of the 1890's
stabilized Republican political and economic dominance over the nation and
legalized one party white Democratic rule in the South; the economic depression of the 1930's mobilized large numbers of new ethnic voters,
brought northern blacks toward the Democrats and made the Democratic Party
the creator of a new social welfare state.[21]

These realignments occur through conversion when individuals
change their voting behavior or choice of parties, by mobilization when
large numbers of new voters, members of an immigrant group, or their
children, are activated by a political crisis, or by invention when new
parties arise and reshape the partisan universe. Political mobilization
and the rise of new parties are also important in explaining realignments
because the political science literature argues people most conventionally

develop their partisan identification based on political socialization, that is learning their politics along with religious, educational and other social norms and values in the context of home and family. Even when this socialization process has not changed significantly, political mobilization of new voters, the invention of new parties such as those formed by exit from an existing party, and an economic or other societal crisis such as an attempted change in status by a previously subordinated group, may precipitate dramatic changes in the operation of the party system.22/

Important new mobilization occurred in the 1960's when southern black voters entered the electorate for the first time and in turn stimulated the mobilization of new white voters. Analysts originally interpreted this as a strengthening of existing dominance of the electorate by the Democratic Party, but another pattern has now become apparent; when blacks entered the Democratic Party they held more liberal views than most of the rest of the electorate. Southern whites with the most conservative views and in opposition to racial reform, and southern whites newly mobilized by these reforms moved toward independent or Republican positions. Nationally there was a strong backlash among whites to the civil rights reforms, to the war on poverty combined with the urban rebellions of the 1960's as reflected in northern support for George Wallace's presidential campaigns in 1968.

White voters respond to questions about their partisan identification, that they are Democratic more often than not, although the overall balance has shifted in recent years. In a recent work John Petrocik suggests that Republican partisan identification may have surpassed Democratic identification in 1984. His data show the expression of Republican partisan identification by the electorate increased significantly in late 1980, but quickly returned to a strong preference for the Democrats after the November 1980 election. Changes in partisan identification have occurred as voters have elected a Democratic president only twice in the last 20 years, and white voters have moved more decisively toward the Republican Party during that era than was the case in the past. It is not clear however whether a majority of the electorate now prefers the Republican Party.23/

The interesting question which is also one of vital importance for black voters is whether their mobilization produced a national realignment in reaction to the creation of a southern black electorate and to the development of a policy agenda of interest to blacks throughout the nation by the Democratic Party.

B. Black Partisan Alignment

How did blacks, voters or not, so loyal to the Republican Party for nearly half a century, become Democrats? The Democrats won blacks through a combination of coercive and positive incentives, and through the cooperation of the Republicans who voluntarily relinquished their alliance with black voters.

When blacks began to vote in the post-civil war era, they supported Republicans and that pattern persisted until the 1930's. But there

-94-

were important exceptions. In cities such as New York, Memphis, Cincinnati and Atlanta, and the state of Virginia, or at the national level in the 1912 presidential election, where blacks voted, ambitious white leaders in local Democratic parties interested in solidifying their electoral status, tied blacks into asymmetrical political arrangements. Knowing that the Republican Party took blacks for granted, they welcomed black voters, but failed to reward them equally. In a number of specific locations, blacks voted with the Democratic Party in an effort to enhance their political power, but that failed.24/

By the mid 1920's the constitutional reforms of the late nineteenth and early twentieth century began bearing political fruit as southern Democrats won office at local and state levels and began to climb congressional seniority ladders to chair committees. The Republican Party, trying to compete with the Democratic Party for the Solid South, disavowed its alliance with black voters, reduced the size of black delegations at presidential conventions and rearranged its alignment on racial issues to increase its attractiveness to whites.

The Democratic Party became dramatically more important to the nation in the depression of the 1930's. The Roosevelt Administration created and dispensed goods and services in vast quantities to the severely impoverished, making the party highly attractive to black voters. In a city such as Chicago, the Democratic Party nearly simultaneously captured control of the city bureaucracy and locked into place a complex, highly effective political machine which controlled office by controlling the distribution of goods and services. "...the social and economic position of most people in the second ward was such that they could not easily afford political loyalties which no longer provided material benefits." 25/ Blacks, therefore shifted their alignment in cities like Chicago although they were not in full agreement with the political position of the party at either the national or local level. All blacks did not turn Democratic in the 1930's however; 20-25% of northern blacks identified with the Republican Party during the Eisenhower Administration, while 17% to 32% actually voted Republican. Full conversion of the black population into active, positive Democrats occurred only in the 1960's when the party resolved the contradiction of a liberal national party co-existing with a racially restrictive regional party. Then southern black and northern black identification turned almost universally Democratic and participation rose to levels equal with whites' by the 1980's.26/

A number of sources suggest blacks made the transition to Democratic identification in the 1930's, with the process completed by the 1940's but as recently as the 1952, 1956 and 1960 presidential elections, 17%, 32%, and 28% of black voters supported the Republican presidential candidate. In the 1960's, positive incentives, civil rights reforms initiated by the Democratic Party and negative incentives articulated in the Goldwater candidacy, sharply increased black identification with the Democratic Party while all other voters moved away from the Democratic or Republican parties or became considerably less partisan altogether. For blacks "the intrusion of race has given the party sytem a salience it previously lacked. This salience...has had the greatest effect where there is the most room for an expansion of the black electorate, in the South." So while blacks were strongly identified with Democrats by the

1940's and 1950's, full identification of 85% or more that we think of as standard for black voting, and in the South full mobilization to Democratic partisanship, came about only after the mid 1960's.[27]

While the pattern of one party dominance has been strong in the past, more careful examination of some of the historical work on black participation shows greater complexity: that black Democrats often competed with black Republicans in some cities and with a variety of black third party activists, that the black alliance with the Democratic Party, strong in the 1940's, slightly less in the 1950's, reached full power only in the 1960's and afterwards, encouraged by a combination of Democratic policy appeals and Republican conservatism.

C. Strategic Conflict: Options And Policy Outcomes

Here lies the heart of the complex set of choices that black political leaders face today. Although they have faced such problems on other occasions in the past they have not done so with a fully mobilized and activated black electorate behind them. Both parties offer an unpalatable range of policy options, or one offers none and the other, accepting the black vote as a given, proposes fewer positions within the party and offers less attractive substantive benefits knowing its allies have no credible or obvious reasons for exit. In the absence of competition for the black vote, the Democratic Party is moving back toward a modernized version of its historically traditional constituency, southerners and white males, just as the Republican Party moved toward them in the early twentieth century by reducing its attachment to black voters.

So also the Democratic Party recently created electoral thresholds which minimize the impact of smaller groups, most obviously black and especially the Jackson rainbow coalition's leverage within the party: it selected Comptroller of the State of Illinois Roland Burris as black vice-chair for the Democratic National Committee, rather than former vice chair Mayor Richard Hatcher who had been nominated by the Black Democratic Caucus; it named Don Fowler, a white party official from South Carolina the chair of the Fairness Commission over Jesse Jackson's choice, Maynard Jackson, and it passed certain rules for that same commission and reduced the role of the minority caucuses in party committees.[28] Reports from Washington informants suggest that Democratic Party workers treat blacks within the party with annoyance and contempt as if blacks lost the election for the party. Whites for example, stop talking when blacks walk into the room.

Now this is an interesting postion; blacks must calculate the costs and benefits of remaining loyal, of loyalty with some expression of voice, or of exiting from the party. If they exit for the Republican Party, there are inherent pitfalls in such a strategy as the following cases show. In 1898 the United Colored Democracy under Boss Croker of New York mobilized, even coerced black participation; blacks' role in the Democratic Party was a dependent one in which they had no control over policy. In the 1912 Presidential election black leaders attempted to use a balance of power strategy when the Democratic candidate Wilson, and the Republican William Howard Taft, faced a credible third party candidacy,

Teddy Roosevelt of the Progressives. Blacks including W.E.B. DuBois and the NAACP moved to support Wilson who along with Roosevelt made some efforts at winning the black vote. Roosevelt's initiatives didn't last through the campaign and Wilson moved to segregate the civil service after his election. Finally after the 1976 Presidential election Jesse Jackson attempted to coerce President Carter into providing policy benefits to black voters as a reward for their strong Democratic support. This was an awkward and essentially ineffective strategy as any sanctions threatened were primarily electoral and not directly available until the next presidential election, when presumably the Republican alternative would coerce blacks back into the Democratic alliance. The threat of exit was therefore not credible; using an exit threat when blacks have no real electoral option only leaves blacks in an even weaker position politically. The party against which the threat is used, is reinforced in its original evaluation of the group's loyalty when the exit threat fails.29/

Attempting independent strategies, whether within a regular party structure or outside of it, has certain benefits and risks and is more likely to be successful under certain conditions. Hanes Walton summarized these in a comparison of black political machines: "...the independent machine distributed mainly intangible incentives, while the subordinate machine distributed mainly tangible benefits."

"In regard to the formation of both machines, the independent machine seemed to arise in a milieu when weak party or machine control existed over the black electorate; the subordinate machine arose in areas where strong party or machine control existed. However, some independent machines began as Dawson's (the late south side Chicago Congressman William Dawson who led a submachine in five black wards from the 1940's through the early 1970's) did, but became subordinate in order to remain viable; some subordinate machines on the other hand, like the one in Memphis became independent due to the collapse of the major white machine. Finally, the independent machine [the late Adam Clayton Powell's; he was congressman from Harlem and pastor of Abyssinian Baptist Church from the 1940's through the early 1970's, and chaired the House Education and Labor Committee in the 1960's] tended to be much more personalized than the subordinate, and depended more or less upon one individual than upon a well-built bureaucracy."30/

I reach several conclusions from an evaluation of black independent efforts. First an independent, personalized candidacy is much more likely to mobilize black voters. Secondly, only in eras when one or both of the political parties are weak is that candidacy likely to be effective. Third, black leaders must calculate which set or mix of tangible and/or intangible benefits they hope to gain from the campaign. An independent extra party campaign is less likely to generate tangible rewards though the candidate would certainly seek to win them, and more likely to produce intangible rewards such as higher participation, efficacy and group self-confidence. Fourth, black leaders must calculate whether such an effort: exit from the Democratic Party, via an independent campaign (or an exit from the Democratic into an alliance with the Republican Party) might not, lead into a subordinate relationship, where the other party eager for votes accepts the coalition, but offers no benefits as has happened on the occasions described above.

D. Scenarios

Black leaders must deal with three basic factors regardless of the partisan choices they make.31/ First what is the electoral balance? what are the preferences of the voters: Democratic, Republican or Independent, and most importantly is the white vote split evenly or not between the two major parties? Electoral balance is an important variable in determining the significance of the black vote.

Secondly, what are the policy appeals of the competing parties? What substantive representation is found in the policies proposed by the presidential candidate, or even if not formally proposed, what is the policy with which the candidate is most conventionally associated? Finally, how is that policy likely to be implemented; in other words is it possible that a policy attractive to blacks, once proposed is likely to be implemented? These are separate, distinct issues yet black leaders must be prepared to respond to the first and plan for the creation of the second and third. Next, I will calculate how these are likely to operate in three different political alternatives: Republican alliance, continued alliance with the Democratic Party, and an exit-Independent Strategy.

In the first option, in which blacks exit from the Democratic Party and form an alliance with the Republican Party, and in which the electoral balance is split, the black vote is very important. To construct a public policy with strong substantive appeal to black voters, the moderate sectors of the Republican Party would have had to capture the presidential nomination. A Republican nominee from the moderate sectors of the Republican Party of the likes of Robert Dole and Howard Baker, would support voting rights and affirmative action programs, but would not support increased economic social welfare programs. The deficit is important to these Republicans: they favor a tax increase, but not a spending increase for social welfare issues.

The more likely outcome (even after an alliance with the Republican Party) is that the party would select a nominee closer to the ideological heart of the party and its conservative activists, a Bush, or Kemp; in the general election when the nominee would have to appeal more broadly to the electorate, more moderate views might prevail but even these would not have great substantive appeal to black voters. A confounding factor to an alliance with greater numbers of black voters is that leading black Republicans have expressed strong anti-affirmative action positions, and have limited civil rights to political rather than economic dimensions, making it difficult for the party to disavow this group in order to appeal to the broader black population. In terms of implementation, the likely nomination of an ideological conservative (by black standards) would make the implementation of policy substantively attractive to blacks highly unlikely. In the best case, this new group would have to roll back all the policies implemented during the Reagan Administration; in the more probable outcome, it would be unwilling to do so.

In the second type of alliance, a continued relationship with the Democratic Party, blacks have two choices: loyalty without voice or loyalty with voice. If the white electorate is predominantly and overwhelmingly Republican, then the Democratic Party loses. If the white electorate is

-98-

split, or is predominantly Democratic, then the party in alliance with black voters wins.[32/]

Creating public policies to appeal to blacks is problematic because of racial concerns and tax and deficit problems; whether whites accept racial reforms is complicated by the fact that they cost money under any of the above possibilities. This problem is more important for the Democrats because of the prominence of black voters. If blacks do not address these issues strongly, the party will subordinate them to the economic and racial concerns of white voters.

Implementation becomes even more problematic in creating a governing coalition which can successfully implement the proposed policies; rolling back the Reagan reforms in a Democratic Adminstration is only modestly easier than in a Republican one. Financial and administrative issues abound because of the changes in the previous eight years. Policy discussions within the Mondale staff for the transition team reportedly focussed on the same parameters of budget deficits as the Reagan Adminstration's later did.

In the second type of posture within the Democratic Party alliance--loyalty without voice--electoral balance is the same as discussed above. However the creation of a substantive program is still problematic if not more so because the party can assume black loyalty, warn of the loss of the white vote, and therefore emphasize the need for blacks to subordinate their policy concerns to the broader goals of the party and of winning elections. Having subordinated these issues during the campaign for office, the governing Democrats will be even less likely to address and implement them in the more complex policymaking environment.

There are also several possibilities in the independent strategy: a third party option which includes an independent black party, or a coalition party formed with non-black groups. An electorate balanced between the parties advantages a third party of whatever form not at all. Third parties' influence increases only if voters decrease their association with either of the two major parties and focus in a more structured way on the type of third party blacks would also find attractive. Voters may weaken their identification with one of the major parties without also reorienting towards a third or alternative party.

Presumably blacks would create a strong substantive program in this scenario because they form a relatively greater portion of the party's constituency. They would join with other dissatisfied segments of the Democratic/Republican parties or recent independents, who, on the whole, would be more liberal than the rest of the electorate. This group would construct policy alternatives distinctive from the racial and economic constraints used within the conventional parties.

Probably the most difficult task for a third party would be to decide whether to attempt to win the presidency or other offices, or to influence the campaign/electoral/policy environment enough to reshape policy no matter who wins. Influencing the implementation of policy regardless of who wins is perhaps most difficult in this third party option because it is somewhat less likely than the traditional parties to have a large group of professionals and policy experts to staff administrative positions.

The cost of setting up an organization for a black political party is quite high and the ideological demands of the broad spectrum within the black community can be problematic when the main goal or concern is an electoral one. Some sectors of black activists find electoral politics highly attractive, while others reject it as useless or counter to black interests. The party option might make focussing on an electoral arena very difficult. A third party coalition has costs of organization similar to a black party; but its specifically electoral focus makes it more likely to be successful in influencing the electoral process, but it may have some difficulty in creating and implementing policy.

The independent campaign by a black candidate is also an interesting and possibly rewarding option. Here the choice makes the action more critical; the Democratic Party cannot win an election without the black vote. "No Democratic president and no individual who aspires to national leadership in the Democratic Party could alienate blacks as a group." [33/] The exit option creates a stronger bargaining position for blacks, but also creates other problems. How is the independent black campaign presented - does it focus primarily on racial issues; does it include a mix of nationalism and economic concerns, from the left and/or right but is it positioned to appeal to whites along a wide range of the electoral continuum?

The Democratic Party may respond over time in several ways. It may move to follow blacks but without enough white votes the party will lose so the substantive appeal creates a situation in which there are no implementation problems. This strategy compares to the 1964 Republican and the 1972 Democratic campaigns. In 1964, the Republicans nominated Senator Barry Goldwater of Arizona, a conservative at the far right of the party and thus to the right of most of the electorate. In 1972, the Democratic Party nominated Senator George McGovern of South Dakota, whose policies located him at the far left of the party and therefore of the electorate. Since Johnson won overwhelmingly in 1964, and Nixon in 1972, the two elections mirrored the other one from opposite ends of the electoral spectrum, and in each case the extreme candidate lost. Secondly, the party may move right (away from blacks) to capture the broad middle of the electorate which hasn't changed position significantly, but which seems to have moved right in its support for a charismatic President Reagan; in this case the party wins, blacks lose, and they have no influence over the formation or implementation of policy. Blacks are isolated ideologically and politically.

Finally, the party may attempt a status quo bridge of the left and right. If a black independent appeals to the left to moderate wings of Democratic and the moderate portions of the Republican Party then an independent candidacy which focuses on substantive racial and economic concerns of blacks differs from the Democratic Party but in a way which is attractive to a significant number of whites. Because such a campaign might generate increased electoral support, it may force the party to address substantive issues in a substantive appeal to voters and lead to an eventual implementation phase.

V. CONCLUSION

The chances of a simple black realignment, a shift to the Republican Party, are by all qualitative and quantitative indications, improbable. Black voters are so Democratic that a shift to the Republican Party is both structurally and ideologically unlikely. Black elites however have become more responsive to criticism from the right that the black population is out of step with the rest of the country, and to invitations from moderate Republicans to join the party. Black voters and political leaders may find the Republican Party increasingly attractive for pragmatic rather than ideological reasons. If moderate Republicans move more aggressively and convincingly to attract blacks, the shift to the Republicans could have an ideological as well as a pragmatic dimension. The National Black Republican Council's recent program in honor of former President Nixon sent a very clear message to the Republican Party that the party must be more responsive to substantive concerns of blacks such as affirmative action.

Realignment which involves shifts to a black party will move small rather than large portions of the black electorate as it has in the past. A third party coalition or an independent black campaign seem most promising because they increase blacks' influence over the policy dimensions and they threaten the Democratic Party's critical control over black voters. Even in the most optimistic of outcomes however, these two strategies are fraught with complicated problems which are not all that likely to be successful. The question is whether blacks would gain or lose by the status quo, or by one of these alternatives.

We need not assume that realignment means all blacks will shift uniformly. What seems more likely is the development of a more complex pattern of relating to the party system by black voters although there is only marginal evidence of that at the moment. Different segments of the black population may choose varying options, creating a much more diverse group of partisan voters than has been the case in the past. That is a significant form of realignment in and of itself. Even a diversification will create a situation which will make presidential campaigns more competitive.

The mixed strategy in some ways is most logical. In the same way that recognition of slavery in the constitution, and the conflict over the expansion of slavery led to civil war, shaped and reshaped the American political universe in the past, full political incorporation and mobilization of black voters forces the question of black economic citizenship squarely onto the political agenda. Political incorporation may therefore lead to a very different partisan alignment, as well as to a different pattern of partisan behavior by blacks and whites than has heretofore existed.

An important even critical conclusion to this article is to reflect briefly on the question with which this article began and on what it implies. First, I think it's highly problematic to prescribe realignment; even if one were to do it, I am not sure the prescription would be taken. Black leaders are selected by voters or by specialized sets of interests for day to day governance and for the creation and implementation of public policy. Whether it is possible for this same group also to evaluate broader questions of partisan alliance is highly problematic. Voters respond to these questions based more on their individual calculations and less on what they hear from political leaders. The Jackson campaign itself proved this point in cities like Detroit, Philadelphia and Chicago, where much as they tried, black elected officials were unable to direct or control the flood of voters who turned out for Jackson.

Black elites should certainly evaluate the possibilities discussed in this article, but prescriptive action seems both dangerous and unwarranted; black voters will be able to calculate the rewards from the alternatives offered through their own evaluation.[34/] Changes in partisan identification will arise from the results of their deliberations.

Finally, the most important information I can provide in concluding this article is the strong clear attitudes of the black population. Both the JCPS/Gallup survey and the NBES found strong Democratic partisanship, and some interest in third party or black independent campaign alternatives. The NBES shows that when blacks are asked to agree or disagree on whether discrimination is no longer a problem, 64.9% disagreed strongly and 19.8% disagreed somewhat. Those least likely to disagree strongly (49%) had no high school degrees, and earned the lowest incomes $0-$10,000 (50.7%). Blacks with university degrees and with incomes above $30,001 disagreed most often, 84.9% and 81.3% respectively, that discrimination was no longer a problem. While there is strong variation by education and income in levels of disagreement, all felt that discrimination was still a problem. Republicans, though there were very few in the survey, as well as Democrats agreed that discrimination was a problem.

To resolve this gap, blacks would have to shift their ideological positon dramatically, the rest of the electorate would have to move toward blacks, or both would have to move toward each other. Whether the Republican Party chooses to compete with the Democratic Party, whether the Democratic Party seeks to link black voters more securely through greater substantive appeals, or whether black voters set out on a search for new types of partisan arrangements, will determine the shape of the American electoral universe for the remainder of this century.

FOOTNOTES

*I would like to thank Ronald Brown, Vivian Carpenter, Shirley Hatchett, James Jackson, Roger Kanet, John Petrocik, Darryl Piggee, Michael Preston, Linda Shepherd, Denis Sullivan, and Linda Williams for their ideas, suggestions and information, all of which contributed significantly to this article.

1. Cavanaugh, Thomas E. "The Black Vote in the 1984 Presidential Election," presented at the 1985 American Political Science Association, August 29–September 1, 1985, New Orleans, Louisiana. John R. Petrocik, PARTY COALITIONS REALIGNMENTS AND THE DECLINE OF THE NEW DEAL PARTY SYSTEM, Chicago: University of Chicago, 1981. Norman Nie, Sidney Verba and John Petrocik, THE CHANGING AMERICAN VOTER, Cambridge: Harvard University Press, 1979, and Robert Axelrod, "Where the Votes Come From: An Analysis of Electoral Coalitions, 1952–1968" AMERICAN POLITICAL SCIENCE RE-VIEW, 66 (pp. 11–20) and Robert Axelrod, "Communication," AMERICAN POLITICAL SCIENCE REVIEW 76 (1982 393–396).

2. Walters, Ron "Black Democrats: Time For a Third Party?" THE NATION, November 2, 1985, 440 and 442. For a detailed description of this response see for example, Juan Williams, "The Vast Gap Between Black and White Visions of Reality," The Washington Post, March 31, 1985. Conversations with friends who are political observers in Washington confirm many of these points.

3. See transcript of Robert Dole's address to the National Urban League July 22, 1985, published as "We Can Work Together," FOCUS, 13 (August 1985), 3, 5. Also Letter to the author from John E. Jacob, President and Chief Executive Officer, National Urban League, October 11, 1985. On Jackson's activities in the mid 1970's see, Dianne Pinderhughes, "The Limits of Electoral Lobbying," presented at the National Conference of Black Political Scientists, Atlanta, Georgia, March 1980.

4. For varying presentations of Barnett's concepts of hierarchy and collectivism see Marguerite Ross Barnett, "A Theoretical Perspective on American Racial Public Policy," PUBLIC POLICY FOR THE BLACK COMMUNITY, Ed. Marguerite Ross Barnett and James A. Hefner, New York: Alfred Publishing Company, Inc., New York, 1976, 1–54; "The Congressional Black Caucus: Illusions and Realities of Power," THE NEW BLACK POLITICS: THE SEARCH FOR POLITICAL POWER, Ed. Michael B. Preston, Lenneal J. Henderson, Jr. and Paul Puryear, New York: Longman, 1982, 28–54; and "The New Federalism and the Unfinished Civil Rights Agenda," BLACK LAW JOURNAL 8 (1982) 375–386.

5. Conversation with Roger Kanet, Department of Political Science, University of Illinois, Urbana, November 11, 1985.

6. See Robinson, Pearl "Whither the Future of Blacks in the Republican Party?, POLITICAL SCIENCE QUARTERLY, 97 (Summer 1982) 207-231, and the same pattern cited and discussed in Dianne M. Pinderhughes, "The Black Vote: The Sleeping Giant," THE STATE OF BLACK AMERICA 1984, New York: The National Urban League, January 1984, 78.

7. The JCPS/Gallup survey was conducted in July-August of 1984 of 902 blacks and 1365 whites, as reported in Thomas E. Cavanaugh, "The Black Vote in the 1984 Presidential Election," presented at the American Political Science Association, New Orleans, La., August 29-September 1, 1985. National Black Election Study, Institute for Social Relations, University of Michigan. I would like to thank James Jackson, Ronald Brown, Shirley Hatchett and Linda Shepherd for making the NBES data available. The National Black Election Study reports data from a telephone survey of the black population including tests administered before and after the 1984 election. The survey is of 1293 individuals questioned immediately after the 1984 presidential election. It is not a representative sample of the entire black population, but of the black population which has telephones. This has certain consequences for the characteristics of the resulting sample: people without phones are more likely to be black, to be poor and to be from the South. So because the black population is less likely to have phones the black population which does have them and which is sampled in this study is of a specific character. It is much more likely to be educated: 26% have some college without a degree, and 17.3% have a university degree, higher income 17.1% earn $20,001 to $30,000 and 22% $30,001 or more. The sample is also 38.8% male and 61.2% female which Shirley Hatchett reports is characteristic of contemporary surveys by the Census Bureau as well as an earlier study conducted by the same Michigan researchers. This may reflect the increase in black women who head households, and the fact that some significant portions of the black male population are institutionalized (in prison).

    The researchers worked initially with an equal probability design, random digit dialing, but moved to a disproportionate design aimed at sampling first from large cities, second from states with a large black population, the South, and finally from the remainder of the United States. The researchers "attempt[ed] to isolate areas with high proportions of telephone users who are black. Large sampling fractions are then applied to those strata, relative to those with lower proportions black." "Telephone Sample Design For The Black Household Population," Kathryn M. Inglis, Robert M. Groves, Steven G. Heeringa, The University of Michigan. Paper presented to the American Statistical Association Meeting, Las Vegas, Nevada, August 1985, 1. The sample was then weighted to balance the overselection of telephone numbers from northern cities and from southern states. The sample reflects blacks who have telephones and therefore includes a higher proportion of educated, higher income households. Among those with phones, blacks have a high rate of shut-offs or temporary disconnections.

8.   NBES; Cavanaugh, 26.

9.   Booker, Simeon "Black GOP Businessman Laud Ex-President Nixon At
     Gala Dinner in New York," JET MAGAZINE, November 4, 1985, 6-7,
     10. There is typically not a great difference in participation
     by socioeconomic status among blacks. See, for example, Sidney
     Verba and Norman Nie, PARTICIPATION IN AMERICA, New York: Harper
     and Row Publishers, 1972.

10. Jackson's candidacy has been discussed on numerous occasions by
     black intellectuals and political activists. See for example,
     Robert Smith and Joseph P. McCormick II, "The Challenge of a
     Black Presidential Candidacy (1984): An Assessment," NEW DIREC-
     TIONS, April 1985, 24-31 Thomas E. Cavanaugh and Lorn Foster,
     JESSE JACKSON'S CAMPAIGN: THE PRIMARIES AND CAUCUSES, Washington:
     Joint Center for Political Studies, 1984. A number of conferences
     addressed the subject: Joint Center for Political Studies, re-
     ported as "Black Politics after the 1984 Elections," April 30,
     1985 FOCUS 13 (October 1985) 5-8; also see "Black Electoral
     Politics: Chicago and the U.S.," Lucius J. Barker, Guest Editor,
     PS (Summer 1983), 480-507 including articles on a black presiden-
     tial candidacy by Marguerite Ross Barnett, Ronald Walters, Mack
     Jones and Paula McClain. Also see Henry A. Plotkin, "Issues in
     the Campaign," THE ELECTION OF 1984, REPORTS AND INTERPRETATIONS,
     Ed. Marlene Michels Pomper, Chatham, New Jersey: Chatham House
     Publishers, 1985, 44-48, for his discussion of Jackson's impact
     on the campaign.

11. Walters, "Black Democrats: Time For a Third Party?" THE NATION,
     440, 442; Plotkin, "Issues in the Campaign," 47. This occurred
     after the highly publicized photograph of Jackson embracing Yasir
     Arafat, and made him the subject of criticism from Jewish and
     other voters.

12. Cronon, E. David BLACK MOSES: THE STORY OF MARCUS GARVEY AND THE
     UNIVERSAL NEGRO IMPROVEMENT ASSOCIATION, Madison: University of
     Wisconsin Press, 1969; see Harold Cruse THE CRISIS OF THE NEGRO
     INTELLECTUAL, New York: William Morrow and Company, Inc., 1967,
     for discussions of Marcus Garvey and Black Nationalism throughout
     the book. Cruse also examines earlier conflicts between blacks
     and Jews in the chapter "Negroes and Jews - the Two Nationalisms
     and the Bloc(ked) Plurality," 476-497. Also see Dianne M.
     Pinderhughes, RACE AND ETHNICITY IN CHICAGO POLITICS: A REEXAMI-
     NATION OF PLURALIST THEORY, Champaign, Illinois: The University
     of Illinois Press, 1986, Chapter 5, for a discussion of the com-
     plex and conflicting dimensions of political philosophies within
     black politics, and also see C. Eric Lincoln, THE BLACK MUSLIMS
     IN AMERICA, Beacon Press, 1973.

13. Walton, Jr., Hanes INVISIBLE POLITICS, BLACK POLITICAL BEHAVIOR,
     Albany, New York: State University of New York Press, 1985, 141.

14. BLACK ELECTED OFFICIALS A NATIONAL ROSTER 1984, New York: Joint Center for Political Studies, UNIPUB A Division of R.R. Bowker Company, 1984, 17 for increase in black elected officials. Cavanaugh, 19.

15. Hirschmann, Albert O. EXIT, VOICE AND LOYALTY, RESPONSE TO DECLINE IN FIRMS, ORGANIZATIONS AND STATES, Cambridge: Harvard University Press, 1970.

16. New York Times, May 5, 9, 1985. Conversation with Darryl Piggee, October 1985.

17. PROJECTIONS OF THE POPULATION OF VOTING AGE FOR STATES: NOVEMBER 1982, Current Population Reports, U.S. Department of Commerce, Bureau of the Census, 2.

18. New York Times, October 15, 1985.

19. National Black Election Study; Cavanaugh "The Black Vote in the 1984 Presidential Election," Paper presented to the American Political Science Association, August 29-Septermber 1, 1985. 17.

20. Walters, "Black Democrats...," November 2, 1985.

21. Petrocik, PARTY COALITIONS AND REALIGNMENTS..., Chicago 1981; also Denis Sullivan, Richard Winters, Robert T. Nakamura, HOW AMERICA IS RULED, New York: John Wiley and Sons, 1980, 162-169.

22. Petrocik, ibid; Kristi Andersen, THE CREATION OF A DEMOCRATIC MAJORITY, Chicago: The University of Chicago Press, 1979.

23. Petrocik, John R. "The Post New Deal Party Coalitions and the Election of 1984," Paper presented at the American Political Science Association, August 29-September 1, 1985, New Orleans, La., 10.

24. Walton, Jr., Hanes BLACK POLITICS: A THEORETICAL AND STRUCTURAL ANALYSIS, Philadelphia: The Lippincott Company, 1972, and THE NEGRO IN THIRD PARTY POLITICS, Philadelphia: The Dorrance Company, 1969. For other sources on black parties see Ron Daniels, "National Black Political Assembly, Building Independent Black Politics in the 1980's," BLACK SCHOLAR 15 (July/August 1984) 34-44, reprinted from 1980 edition on the assembly formed after the 1972 black convention in Gary; Chuck Stone, "Black Politics, Third Force, Third Party or Third Class Influence," BLACK SCHOLAR 15 (July/August 1984) 2-7, and Ronald Walters, "Strategy for 1976: A Black Political Party," BLACK SCHOLAR 15 (July/August 1984) 14-25, a reprint of an earlier article on the 1976 presidential campaign.

25. Andersen, 106. See Dianne Pinderhughes, RACE AND ETHNICITY IN CHICAGO POLITICS, for a description of coercive partisan shift.

26. Axelrod, "Communication," 1982, 393. Petrocik, pp. 82-83, and 88-89. For a contemporary analysis of survey data on black partisanship and independence, see Ronald Brown, James S. Jackson, Shirley Hatchett and Linda Shepard, "Support for a Black Political Party, Black Political Independence in the 1980's and Beyond," presented at the 1985 American Political Science Association, New Orleans, Louisiana, August 28-September 1, 1985.

27. For sources on changes in black partisan identification, see Petrocik, 1981; and Norman Nie, Sidney Verba and John Petrocik, THE CHANGING AMERICAN VOTER, Cambridge: Harvard University Press, 1979, Walton, 1972. For information on black support for Democratic presidential candidates see Axelrod, 1982, 393-396, and quotation from Petrocik, 1981, 107-108.

28. Walters, 1985, 440, 442.

29. 1912 election, Walton, 1969; New York, Walton, 1972; Jackson and Carter, Pinderhughes, 1980.

30. Quote from Walton, 1972, 68-69. See William J. Grimshaw, BLACK POLITICS IN CHICAGO: THE QUEST FOR LEADERSHIP 1939-1979, Chicago: Loyola University of Chicago, 1980 for a critical analysis of the Dawson machine; see Dianne M. Pinderhughes, RACE AND ETHNICITY IN CHICAGO POLITICS, 1986 for an examination of the formation of the Chicago machine and of black participation in it.

31. I would like to thank my colleague, Professor Michael Preston of the Department of Political Science of the University of Illinois, Urbana-Champaign for helping me sort out the types of alliances likely to develop and the possible outcomes from the alliances.

32. The reader should know that this is a highly simplified discussion of electoral patterns; deviating elections can occur for example when voters who are otherwise Democratic or Republican vote for the other party because of short term forces such as the personality of the candidate or of other specific issues.

33. Petrocik, 1981, 97.

34. Some observers have already argued that black leaders do not represent the black public because of reported differences in political attitudes. See Linda S. Lichter, "Who Speaks for Black America?" PUBLIC OPINION, (August/September 1985), 41-44, 58; also see the Statement by Eddie N. Williams, President of the Joint Center for Political Studies, October 4, 1985, which comments on the Lichter article and notes a number of methodological difficulties with her survey.

TABLE 1

Party Identification by Income

Income	Strong Dem	Weak Dem	Ind Dem	Ind Ind	Ind Rep	Weak Rep	Strong Rep	Other & Apol	Revised Total
1-10,000	51.1%	16.3	10.0	6.6	2.7	3.3	2.1	7.9	100% (331)
10,001-20,000	46.3%	23.6	14.8	4.5	3.4	4.0	1.7	1.7	100% (352)
20,001-30,000	57.0%	20.5	12.5	3.5	2.5	1.5	0.5	2.0	100% (200)
30,001-40,000+	59.8%	12.1	12.1	8.6	1.6	0.0	1.2	4.7	100% (256)
Revised Total	52.6% (599)	18.3 (209)	12.4 (141)	5.9 (67)	2.6 (30)	2.5 (28)	1.5 (17)	4.2 (48)	100% (1139)

Source: National Black Election Study

'Revised' Total indicates number surveyed after weighting

TABLE 2

Evaluation of Jackson Campaign by Income

Income	Good Idea	Bad Idea	Rev. Total
0-10,000	78.0%	22.0	100% (350)
10,001-20,000	76.8%	23.2	100% (360)
20,001-30,000	88.9%	11.1	100% (200)
30,001-40,000+	90.4%	12.1	100% (257)
Revised Total	82.3% (925)	17.1 (199)	100% (1124)

Source: National Black Election Study

Question:
Do you think it was a good idea or bad idea for Jesse Jackson to have run for the Democratic nomination for President?

TABLE 3

How Hard the Democrats Work on the Issues by Sex & Income

Males	Very Hard	Fairly Hard	Not too Hard	Not Hard at All	Revised Total
0-10,000	25.8%	51.7	19.1	3.4	100% (89)
10,001-20,000	21.3%	51.5	18.4	8.8	100% (136)
20,001-30,000	23.2%	45.1	28.0	3.7	100% (82)
30,001-40,000+	14.5%	54.2	23.7	7.6	100% (131)
Revised Total	20.5% (90)	51.1 (224)	21.9 (96)	6.4 (28)	100% (438)

Females	Very Hard	Fairly Hard	Not too Hard	Not Hard at All	Revised Total
0-10,000	36.6%	39.1	20.2	4.2	100% (238)
10,001-20,000	34.0%	40.1	17.0	9.0	100% (212)
20,001-30,000	22.0%	57.6	17.8	2.5	100% (118)
30,001-40,000+	31.5%	49.2	16.9	2.4	100% (124)
Revised Total	32.4% (224)	44.4% (307)	18.2% (126)	5.1% (35)	100% (692)

Source: National Black Election Study

TABLE 4
Black Professionals and Managers
1960-1980

Occupation	1960	1970	% increase	1980	% increase Over 1960
Total Employed	6,087,47[1]	7,361,143	20.9%	8,854,048	45.4%
Managers & Prof Specialists	88,098	170,035	93.0%	1,317,080	1395.0%
Teachers	132,139	223,263	68.9%	354,176	170.3%
College Profs & Instructors	7,483	16,810	124.6%	29,917	299.7%
Lawyers & Judges	2,440	3,399	39.3%	14,839	508.1%
Physicians & Surgeons	4,996	6,106	22.2%	13,391	168.0%
Social Scientists	1,076	3,088	186.9%	11,708	801.1%
Social & Welfare Workers	10,372	33,869	223.0%	82,957	699.8%

Source:
1. Table 3, "Race of Employed Civilian Labor Force," U.S. Census of Population, 1960, Subject Reports, Occupational Characteristics, 1963, 21-22. (14 years and over)
2. Table 273, "Occupation of Employed Persons," U.S. Census of Population 1970, Detailed Characteristics, U.S. Summary, 1973, 1-739-745. (16 years and over)
3. Table 278, "Detailed Occupation of Employed Person by Sex, Race and Spanish Origin," U.S. Census of Population 1980 Characteristics of Population, Detailed Population Characteristics, June 1984, 1-196-197. (16 years and over)

TABLE 5
Vote For President By Sex and Income
1984

Males	Reagan	Mondale	Other	Revised Total
0-10,000	9.3%	90.7	0	100% (54)
10,001-20,000	13.0%	84.3	2.8	100% (108)
20,001-30,000	12.1%	86.4	1.5	100% (66)
30,001-40,000+	11.1%	88.9	0	100% (133)
Revised Total	11.6% (39)	87.2% (293)	1.2% (4)	100% (336)

Females	Reagan	Mondale	Other	Revised Total
0-10,000	8.2%	91.2	0.6	100% (159)
10,001-20,000	9.0%	91.0	0	100% (144)
20,001-30,000	6.5%	91.3	2.2	100% (92)
30,001-40,000+	6.4%	92.6	1.1	100% (94)
Revised Total	7.8% (38)	91.4% (447)	.8% (4)	100% (489)

(The numbers in parenthesis indicate total number of respondents in that category).

Source: National Black Election Study

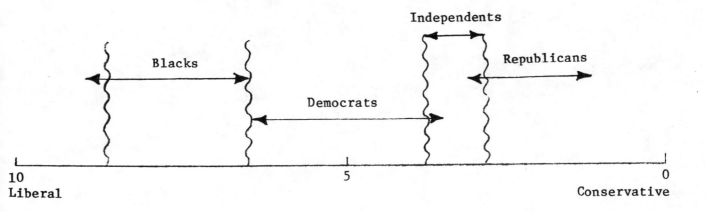

Chart I
The American Electorate

10
Liberal

5

0
Conservative

NATIONAL HOUSING POLICIES AND BLACK AMERICA: TRENDS, ISSUES, AND IMPLICATIONS

By

John O. Calmore

> Policy words are important only insofar as they may be translated into living reality. Thus an understanding of the potential for this transformation is possible only from an understanding of the social condition that gave rise to the policy, and the nature and extent of the social evil to which the policy is directed.[1]

I. INTRODUCTION

The "disadvantageous distinction"[2] of being black in America probably presents its most diverse, complex, and intractable problems in our attempts to secure viable property rights and housing opportunities. Problems associated with where we live, under what conditions, and why have plagued Black America since slavery. Indeed the continual push for equal treatment and real housing opportunities has been Black America's Sisyphean rock. While this rock has grown appreciably lighter for some, its general tendency nonetheless is to persist in rolling back to the bottom of our hill. And this tendency impacts most severely on the 36% of poor black Americans. It is for this reason that, in a normative sense, we can no longer expect to advance housing opportunities for Black America with- out primarily addressing the need to meet the housing deprivation of Black America's poor.

While virtually all socio-economic indices point to the need for an enlarged commitment to low-income housing and to fair housing, and while cutbacks in subsidized housing began under the Ford and Carter Administrations, the Reagan Administration has not merely cutback further on that commitment, but has derailed it.[3]

Throughout the 50-year history of federal housing programs, Congress has sought to increase the number of units which are subsidized and the amount of subsidies available in order, eventually, to enable every American family to secure a decent home in a suitable living environment. Two decades ago, Congress declared that this goal could be achieved in ten years by the construction or rehabilitation of six million units of housing for low and moderate income families.[4] Since then the government has spent over $100 billion on housing programs presently aiding over 15 million people, yet decent, safe, and sanitary housing remains beyond the means of another seven million households.[5]

Since 1981 and the coming of Ronald Reagan, funding for adding to the supply of low-income housing has been radically reduced and occasionally knocked down to an annualized rate of zero, when pipeline purges, recaptures and rescissions are taken into account. Although ultimately rejected by Congress, the Administration's budget for fiscal year 1986 proposed an absolute halt to the authorization of new units for two years.

This proposal was presented at a time when waiting lists for public housing and other subsidized projects across the nation are years long, when most housing authorities regularly suspend taking applications for the Section 8 Existing Housing Program because demand so exceeds the few slots available and, when housing authorities which do open up the application process get deluged with thousands of applicants for the few slots that are available. At the same time the number of individuals and families across the nation who have no homes at all is outrageous and growing.[6]

Congressman William Gray, the present House Budget Committee Chairman, correctly criticized the proposed housing moratorium. In March, 1985 he stated, "These drastic domestic program reductions, such as are recommended for housing and community development programs are not based on reducing the federal deficit. In reality, the decrease...is more than offset by the increase in defense programs and represents a shift in federal priorities rather than true deficit reduction."[7] The "centerpiece" of the nation's housing program under Reagan has dwindled to an inadequate private market voucher system that reduces the low-income housing problem to the lack of ability to pay rent. Increasing the supply, preserving the existing supply, protecting tenant rights and co-ordinating housing and community development are diminished concerns.

While racial discrimination in housing remains widely prevalent, "where it is even more deeply entrenched and stubborn than elsewhere,"[8] President Reagan operates on the assumption that the future, colorblind society has already arrived. As Martin Sloane points out, from 1981 until the present, the government has been in a period of retrenchment, severely reducing its activities to affirmatively enforce or further fair housing. Appearing recently before the U.S. Commission on Civil Rights Sloane stated:

> The Federal Government currently exhibits no enthusiasm in carrying out statutory and constitutional mandates of nondiscrimination in housing. Indeed, the Government, measured by its actions during the present administration, appears to be engaged in an effort to dismantle the very legal and programmatic structure by which the fragile foundation of fair housing has been painfully built over the past three decades.[9]

In light of these policy trends and others, we will examine emerging issues and implications for the housing state of Black America. The following topics will be discussed: (1) the growing link between racial discrimination and social disadvantage; (2) the problem of housing deprivation; (3) the paradigm shifts in national low-income housing programs; (4) the dysfunctions of integration imperatives, and (5) the need to achieve a fair housing goal of "spatial equality" and community enrichment.[10]

II. DISCRIMINATION AND SOCIAL DISADVANTAGE

With respect to housing, the present state of affairs is particularly distressing because racism has combined so synergistically with class oppression. For Black America fair housing and low-income housing must now be considered in combination.[11] Often the best, and sometimes the only proof of racial discrimination is proof of the correlation between economic inequality and race. As stated by Professor Horwitz, because America treats and accepts inequality as both an incentive and reward for talent and industry, we are faced with trying to distinguish between the indistinguishable. We are asked to tolerate social and economic inequality even though it is the best evidence of racial discrimination.[12] Thus, Father Drinan, a co-author of the Fair Housing Amendments Act of 1980, perceptively inquires: "Can 'fair' housing come about if the economic disparity between white and black citizens is not first lessened?"[13]

The wrong answer to Father Drinan's question is reflected by President Reagan's low-income housing retrenchment. In hearings before the U.S. Commission on Civil Rights, on November 13, 1985, Jane McGrew, General Counsel of the United States Department of Housing and Urban Development under the Carter Administration, stated:

> The lack of federal funds for assisted housing produc-
> tion and acquisition is a significant impediment to
> fair housing or even decent housing. Litigation and
> public housing audits are pointless unless the re-
> sources are available to provide remedies. Housing
> vouchers and Section 8 certificates do not, in prac-
> tice, accomplish desegregation or integration unless
> families are personally assisted in finding units out-
> side impacted areas. The current allocation of this
> nation's resources for housing is not commensurate
> with need or our professed desire to achieve fair
> housing.[14]

Writing in a recent edition of the New York Times Magazine on the topic "What Constitutes a Civil Right," Morris Abram, the present vice-chairman of the Commission provides another wrong answer, stating that during President Johnson's administration the civil rights movement became "fractured and confused" by treating economic claims as civil rights and holding to an idea of "rights" that included economic entitlements--a "right" to shelter, a "right" to health care, a "right" to day care for children. According to Commissioner Abram, "The movement demanded these rights even though none of them are to be found in the Constitution. By treating economics as civil rights, the new movement lost dawning societal consensus. When economic and social goals were asserted as civil rights, the movement lost a certain moral force and its unity was fractured."[15] In 1986 and beyond, Black America's civil rights agenda must embrace precisely the idea of rights that Mr. Abram rejects expressly and the Administration rejects implicitly.

Although in absolute numbers there are more whites than blacks mired in poverty, blacks carry a dramatically disproportionate burden of po-verty. Almost 36% of all blacks - more than one out of every three - lived in poverty in 1983. This represents the highest black poverty rate since the Census Bureau began collecting data on poverty in 1966. An additional 1.3 million blacks became poor from 1980 to 1983. Almost half

(47%) of all black children, over half of all blacks living in households headed by a woman, over one-third of the black elderly, over one-third of all adult women of prime working age, and nearly one-fourth of all black men of prime working age, are now in poverty. Since 1980, the gap between black and white poverty has widened further. The proportion of blacks falling into poverty since 1980 is almost double that of whites who fell into poverty during this period. In other words, although blacks make up 12% of the U.S. population, they comprised 22% of those becoming poor since 1980. Thus blacks were nearly twice as likely to have fallen into poverty since 1980 as other Americans were.[16]

Because of the disparity here, many times blacks' claims for substantive distributive justice are essentially race claims. Many times, however, what begins as a claim concerning the _effects_ of racial discrimination gets transformed in constitutional analysis into a complaint not of racial injustice but economic injustice and then denied in judicially and legislatively reformulated terms. This means, then, that the victim of racial discrimination must hold out until the nation embraces the utopian notion that everyone is entitled to distributive justice.[17]

III. THE HOUSING DEPRIVATION PROBLEM

Black America's housing problems are those of deprivation, compounded by racial discrimination and disproportionate economic class subjugation. Social response to housing deprivation has proven to be problematical not only because of the implications of race and class, but also because the problems have so many dimensions and because the concept of "housing" is so complex.[18]

While shelter is certainly a principal component in defining "housing", the concept of housing entails much more. Housing refers to a collection of things packaged together, not just four walls and a roof overhead. The collection includes a specific location with respect to employment and services, environmental amenities, neighbors and neighborhood, property rights, privacy considerations, opportunities for income and investment, and emotional or psychological symbols and supports. This collection and more are "bundled" together. Economists characterize the bundle as "a heterogeneous set of attributes which must be consumed jointly."[19] The importance of seeing housing as more than shelter is important.

This idea of housing as a bundle of disparate but inseparable elements prompts a recognition of the complexity that must underlie action, planning, policy, and practice if they are to be effective and avoid unanticipated side effects. As Professor Montgomery points out, "Action of any kind directed at any one or more aspects or attributes of the housing bundle will have repercussions on other parts of the bundle. These repercussions may defeat the original objective of the action or involve side effects too costly to be worth achieving that objective however valuable in and of itself."[20] The bundle concept helps insure that analytical thinking about housing will consider this interconnectedness and its implications.

One facet of the housing deprivation problem occurs when housing markets fail to meet the needs of population groups that are unable to compete effectively. Among such groups are blacks and other nonwhites who are restricted to substandard dwellings and undesirable neighborhoods because of discriminatory, exclusionary market practices. Also included among these groups are those whose incomes are inadequate to enable them to obtain "decent, safe and sanitary housing" or who must spend an excessive proportion of their incomes to obtain such housing, forcing them to forego adequately meeting other basic needs.[21] Some blacks are able to mitigate the damage of poverty. The fortunate few in federally assisted or subsidized housing, at least, are relieved of their rent-paying burden because most of the government housing programs restrict tenant contribution to rent to no more than 30% of the tenant's adjusted income. The housing deprivation problem of poor people, however, expands beyond this. Grigsby and Rosenburg identify at least 12 dimensions of the housing problem of the poor:

> Lack of adequate housing, space, quality, and furnishings; poor neighborhood environment; excessive housing costs relative to family income; lack of security of occupancy; restrictions upon choice of tenure; restricted locational choice; lack of special housing services for the physically handicapped; racial discrimination; excessive housing cost relative to quality and quantity of space received; and the stigma attached to receiving housing assistance.[22]

Title VIII of the 1968 Civil Rights Act declares that it is the policy of the United States to provide for "fair housing" throughout the nation. The statute bars both private and public discrimination in the sale or rental of housing.[23] Section 1982, enacted originally in 1866 by the Reconstruction Congress, provides: "All citizens of the United States shall have the same right...as enjoyed by white citizens to inherit, purchase, lease, sell, hold and convey real and personal property."[24]

Although "fair housing" is national policy, the 1968 Act does not define the term.[25] Thus, this policy has been given a wide variety of meanings. President Richard Nixon defined the term as "the achievement of a condition in which individuals of similar income levels in the same market area have a like range of housing choices available to them regardless of their race, color, or national origin."[26] In 1970, the Commission on Civil Rights, speaking in broader terms, stated that a goal of fair housing would be to increase the accessibility of nonwhites to housing throughout the metropolitan areas.[27] Professor Chandler argues that a possible goal of national policy "should be to undo the results of officially approved housing discrimination between the years of 1930 and 1962. This goal would include the achievement of residential integration of the metropolitan areas of the nation, thereby cojoining the 1949 goal of 'a decent home and a suitable living environment for every American family' with the apparent 1968 goal of removing racial barriers to home acquisition."[28] Additionally, we should note, even the most conservative definition of fair housing will necessarily regard eradicating discrimination.

Karl Taeuber says, however, "...despite court rulings and legislation clearly outlawing virtually all types of racial discrimination in housing, past patterns persist, and every investigation uncovers evidence that old impediments to free choice of residence by blacks continue."[29] He refers to the following practices:

1. Racially motivated site selection and tenant assignment policies in public housing.

2. Racially motivated site selection, financing, sales, and rental policies of other types of government-subsidized housing, e.g., Federal Housing Administration and Veterans Administration insurance programs.

3. Racially motivated site selection, relocation policies and practices, and redevelopment policies in urban renewal programs.

4. Zoning and annexation policies that foster racial segregation.

5. Restrictive covenants attached to housing deeds.

6. Policies of financial institutions that discourage prospective developers of racially integrated private housing.

7. Policies of financial institutions that allocate mortgage funds and rehabilitation loans to blacks only if they live in predominantly black areas.

8. Practices of the real estate industry such as: (a) limiting the access of black brokers to realty associations and multiple listing services; (b) refusals by white realtors to cobroker on transactions that would foster racial integration; (c) "blockbusting," "panic selling," and racial steering; (d) racially identifying vacancies, overtly or by nominally benign codes (e.g., advertising housing according to racially identifiable schools or other neighborhoods); (f) reprimanding or penalizing brokers and salesmen who act to facilitate racial integration.

9. Racially discriminatory practices by individual homeowners and landlords.[30]

In Alan Freeman's article, "Legitimizing Racial Discrimination Through Antidiscrimination Law: A Critical Review of Supreme Court Doctrine,"[31] he points out that the concept of racial discrimination may be approached from two very different perspectives, either that of the "victim" or the "perpetrator." From the former view, racial discrimination describes the actual conditions associated with being victimized by a racist society: the lack of money, jobs, quality education, and affordable, decent housing. The perpetrator's perspective makes antidiscrimination law indifferent to the victim's conditions because it narrowly focuses on remedying the acts, or series of acts, inflicted on the victim by an identifiable wrongdoer. The overall life situation of the victimized group is largely ignored. Whereas from the victim's perspective, remedial measures require an affirmative effort to eliminate the oppressive conditions, from the perpetrator's perspective, the goal is merely to neutralize the wrongdoer's improper conduct. With the host of historical and institutional factors conspiring toward discrimination in the housing of nonwhites, the effort to neutralize the acts of wrongdoers is virtually impossible, except in rather isolated, individual cases.[32]/

According to Professor Freeman:

> Central to the perpetrator's perspective are the twin notions of "fault" and "causation."
>
> The fault concept gives rise to a complacency about one's own moral status: it creates a class of "innocents," who need not feel any personal responsibility for the conditions associated with discrimination, and who therefore feel great resentment when called upon to bear any burdens in connection with remedying violations.
>
> Operating along with fault, the causation requirement serves to distinguish from the totality of conditions that a victim perceives to be associated with discrimination and those that the law will address. These dual requirements place on the victim the nearly impossible burden of isolating the particular conditions of discrimination produced by and mechanically linked to the behavior of an indentified blameworthy perpetrator, regardless of whether other conditions of discrimination, caused by other perpetrators, would have to be remedied for the outcome of the case to make any difference at all.[33]/

As Professor Dorn points out, equal opportunity can lead to racial equality only if the races are substantially equal at the time the rule is applied, because America's current working concept of equality of opportunity is so biased in favor of the advantaged. The doctrine's development and application have focused on permitting all social groups to compete in the political, social, and economic marketplaces, but the concept is unrealistic in its assumption that such groups compete unencumbered by handicaps at the beginning.[34]/ If fair housing is to be truly that, and if equal opportunity is to be truly that, then the nation simply cannot buy into the perpetrator perspective. Such a perspective ignores racism's legacy and its institutional manifestations while freezing in the effects of past discrimination, effectively handcuffing the reach of effective remedial action.

IV. EVOLVING POLICY AND RECURRING THEMES IN FEDERAL HOUSING PROGRAMS

A. Congressional Policy Declarations

In 1949, Congress laid the cornerstone of national housing policy as "the realization as soon as feasible of the goal of a decent home and a suitable living environment for every American Family."[35/] An earlier policy declaration contained in the United States Housing Act of 1937 committed the nation "to remedy the unsafe and insanitary housing conditions and the acute shortage of decent, safe and sanitary dwellings for families of low income in rural or urban communities, that are injurious to the health, safety and morals of the nation."[36/] Reaffirming this policy in 1968, Congress directed that "the highest priority and emphasis should be given to meeting the housing needs of those families for which the national goal has not become a reality."[37/]

The Housing and Community Development Act of 1974, as amended, was passed in recognition of critical social, economic, and environmental problems facing the nation's urban communities.[38/] The identified problems arose from (1) the growth of population in metropolitan and other urban areas and the concentration of poor people in central cities; (2) inadequate public and private investment and reinvestment in housing and other physical facilities, and inadequate public and social services, resulting in growing and persistent urban slums and blight and deterioration in the quality of the urban environment; and (3) inflated energy costs which were seen as having undermined effective local housing and community development activities. Congress declared, therefore, inter alia, a need to establish viable urban communities through the systematic and sustained action by federal, state and local governments; substantial expansion of and greater continuity in the scope and level of federal assistance; and increased private investment.[39/]

Congress declared that the primary objective of the Act was "the development of viable urban communities, by providing decent housing and a suitable living environment and expanding economic opportunities, principally for persons of low and moderate income." Consistent with this primary objective, Congress enumerated nine supporting objectives:

1. the elimination of slums and blight and the prevention
    of blighting influences and the deterioration of pro-
    perty and neighborhood and community facilities of im-
    portance to the welfare of the community, principally
    persons of low and moderate income;

2. the elimination of conditions which are detrimental to
    health, safety, and public welfare, through code en-
    forcement, demolition, interim rehabilitation assist-
    ance, and related activities;

3. the conservation and expansion of the nation's housing
    stock in order to provide a decent home and a suitable
    living environment for all persons, but principally
    those of low and moderate income;

4. the expansion and improvement of the quantity and qua-
    lity of community services, principally for persons of
    low and moderate income, which are essential for sound
    community development and for the development of viable
    urban communities;

5. a more rational utilization of land and other natural
    resources and the better arrangement of residential,
    commercial, industrial, recreational, and other needed
    activity centers;

6. the reduction of the isolation of income groups within
    communities and geographical areas and the promotion
    of an increase in the diversity and vitality of neigh-
    borhoods through the spatial deconcentration of housing
    opportunities for persons of lower income and the re-
    vitalization of deteriorating or deteriorated neighbor-
    hoods to attract persons of higher income;

7. the restoration and preservation of properties of spe-
    cial value for historic, architectural, or esthetic
    reasons;

8. the alleviation of physical and economic distress
    through the stimulation of private investment and com-
    munity revitalization in areas with population out-
    migration or a stagnating or declining tax base; and

9. the conservation of the nation's scarce energy re-
    sources, improvement of energy efficiency, and the
    provision of alternative and renewable energy sources
    of supply.[40]

In light of this evolution of national housing policy, one appreciates
the devastating nature and extent of the Reagan retrenchment. For, now,
virtually none of these policy findings or goals pertain to the Administration's housing and urban development program.[41]

B. Recurring Themes in Housing Programs[42]

Federally assisted housing has made varying responses to the
problems of housing deprivation, primarily through government intervention
in housing markets. The problem focus has generally been placed on (1)
urban blight and substandard housing; (2) the rent paying burden; (3) the
inadequate supply of low-income housing; (4) the quality or habitability
of low income housing; (5) the socio-economic disabilities associated with
concentrations of low-income and nonwhite families; (6) the stigma associated with living in federally assisted housing; and (7) restrictions
in locational choice or housing opportunities due to low-income, racial,
welfare, or family status.

Problem (1) has been addressed through a succession of urban development programs such as code enforcement, slum clearance, urban renewal, Community Development Block Grants (CDBG) and Urban Development Action Grants (UDAG). Problem (2) has generated the fundamental response of the rent subsidy whereby the subsidized tenant pays up to 30% of income for rent. The programs have been directed at subsidizing the price of housing and its production, through demand-side and supply-side subsidies.

Problem (3) has prompted programs directed at either new construction or substantial rehabilitation. To encourage development and rehabilitation, subsidies were paid directly to the project owner and tied to the housing units subsidized rather than to the individual tenant. Ownership could either be in the hands of public housing authorities or private sponsors. For the latter, guaranteed subsidy payments and federally-insured below market interest rate mortgages, secured by long term contracts between the owner and HUD, were aimed at enabling owners to secure financing to build or rehabilitate housing units. These programs, thus, illustrate supply-side subsidies.

The quality of housing, problem number (4), has been dealt with by rehabilitation grants or subsidy programs and requirements that the assisted housing meet certain regulated quality standards. Problem (5) has produced requirements to deconcentrate the beneficiaries through site selection requirements and economic and racial mix policies. The stigma problem, number (6), has fostered policies of leasing individual units from the private sector's existing or rehabilitated housing market and thereby avoiding the placement of tenants in housing that has a public housing look or image. Finally, expanding the choice of housing opportunity, problem number (7), has induced policies related to fair housing such as spatial deconcentration, "benign" quotas, affirmative marketing, prohibiting sites in areas already concentrated with assisted housing, the poor, or nonwhites, and regional fair share programs tied to receiving community development block grants.

The recurring themes that transcend the individual policy and programmatic responses have included:

1. obtaining a sufficient supply of decent and affordable housing for all poor people;

2. determining how housing subsidies should be provided-private enterprise or local public housing authorities; new construction or existing units; housing vouchers; etc.;

3. determining who should receive the limited amounts of housing subsidies;

4. determining how much should tenants pay and how deep should the government subsidy be;

5. determining what the relation should be between housing and urban development;

6. determining how much state and local control should be granted in the administration of federal programs; and

7. determining what "fair housing" is and what the government's role should be in acting to further it.

C. The Reagan Paradigm Shifts

Historically, HUD has administered programs aimed at increasing or improving the low-income housing supply. Subsidies on behalf of tenants were project-based, paid either to a local public housing authority or a private owner. Payment contracts would run from 15 to 40 years. Thus, federal involvement was intensive and its commitment was long-term. The Reagan paradigm shifts in federal housing call for a move from project-based subsidies to housing allowances, and a radical reduction in federal spending for housing assistance. As John Nolan wrote in the spring of 1982:

> Several recent actions at the federal level represent a fundamental shift in the role that the nation's highest level of government will play in pressing for "a decent home and suitable living environment for all Americans." Congress acted in 1981 to reduce federal spending for housing by nearly 50% and to shift the emphasis of federal programs to subsidies for existing housing rather than for the construction of new housing units.

> These actions contrast markedly with the federal housing programs of the 1970s and early 1980s. For fiscal year 1981, for example, Congress approved funding for 280,000 assisted housing units, fully half of which were to be newly constructed or substantially rehabilitated housing.[43/]

In 1979, 440,000 households were added to those assisted under all programs. New recipients of federally assisted or subsidized housing fell to 136,000 in 1983 before rising to 183,000 in 1985. In a compromise with senate Republicans, the Reagan Administration dropped its two-year moratorium on all new commitments. On November 13, 1985, Congress approved the Fiscal 1986 HUD appropriations bill (H.R. 3038) which provides funding for 97,000 assisted units, 86,000 fewer than the current level. The bill also cuts the CDBG and the UDAG programs, respectively by 10 and 25%. Most of the units are for the Section 8 Existing Housing Certificate Program (32,000) and the free standing voucher program (36,000). The bill appropriates funds for only 5,000 new public housing units.[44/]

In addition to reducing funding levels, the Administration has attempted to purge the pipeline of already approved units in the public housing, Section 8 New Construction and Substantial and Moderate Rehabilitation Programs. By the end of fiscal year 1986, HUD will have excluded funding for 70,000 federally assisted or subsidized units that had previously been allocated. As a consequence of the funding reductions and pipeline purges, the number of housing units for additional households that have and will eventuate in the federally subsidized housing programs during the mid-1980s will amount to less than half those units provided during the late 1970s and early 1980s.[45]/

During the first half of the 1980s, HUD and Congressional action have shifted the balance from subsidizing newly constructed or substantially rehabilitated buildings toward subsidizing existing units already on the market. Since 1980, for example, virtually no funds have been appropriated for section 8 new construction or substantial rehabilitation. In 1983, Congress repealed the statutory authority for additional units under these programs. The new construction funding has largely been restricted to Section 202 housing for the elderly and handicapped, although the identified need is for family housing, a particularly acute need for nonwhites. The supply problem has been exacerbated further by efforts that counter preserving the existing inventory of federally subsidized housing. As the National Housing Law Project summarizes:

> The Administration's opposition to project-based federal housing subsidies has not been limited to a strategy of preventing additional project-based subsidies from being approved. On numerous fronts the Administration has been moving to get out of its long-term commitments to projects which are already subsidized under various federal programs. Thus, for example, HUD has been encouraging the demolition or sale of public housing projects, including sales to tenants, by having the governing rules loosened, by issuing policy statements in favor of local effort to demolish or sell projects and, finally, by creating financial pressures on housing authorities to sell or demolish. Similarly, with the private programs, HUD has encouraged legislative changes loosening the grounds for allowing prepayment of the mortgages, has taken no steps to prevent Section 8 landlords from deciding not to renew their project-based Housing Assistance Payments (HAP) contracts, and has pursued property disposition policies that eliminate the federal government's commitment to subsidize projects in the future.[46]/

D. The Reagan Centerpiece Program: Housing Allowances

In October 1981, President Reagan's Commission on Housing concluded that affordability rather than an inadequate supply of housing was the major problem facing poor families. It thus recommended "that the primary federal project for helping low-income families achieve decent housing be a consumer-oriented housing assistance grant."[47]/ The Administration and HUD have adopted this as the program "centerpiece" for federally assisted housing. Last spring, a five-year, $1 billion demonstration voucher program began in San Antonio, Texas. Administration officials have stated that it is their hope and plan that "in the 1990s vouchers will replace virtually all federally assisted housing programs, which now cost about $10 billion each year. They believe this will help make the poor far more mobile than they have been since the 1930s and, in the process, help blacks break away from the isolation of the inner cities."48/ After 1990, the multibillion-dollar housing assistance programs enacted by prior administrations will expire and thus the Administration expects, no matter who is President, that in the next decade housing allowances for renting on the private market will be the principal, if not exclusive, means of helping families who cannot afford adequate, market-rate housing.49/

While housing allowance programs are not new,50/ the degree of emphasis now being placed on vouchers is a radical paradigm shift in federal housing policy. Based on conclusions reached from a consideration of earlier experiments in housing allowances:

> [I]t may be fairly stated that housing allowances are, at best, only a partial response to the housing problems of low-income households. Where the supply of housing is inadequate, where deterioration is widespread, and where costs are particularly high, the allowance approach is simply not enough to redress the major shelter needs of the poor. If housing standards are not used, participation will be acceptable, but public funds will be used to subsidize substandard housing. If decent, safe, and sanitary conditions are required, participation among the occupants of substandard housing will decline markedly. In either event allowances are not deep enough to cause the market to increase the supply of housing for the poor.51/

The present voucher program will be administered through local public housing authorities and will involve mandatory housing quality standards.52/ But it will significantly shift program costs from the federal government to the voucher recipients. First, the rent subsidy is limited to the difference between the tenant contribution of 30% of adjusted income and a federal payment standard, somewhat similar to the Section 8 fair market rent (FMR). Unlike the FMR, however, the participating landlord will be allowed to charge a rent in excess of the federal payment standard. Thus, the tenant will pay not only the 30% of income contribution, but also any difference between the charged rent and the lower payment standard. Moreover, the housing authority may only adjust the payment standard once every other year and is not even required to do so that often. As a result, rent increases will have to be paid out of the tenants' already shallow pocket.53/ These are minor problems, however.

Based on the earlier experiments with housing allowances, when stringent housing standards were introduced as a program requirement (as in the present program), there was a disproportionate reduction in participation of nonwhite families, large households, and poorer people. The program, moreover, seems to disregard the continuing prevalence of discrimination, not just against nonwhites, but also against the handicapped,

-127-

single parent families, families with children, and the poorest of the poor.[54/] As Chester Hartman has warned:

> The housing allowance is only part of a good idea.
> It fosters the principle of individual choice in the
> housing market, which is a critical component of hous-
> ing satisfaction, but it takes no steps to ensure that
> market conditions will be such that the low-income
> consumer can truly have free choice or satisfaction.
> With the present realities of housing conditions and
> the housing market, freedom of choice can only be en-
> hanced by more government intervention, not less. As
> Miles Mahoney, former commissioner of Community Affairs
> of Massachusetts, noted, "unless the government is, in
> fact, willing to intervene forcefully in the workings
> of the private market, the housing allowance program
> will prove to be no more than yet another subsidy pro-
> gram for the private sphere-the poor will benefit only
> marginally and the near poor will likely be harmed."
> Housing allowances are a backward step, as they are
> being developed, for they will not improve the housing
> conditions of the poor and will postpone the basic
> changes that are needed in the housing system if all
> Americans are to be decently housed.[55/]

This housing program really offers neither help nor hope. It is at best a cruel hoax and a turning away from the federal commitment to help shelter the poor.

V. FAIR HOUSING AND THE INTEGRATION IMPERATIVE

A. The Title VIII Mandate

The first Title VIII controversy decided by the Supreme Court was the 1972 case of Trafficante v. Metropolitan Life Insurance Co.[56/] A black and a white tenant living in a San Francisco apartment complex housing about 8,200 residents were held to have standing to sue their landlord for racially discriminating against nonwhites. Thereby the tenants allegedly lost the social benefits of living in an integrated community, missed business and professional advantages that would have accrued from living with nonwhites, and suffered from being "stigmatized" as residents of a "white ghetto." Upon these ironic facts, the U.S. Supreme Court confirmed the integration imperative of Title VIII. In assessing the injury of the plaintiffs, the Court cited Senator Mondale, the principal sponsor of Title VIII, who had stated that the reach of the law was to replace the ghettos "by truly integrated and balanced living patterns."[57/]

Other aspects of the Act's legislative history further reflect the integration imperative. Among House members, Congressman Celler, then chairman of the Judiciary Committee, addressed the need to counter the "blight" of segregated housing and Congressman Ryan envisioned Title VIII as a way to help "achieve the aim of an integrated society."[58/] Additionally, in a case finding "redlining"--the practice by institutions of not making mortgages available in certain areas--to violate Title VIII the court in Laufman v. Oakley Building & Loan Co.[59/] cited the Kerner Commission Report on Civil Disorders which described the adverse effects of racial segregation and isolation stemming from "the formation of racial ghettos."[60/] This report was released about one month prior to the signing of the Fair Housing Act and the legislative history shows that Congress considered the Kerner Commission's finding. As the court stated in Laufman:

> In this case, a realistic examination of the concerns that led to the adoption of this legislation proves a better guide to congressional intent than the dusty volumes of Sutherland on Statutory Interpretation. Primary among these concerns were the rioting and civil disturbances that had rocked the central cores of many of the nation's major cities the previous summer. These disturbances had not only focused attention on the discontent of the people trapped in the nation's ghettos, but had also brought many to the realization that the underlying illness, of which the riots of 1967 were symptomatic, had to be treated if a worse catastrophe was to be forestalled.[61/]

In most cases, the judicial recognition that integration is the ultimate goal of Title VIII merely reflects the anti-discrimination principle. The typical fair housing case involves a black shelterseeker whose efforts to secure housing in a white market area or among white tenants is frustrated by disparate treatment or effect. The integration goal is served by removing the discriminatory barriers that have been put before him or her. Similarly, in the exclusionary zoning cases and others involving the locations of low-income subsidized housing, removing the exclusionary or preventive barriers often furthers the goals of integration. For example, in Resident Advisory Board v. Rizzo, a lawsuit challenged the city of Philadelphia's attempts to block construction of a housing project in a nearly all-white section of that city. The trial court ruled that, inter alia, because 95% of those on the waiting list for public housing in the city were nonwhite, the failure to build such housing had a disparate effect on nonwhites.[62/]

Integrating the nonwhite poor has proven to be problematical, however, and often integration has been dysfunctional. The dysfunction is discussed below in terms of (1) spatial deconcentration and impaction, (2) gentrification and urban revitalization, (3) involuntary displacement, and (4) integration maintenance through such mechanisms as "benign" occupancy controls and steering.

B. Dysfunctional Integration through Spatial Deconcentration and Nonimpaction

In Shannon v. HUD,[63/] HUD was enjoined from using an urban renewal site for a rent supplement housing project because the agency had failed to develop an institutionalized methodology for determining the racial impact of the proposed project. According to the court in <u>Shannon</u>, as a general proposition it would be contrary to national fair housing policy for HUD to permit building a project that would increase the racial concentration in a given area. Importantly, however, the court went on to state:

> ...we [are not] suggesting that desegregation of housing is the only goal of the national housing policy. There will be instances where a pressing case may be made for the rebuilding of a racial ghetto. We hold only that the agency's judgment must be an informed one; one which weighs the alternatives and finds that the need for physical rehabilitation or additional minority housing at the site in question clearly outweighs the disadvantage of increasing or perpetuating racial concentration.[64]

At a minimum, policies seeking to further fair housing must be implemented with sufficient consideration for the balancing factors enunciated in <u>Shannon</u>. For example, in one case before the federal district court in New York City, plaintiffs tried to halt changes in an urban renewal plan which would have increased the number of low-income residents in the area. The court required a stringent burden of proof with respect to the tipping issue because "the proposed racial and economic classifications while intended to preserve the area, would clearly result in a denial of public housing, given the citywide need for such housing and the scarcity of alternative sites within the city."[65]

The <u>Shannon</u> decision prompted a HUD policy response that practically foreclosed the possiblitity of providing federally assisted housing in "impacted areas," that is, those areas with concentrations of poor or nonwhite households or other assisted housing.[66] In October of 1971 HUD published site selection criteria which were designed to force housing subsidy allocations into suburban areas at the expense of inner cities. Section 8 regulations presently provide that a site shall not be located in an area of nonwhite concentration unless sufficient, comparable opportunities exist for housing low-income nonwhite families outside areas of nonwhite concentration or unless the project is necessary to meet overriding housing needs which cannot otherwise feasibly be met. Additionally, a site may not even be located in a "racially mixed" area if the project will cause a "significant" increase in the proportion of nonwhite to white residents in the area. Finally, the site must avoid undue concentration of assisted persons in areas containing a high proportion of low-income persons.[67]

A principal goal of the 1974 Housing and Community Development Act focused on dispersal.[68] The section 8 housing program was intended to be the primary vehicle for achieving the HCDA goal of reducing the isolation of income groups within communities and promoting neighborhood diversity through the "spatial deconcentration" of housing opportunities for persons of lower-income and the attraction of persons of higher income.[69] The goal carried immense dysfunctional baggage. The site

-130-

selection pressures against building in impacted areas combined with the fact that nonconcentrated areas resisted the building of Section 8 new construction. New construction often remained undeveloped and those most in need were shut out. Moreover, the "revitalized" communities' attraction of higher income persons often exacerbated this situation by contributing to the displacement of the urban poor and nonwhites, fueling the process of gentrification. Many of the so-called impacted areas were really transitional areas where the absence of an increased supply of low-income housing meant that the victims of displacement were forced out of an upgrading area and relocated in another impacted area. Thus spatial deconcentration has been characterized as representing a fair housing policy that was "neither fair nor housing" 70/ and one of "symbolic gestures and false hopes." 71/

It is seen that even HUD's special efforts designed to increase spatial deconcentration failed. Look at the results of HUD's plans intended to develop and implement a coordinated areawide strategy for distributing housing assistance in a manner which would promote increased housing opportunities outside areas and jurisdictions containing undue concentrations of low-income or nonwhite households. 72/

One study found that in using a fiscal 1978 bonus of $16.4 million for ten special jurisdictions, 90% of the funds went to deconcentrating assisted housing, but only 10% went to improving mobility. That is, assisted units were placed outside impacted areas, but residents of impacted areas were largely unserved under a implementation of the plan. 73/ In another study, "Assessment of the Impact of the Housing Opportunity Plan Program," urban planners looked at five regions in the program since fiscal 1976. The study found that only 10.5% of the assisted households moved from the inner city to the suburbs, with the Minneapolis-St. Paul region accounting for virtually all of the shift. In other regions, under 3% of the assisted households made such moves, a figure representing less than the national percentage for all households. 74/

It has also been reported that in HUD's analysis of the Chicago Public housing demonstration program of interjurisdictional mobility, moving to the suburbs involved trade-offs between neighborhood quality and locational convenience that only a small fraction of public housing tenants were willing to make. Of the approximately 22,000 eligible families who chose to participate, only 12% voiced a preference to move to the suburbs. 75/

Finally, a 1981 HUD study by Vernarelli, "Integration and Section 8 New Construction," confirmed that nonwhites were substantially underrepresented in Section 8 new construction projects. The degree of underrepresentation in many cases is startling. 76/ The Vernarelli paper demonstrated that HUD's fair housing reliance on site selection policies to expand opportunities for the nonwhite poor was misplaced. Those policies failed to insure that benefits were not merely diverted from nonwhites in impacted areas. In other words, the location of Section 8 new construction had little correlation with the actual provision of new housing choices for the inner-city nonwhite households in need.

In looking at nonwhite occupancy figures, Vernarelli found that 22% of the Section 8 projects had no nonwhite residents and 35% had less than 10% nonwhite residents. Moreover, in 15 out of the 16 areas sampled, the nonwhite percentage of those eligible for Section 8 exceeded the nonwhite percentage within Section 8 new construction projects.

The Vernarelli paper's major conclusion is that although there was movement of nonwhites to projects in white areas, there was a trade-off between serving nonwhite families and locating the majority of assisted housing outside areas of nonwhite concentration: "The Department's efforts to locate the majority of (Section 8 New Construction) housing in non-minority areas appears to have led to a relative low participation rate by minority families."[77]

C. Dysfunctional Integration through Gentrification and Urban Revitalization.

In 1971 the NAACP characterized black survival as an ability to move from the inner city to the suburbs.[78] In 1974 the U.S. Commission on Civil Rights stated that suburban "economic-racial exclusion may well be called the racism of the seventies."[79] But from the 70s to the present many blacks are fighting to remain in inner cities and to resist what Professor McDougall has termed "reverse exclusionary zoning," which is the effort, through urban revitalization, to prevent the low-income and non-whites from remaining in their own neighborhoods.[80]

Increasingly, racial integration of neighborhoods is occurring through the in-movement of whites in the context of urban reinvestment.[81] As discussed above, the policy of spatial deconcentration of lower-income housing opportunities and the attraction of higher income residents, by deemphasizing additional new or rehabilitated low-income housing in nonwhite and poor areas, has fostered the reinvestment-gentrification-displacement cycle.

Reverse exclusionary zoning is tied to the process euphemistically labeled "gentrification."[82] According to Judge Higginbotham:

> Gentrification is a term used in land development to describe a trend whereby previously "underdeveloped" areas become "revitalized" as persons of relative affluence invest in homes and begin to "upgrade" the neighborhood economically. This process often causes the eviction of the less affluent residents who can no longer afford the increasingly expensive housing in their neighborhood. Gentrification is a deceptive term which masks the dire consequences that "upgrading" of neighborhoods causes when the neighborhood becomes too expensive for either rental or purchase by the less affluent residents who bear the brunt of the change.[83]

The typical reverse exclusionary zoning lawsuit is brought by affluent gentrifiers who espouse fair housing concepts to prevent "undue concentration" of nonwhite or low-income persons in the neighborhood that would result if low-income housing were constructed. As the new residents oppose racial and economic concentration in the name of desegregation, "they may prevent the racial and economic reintegration of neighborhoods which have been converted from ethnically and economically diverse communities into upper-middle class preserves."[84/] In such a case, Business Association of University City v. Landrieu,[85/] plaintiffs challenged the construction of Section 8 housing which was to be built within the gentrifying area in Philadelphia, around the University of Pennsylvania and adjacent to a black impacted area. The court upheld HUD's determination that the so-called racially impacted area around the university itself may have actually been impacted in 1970, but had undergone changes due to gentrification and general redevelopment causing a decrease in the black population. Furthermore, the court rejected plaintiffs' contention that the placement of the low-income housing next to a racially impacted area constituted an impermissable concentration as a matter of law. The court concluded that "under the guise of their concern about the poor and minorities, business interests would probably acquire the land, and the poor and minorities might be forced to live in areas far more racially concentrated and poverty-stricken."

As Congress has stated:

> ...The movement of more affluent families back into city neighborhoods constitutes an unprecedented opportunity to promote the neighborhood integration that is the national policy objective of the 1968 Fair Housing Act. The Committee is concerned that neighborhoods may be resegregated at the expense of the present low and moderate-income residents, and it is for this reason that the Housing Assistance Plan of each locality must include specific programs to provide displaced residents with opportunities to relocate within their neighborhoods, and to ensure that existing residents benefit from neighborhood revitalization.[86/]

Of course, however, the Reagan Administration's virtual elimination of federally assisted production programs has worsened this displacement--now even making the pressing case for rebuilding the black community as noted in Shannon is becoming moot because it entails increasing the supply of low income housing. This fact is behind Jane McGrew's questioning, "What is the point of fair housing enforcement?"[87/] The unavailability of replacement housing in the immediate neighborhood has in one case, Mejia v. HUD,[88/] defeated plaintiff's right-to-return claim. In Mejia, the district court concluded that this right meant that displaced residents were entitled to a "reasonable opportunity" to relocate in their immediate neighborhood only when such housing was, in fact, available.

D. Recognizing Displacment and Seeing it as a Race Issue

In Norwalk CORE v. Norwalk Redevelopment Agency,[89/] the court was considering a challenge to an urban renewal relocation plan and stressed that displacement is a race issue because (1) black displacees

-133-

are likely to face a more difficult time than white displacees in finding decent replacement housing; (2) blacks tend to make up a disproportionately higher number of displacees than whites; (3) blacks are more likely than whites to be repeat victims of displacement; and (4) in order to find relocation housing, blacks are more likely than whites to be forced to move out of a city altogether.[90/]

Additionally, the socio-economic and political integrity of the black community is often impaired by displacing urban developmental activity. Commenting on Western Addition Community Organization v. Weaver,[91/] Professor McGee observed: "Characteristically, the area selected [for the redevelopment project] was the cultural, political and economic center of the black community."[92/] In Arrington v. City of Fairfield, Alabama,[93/] blacks sought to enjoin an urban renewal project that would displace them entirely from their community. The Fifth Circuit held that plaintiffs were entitled to litigate their claims on the basis of their right "to reside in the city by owning or renting housing." The circuit court also cited Nashville I-40 Steering Committee v. Ellington, in allowing plaintiffs to represent the "community" in claiming that a highway routing discriminated against blacks by destroying the black business community, injuring black educational institutions, and otherwise impairing the black community.[94/] While the nature of displacement is changing, its racial design and impact is still prevalent in many circumstances. Conditions have not changed so much that displacement should no longer be viewed as a "race issue."[95/]

Displacement has various manifestations, ramifications, and causes. George and Eunice Grier have provided the most cited working definition of displacement:

> Displacement occurs when any household is forced to move from its residence by conditions which affect the dwelling or its immediate surroundings and which:
>
> 1. are beyond the household's reasonable ability to control or prevent;
>
> 2. occur despite the household's having met all previously imposed conditions of occupancy; and
>
> 3. make continued occupancy by that household impossible, hazardous, or unaffordable.[96/]

Legates and Hartman point out that the nature of displacement has undergone fundamental changes during the past decade because there has been a shift from the government-related displacement primarily caused by federal urban renewal and highway programs to displacement caused primarily by rent increases, purely private action such as condominium conversion and unassisted gentrification, hybrid public/private displacement, and displacement that occurs indirectly due to governmental actions.[97/]

As localities seek to avoid the scope of the federally triggered relocation and anti-displacement responsibilities, more and more displacement will be shifted to appear private. HUD and local governments will emphasize procedure over substance, relying on "citizen participation" that is advisory only and on antidisplacement "planning" that will likely be no more adequate than relocation planning has been. Federal programs increasingly emphasize mixed public-private projects and financial leveraging. This will tend to blur the distinction between public and private action: "Substantial numbers of displacees who would have been classified as public displacees under conventional urban renewal programs are not counted in the public workload now."[98]/

E. Dysfunctional Integration through "Benign" Quotas and Steering.

In the summer of 1984 the Washington Post reported on the controversy over benign quotas in terms of the "nation's policy on integration being at crossroads."[99]/ The sides were drawn as follows:

> If [the Justice Department] succeeds in greatly
> narrowing the interpretation of the Fair Housing Act,
> which includes the premise that quotas, benign steering
> and other integration maintenance techniques are il-
> legal, residence patterns in the nation will be pro-
> foundly changed. Critics say resegregation will take
> place in many areas.

> If fair housing groups prevail, the outlook is
> for growing use of quotas and other means of maintain-
> ing an integrated population in federally assisted
> housing areas and, to some extent, in suburban sub-
> divisions.[100]/

Although I suspect that motives differ, I find myself lining up behind the Justice Department on this issue.[101]/

Both benign quotas and steering are "integration maintenance" techniques designed to create and maintain stable residential balances between whites and nonwhites.[102]/ The focus is on the dynamics of residential segregation:

> Based on the fear of resegregation - "the process by
> which a previously all white community becomes an all
> black community" - these plans seek to limit the pro-
> portion of black residents in order to encourage whites
> to live in the community. The potential limitations
> on black access to housing and the implicit acceptance
> of white prejudice inherent in these programs have
> created a rift among traditional advocates of racial
> integration.[103]/

In other words, the quota is intended to prevent resegregation by limiting the percentage of blacks to just short of the point that would "tip" the housing or community from white to black. Studies show this point to range generally from 20-60%, but conventional wisdom now seems to place it at 30%.[104/]

The case of Otero v. New York City Housing Authority[105/] demonstrates the importance of the tipping factor in the conflict between housing low-income nonwhites and furthering integration. The trial court decision had enjoined the housing authority from renting public housing units to persons other than former black and Puerto Rican occupants of the urban renewal site where the project was built until all present or former site occupants had been accommodated. The district court concluded that the affirmative duty to integrate public housing should not be given effect where it would deprive nonwhites of available and desirable housing.

On appeal, however, the circuit court found that the priority system would create a nonwhite "pocket ghetto" that would constitute a "tipping factor" causing white residents to flee, leading ultimately to the nonwhite ghettoization of the entire community. Because of tipping, the appeals court held that concentrated racial pockets, even within a generally integrated community, resulted in a segregated community contrary to Title VIII. According to the court, effectuating the legislative intent to promote integrated housing cannot be discounted merely because nonwhites are willing to accept segregated housing: "The purpose of racial integration is to benefit the community as a whole, not just certain of its members."[106/]

The Otero decision failed to consider that the denial of public housing to a person solely on the basis of his or her race is likely to prevent that person from finding any decent housing at all. Even if the PHA could find alternative housing for the excluded applicants, there would most likely still be an intolerable delay.[107/] Indeed, it can be argued that the harms of so-called benign housing ceiling quotas are sufficiently severe to render them unconstitutional.[108/]

In Burney v. Housing Authority of City of Beaver,[109/] plaintiffs successfully challenged an integration quota that the public housing authority imposed as the result of a consent decree entered into with the state human relations commission. The court found that the quota violated constitutional equal protection and the Fair Housing Act. Aside from the case being favorable to black plaintiffs, its analysis is excellent.

The decision in Otero was rejected, in part, because it did not adequately address the constitutional personal rights issue raised by restrictions on nonwhite access to subsidized housing. Otero had dismissed this issue by merely asserting that the duty to integrate is not a one-way street and that for the good of the community some nonwhites would have to suffer. In the Burney case the court determined that a constitutional violation existed because it involved purposeful discrimination and the public housing authority failed to meet its burden of justification by proving that the integration quota was necessary and a precisely tailored means of maintaining integration. According to the court:

> "Benign" housing quotas are impermissible if they restrict black entry into low-income housing more than is necessary to prevent tipping and resegregation. When

-136-

the percentage of black residents is kept below the tipping point, the quota imposes unnecessary costs on the black entrants, serving the invidious purpose of exclusion more than the benign purpose of integration. There is no evidence at all before this court to indicate that the defendants' plan includes as many black residents as is compatible with the needs to avoid re-segregation.[110]/

In evaluating the Title VIII claim, the court was insightful enough to recognize that the Fair Housing Act had developed a schism in applying antisegregation and antidiscrimination policies. At the time of its enactment, it was thought that Title VIII's emphasis on antidiscrimination would lead to residential integration. Congress perceived antisegregation and antidiscrimination as complementary. But as the court points out, this is not likely to be the case where tipping is a factor:

> Imposition of a quota would promote the antisegregation (or integration) policy of Tile VIII; refusal to impose a quota would promote the antidiscrimination (or freedom of choice) policy. Neither the language of, nor the legislative history behind, Title VIII resolves the question of which policy must yield when the two conflict.[111]/

While the court in Otero resolved the conflict in favor of the antisegregation policy, the court in Burney ruled that the discriminatory effect of the integration quota could not be justified because the public housing authority failed to show that "[n]o alternative course of action would be adopted that would enable [its] interest to be served with less discriminatory impact."[112]/

Proponents of benign quotas and steering sometimes draw a close connection between integration maintenance and affirmative action, often treating their plans as simply another form of affirmative action.[113]/ For those who oppose affirmative action the linkage here will lead to a quick rejection of integration maintenance. This presumably explains the Justice Department's opposition. But to favor affirmative action should not automatically lead to favoring integration maintenance quotas. Many buy the argument that (1) integration maintenance is affirmative action; (2) if you are with us on affirmative action, then you must be with us on integration maintenance.[114]/ But as Professor Smolla says:

> Integration maintenance is not true "affirmative action." Those who endorse (as I do) the need for affirmative action should think twice before accepting the twist that integration maintenance works on traditional thinking about affirmative remedies. The ameliorative use of race as a remedial device to reverse the lingering effects of centuries of discrimination is laudable. But the use of racial quotas or incentives to create ceilings on the number of Jews, or

Puerto Ricans, or blacks welcome in an apartment complex or neighborhood is a totally different matter.
The stuff of such plans is not access but regress;
they do not employ affirmative invitations, but negative limitations. Even when enacted out of good
faith, such plans violate our fair housing laws and
our Constitution.[115/]

VI. THE GOAL OF SPATIAL EQUALITY

It has been stated that civil rights advocates have found themselves
"unable to argue simultaneously against Jim Crow and for the improvement
of the Negro community."[116/] Black America must now overcome that
inability. An underlying assumption of the civil rights movement was
that "the protection of the law, the heritage of national values, and the
aspirations of the black community formed a functionally cohesive
triad."[117/] When blacks vote against the re-elected President by 91%,
that is some indication that Black America can no longer rely on such an
assumption.[118/]

Efforts to improve life for poor blacks must now be redirected to
create spatial equality in the sense that, even under conditions of segregation, the setting where blacks live should be improved so that blacks
are not disadvantaged because of where they live.[119/] There can be good
schools there; good housing there; access to jobs there. Political power,
moreover, is still dependent on blacks residing in the same community.
Preventing involuntary displacement of poor blacks, whether in the name
of "freedom of housing choice" or "urban revitalization," must be a higher
item on the national black agenda.[120/] As Professor Glasgow says,
"[t]he main policy question, often involving ideological commitment, is
whether blacks should concentrate on combatting institutional racism and
gaining mainstream positions or whether they should focus on revitalizing
the areas of black living."[121/] While the tendency has been to favor
one direction or the other, they are not mutually exclusive.

> The fact is, however, that political activity aimed at
> improving the immediate condition of ghetto-encapsu-
> lated blacks and increasing their capacity for indepen-
> dent functioning, both as individuals and as a com-
> munity, boosts the vitality of all blacks. Critics of
> this approach fail to see, or in some cases cannot ac-
> cept, that most Americans are not really interested in
> correcting the ills of the ghetto. It is therefore up
> to blacks themselves to become a strong force for so-
> cial change of this environment. A crucial lesson to
> be learned about ethnic and minority survival in Ameri-
> ca is that no group has effectively moved from second-
> class or minority status to a self-determined place in
> American society without having in its control some
> economic and social service organizations supplying an
> institutional base.[122/]

While segregation still persists, upwardly mobile blacks continue to measure options within the context of that segregation. As whites have deserted central city areas, new neighborhoods have opened up, and the black middle class has quickly taken advantage of the situation to move there. One result of this, however, is the increase in class differentiation now existing within urban black communities.[123] Professor Hirsch notes that while this phenomenon has always been present to a degree, "the ability of well-to-do blacks to distance themselves from the poor has become much more pronounced in the last decade or two; and spatial distance, throughout American urban history, has generally reflected social, ideological, and political differences as well. The full implications of this movement have yet to be seen."[124]

For the black middle class, the existance of adequate housing and decent housing alternatives to the most impoverished communities is proceeding within the context of persistant racial segregation and this reduces the push to move to all-white or integrated areas. The push to these areas was apparently more valued when they represented the only viable options to deplorable living conditions.[125] According to Professor Hirsh:

> In part, this phenomenon might reflect a new kind of "voluntary" segregation; it is possible that, finally, the centripetal pull of Afro-American "cultural affinities" are being tested and found more enduring than those of the white ethnics. But, given past history, it might also simply reflect the judgment that entry into all-white communities is just not worth the risk or aggravation; and it is certainly no longer necessary to achieve a decent standard of living.[126]

Even the segregated shifts of the black middle class will mean that poor blacks will become increasingly distant and isolated not just from whites, but also from other blacks who are upwardly mobile. For poor blacks their continued segregation, increasingly by class as well as race, "represents a new stage in the evolution of America's black urban communities."[127] As Hirsch states, "If the ghetto has been gilded for some and escaped by others, it shows no signs of disappearing, and, indeed, may now present the dual problems of race and poverty in a more concentrated form than ever before."[128]

A decade ago Kenneth Phillips and Michael Agelasto wrote an article entitled "Housing and Central Cities: The Conservation Approach."[129] The thesis of the article was that it was time for a sober rethinking of government housing policies and programs with a new approach placing primary emphasis on the rebuilding of inner city neighborhoods and the rehabilitation and conservation of the existing housing stock. It is an enlightening article that should now be reread and taken to heart. The thesis, given the Reagan retrenchment, is perhaps more appropriate now than when first articulated. It amounts virtually to the only game in town. As they stated:

> If the deterioration patterns of central city hardcore poverty areas are to be reversed and marginal neighbor-

hoods restored and conserved, realistic, cost effective, broad scale, job-creating, participatory program
approaches must be found. Downtown renewal projects,
benign neglect, and suburban bypass strategies have not
met these criteria. The criticisms and suggestions put
forth in this article are offered in the hope that a
pro-cities commitment will be made and that coordinated
and feasible programs will be developed to restore
urban communities.[130]

If Black America must persist in pushing its rock, let it at least push
the right rock.

VII. CONCLUSIONS

In spite of the foregoing discussion, I recognize the great difficulty
in generalizing about "the state of housing" for a group as diverse as
that of Black America. Housing issues tend to be resolved in light of
local geography and individual predicament. The issues differ in rural
areas from those in urban areas, for families from those of the elderly,
for homeowners from those of renters, for the haves from those of the
have nots. The splintering dichotomization is worsened when the federal
government abandons its long-standing commitment and legitimate responsibility to provide affordable decent, safe and sanitary housing for its
neediest. In light of these considerations, one cannot feel comfortable
making broad recommendations regarding housing policy. One risks being
either presumptious or quixotic. It is basic, however, that this nation's
policy must find foundation in making housing assistance an entitlement
for all who need it and this effort must be federally directed.[131]

The federal role, as well as that of state and local governments, must
increase the supply of affordable housing for all groups, targeting benefits rather than relying on a trickle down theory. The existing supply
of low-income housing must be preserved. Urban reinvestment must not
produce displacement as a natural consequence; it must provide an opportunity for those who have lived in the slums also to live in the revitalized cities. Ineffective integration strategies must not override the
immediate need poor nonwhites have for housing where they reside. Decent
housing for the poor and nonwhites whose locational choice is discrimina-
torily restricted cannot be furthered by tokenism. Rather, decent housing
and community enrichment for them must be viewed as a primary goal, not a
secondary or incidental result of integration. If integrated housing is
pursued to enhance educational or employment opportunities, then one must
make sure that the intended payoffs are indeed available.

In whatever detail, those who claim black leadership roles cannot my-
opically view housing deprivation as merely a manifestation of "personal
troubles" or matters of "personal discontent." Rather, housing deprivation must be viewed as "public issues" and matters of "political discontent."[132]   As Black America pushes its rock, it must do so with the
advice of C. Wright Mills:

Do not allow public issues as they are officially for-

-140-

mulated, or troubles as they are privately felt, to determine the problems that you take up for study. Above all, do not give up your moral and political autonomy by accepting in somebody else's terms the illiberal practicality of the bureaucratic ethos or the liberal practicality of the moral scatter. Know that many personal troubles cannot be solved merely as troubles, but must be understood in terms of public issues--and in terms of the problems of history-making. Know that the human meaning of public issues must be revealed by relating them to personal troubles--and to the problems of the individual life.$\underline{133/}$

: : :

FOOTNOTES

1. Chandler, Fair Housing Laws: A Critique, 24 HASTINGS L. J. 159, 160 n. 8 (1973).

2. Ely, Legislative and Administrative Motivation in Constitutional Law, 79 YALE L. J. 1205, 1228 (1970).

3. See, e.g., Teeley, Subsidies for Housing Will End, Pierce Says, the Washington Post, Nov. 6, 1981, at D11, col. 3; Lindsey, Watts, on 15th Anniversary of the Riots, "Is a Worse Hovel Than It Was," N.Y. Times, Aug. 10, 1980, Sec. 1, at 24, col. 1; Maxwell, Civil Rights Groups Face Tough Challenge in Bid to Regain Power, Wall Street Journal, Sept. 19, 1980, Sec. 1, at 1, col. 1; Rosenbaum, Blacks Would Feel Extra Impact From Cuts Proposed by President, N.Y. Times, June 1, 1981, Sec. 1, at 1, col. 3; and Treadwell & Shaw, Underclass: How One Family Copes, L.A. Times, July 5, 1981, Sec. 1, at 1, col. 1.

4. Herbers, Housing-Aid Debate Focuses on Question of U.S. Duty to Poor, N.Y. Times, May 4, 1985, Sec. 1, at 1, col. 1.

5. Id.

6. NATIONAL HOUSING LAW PROJECT, STATEMENT BEFORE THE SUBCOMMITTEE ON HOUSING AND COMMUNITY DEVELOPMENT OF THE COMMITTEE ON BANKING, FINANCE, AND URBAN AFFAIRS, HOUSE OF REPRESENTATIVES 1-2 (March 7, 1985).

7. Public Housing Development Won't Be Revived After Proposed Moratorium, Pierce Says, HOUSING & DEVELOPMENT RPTR (BNA) 801 (March 11, 1985).

8. Weaver, Keynote Address--Housing Discrimination: An Overview, in U.S. COMM'N ON CIVIL RIGHTS, A SHELTERED CRISIS: THE STATE OF FAIR HOUSING IN THE EIGHTIES 1 (hearings Sept. 26-27, 1983).

9. Sloane, Federal Housing Policy and Equal Housing Opportunity, in A SHELTERED CRISIS, supra note 8, at 134.

10. These topics are merely illustrative and discussion is necessarily limited.

11. See, e.g., Calmore, Exploring the Significance of Race and Class in Representing the Black Poor, 61 ORE. L. REV. 201 (1982); Welfeld, Exercises in Irrelevance: Federal Enforcement of Fair Housing in Federally Subsidized Housing, paper presented before the U.S. Civil Rights Comm'n Hearings on Issues in Housing Discrimination, Nov. 12-13, 1985.

12. Horwitz, The Jurisprudence of Brown and the Dilemmas of Liberalism, 14 HARV. C.R.-C.L. L. REV. 599, 609 (1979).

13. Drinan, Untying the White Noose, 94 YALE L. J. 435, 440 (1984).

14. McGrew, <u>The Federal Fair Housing Enforcement Effort: What's the Point?</u>, paper presented before the U.S. Civil Rights Comm'n Hearings, <u>supra</u> note 11, (summary 2). Ms. McGrew presents an excellent discussion in arguing that federally assisted housing resources are essential to remedy discrimination and promote integration, <u>Id</u>. at 15-17.

15. See also, Abram, <u>What is a Civil Right?</u>, 56 N.Y. ST. B.J. 6 (1984).

16. CENTER ON BUDGET AND POLICY PRIORITIES, FALLING BEHIND: A REPORT ON HOW BLACKS HAVE FARED UNDER THE REAGAN POLICIES 1-4 (1984).

17. Freeman, <u>Legitimizing Racial Discrimination Through Anti-Discrimination Law: A Critical Review of Supreme Court Doctrine</u>, 62 MINN. L. REV. 1049, 1061 (1978). See also Abrams, <u>Primary and Secondary Characteristics in Discrimination Cases</u>, 23 VILL. L. REV. 35, 51-55 (1977) (discussing poverty as a race-linked, secondary characteristic of discrimination).

18. R. MONTGOMERY & D. MANDELKER (eds.), HOUSING IN AMERICA: PROBLEMS AND PERSPECTIVES 1 (2d ed. 1979).

19. <u>Id</u>.

20. <u>Id</u>.

21. D. MANDELKER, C. DAYE, O. HETZEL, J. KUSHNER, H. MC GHEE, & R. WASHBURN (eds.), HOUSING AND COMMUNITY DEVELOPMENT: CASES AND MATERIALS 2 (1981).

22. Grigsby & Rosenberg, <u>Urban Housing Policy</u>, in HOUSING IN AMERICA, <u>supra</u> note 18, at 134.

23. See generally, Calmore, <u>Fair Housing and the Black Poor: An Advocacy Guide</u>, 18 CLEARINGHOUSE REV. 606 (Nov. 1984 Special Issue). Basic texts are J. KUSHNER, FAIR HOUSING: DISCRIMINATION IN REAL ESTATE, COMMUNITY DEVELOPMENT AND REVITALIZATION (1983) and R. SCHWEMM, HOUSING DISCRIMINATION LAW (1983).

24. 42 USCA 1982. See also Smedley, <u>A Comparative Analysis of Tile VIII and Section 1982</u>, 22 VAND. L. REV. 459 (1969).

25. In S 139, Senator Orin Hatch introduced legislation on Jan. 3, 1985 to revise the express policy of Title VIII to provide for "equal access to" instead of "fair" housing. The bill states this policy does not mean assurance of housing for any particular proportion of individuals of a certain race. The bill also limits Title VIII's coverage to actions taken with a discriminatory intent rather than those having a disproportionate disadvantageous impact. This bill is quite unfriendly to Black America.

26. Statement by President Richard M. Nixon on Federal Policies Relative to Equal Housing Opportunity, New Release, June 11, 1971.

27. UNITED STATES COMM'N ON CIVIL RIGHTS, FEDERAL CIVIL RIGHTS ENFORCEMENT EFFORT 446 (1970).

28. Chandler, *supra* note 1, at 164 n. 36.

29. Taeuber, *Demographic Perspectives on Housing and School Segregation,* 21 WAYNE L. REV. 833, 841 (1975). See also Kushner, *Apartheid in America: An Historical and Legal Analysis of Contemporary Racial Segregation in the United States,* 22 HOW L. J. 547 (1979).

30. Taeuber, *supra* note 29, at 841-42.

31. Freeman, *supra* note 17.

32. *Ibid*. at 1052

33. *Ibid* at 1054-55.

34. E. DORN, RULES AND RACIAL EQUALITY 139-40 (1979).

35. 42 USCA 1441 (West 1978).

36. 42 USCA 1401 (current version at 42 USCA 1437).

37. 42 USCA 1701t.

38. 42 USCA 5301.

39. *Id.*

40. *Id.*

41. See generally Herbers, *supra* note 4.

42. See generally NATIONAL HOUSING LAW PROJECT, HUD HOUSING PROGRAMS: TENANTS' RIGHTS (1981 and 1985 Supplement). Themes are discussed in Chapter 1.

43. Nolon, *Reexamining Federal Housing Programs in a Time of Fiscal Austerity: The Trend Toward Block Grants and Housing Allowances,* 14 URB. LAWYER 249, 249-50 (1982).

44. See HOUSING AND DEVELOPMENT RPTR (BNA) 494 (Nov. 18, 1985).

45. NATIONAL HOUSING LAW PROJECT (1985 Supplement), *supra* note 42, at 1/2.

46. *Id.* at 1/4-1/5.

47. THE PRESIDENT'S COMMISSION ON HOUSING, INTERIM REPORT 3 (1980).

48. Herbers, *Mobility for the Poor Sought in Housing Plan,* N.Y. Times, June 1, 1985, Sec. 1, at 9, col. 1.

49. *Id.*

50. See, e.g., R. MONTGOMERY & D. MANDELKER, *supra* note 18, *A Note on*

Federal Housing Subsidy Experience and the Housing Allowance Alternative, at 312.

51. Nolon, _supra_ note 43, at 276-77. The President's Commission on Housing recognized that housing allowances do not increase the supply of housing and thus passed the buck to "reliance on the experience and flexibility of state and local agencies to finance and produce housing, including both rehabilitation and new construction." Interim Report, _supra_ note 47, at 6. The Report also relies on the "trickledown" or "filtering" theory of housing occupancy, sug- gesting that its recommendations related to increasing the supply of housing for middle and upper income families will enable the poor also to find and afford better housing. _Id._

52. NATIONAL HOUSING LAW PROJECT (1985 Supplement), _supra_ note 42, at 1/6-1/7. (See also 42 USCA 1437)

53. _Id._ at 1/7.

54. Hartman, _Housing Allowances: The Grand Delusion_, in R. MONTGOMERY & D. MANDELKER, _supra_ note 18, at 322.

55. _Id._ at 323.

56. 409 U.S. 205 (1972).

57. _Id._ at 211.

58. 114 CONG. REC. 9559 and 9591 (1968).

59. 408 F. Supp. 489 (S.D. Ohio 1976).

60. REPORT OF THE NATIONAL ADVISORY COMMISSION ON CIVIL DISORDERS 1 (1968) (concluding that America was "moving toward two societies, one black, one white--separate and unequal." The Report recommended that a comprehensive open housing law be enacted.)

61. _Laufman, supra_, 408 F. Supp. at 496-97.

62. 564 F. 2d 126 (3d Cir. 1977).

63. 436 F. 2d 809 (3d Cir. 1970).

64. _Id._ at 822; _accord._, _Gautreaux v. Romney_, 448 F. 2d 731, 740 (7th Cir. 1971).

65. _Trinity Episcopal School Corp. v. Romney_, 387 F. Supp. 1044 (S.D. N.Y. 1974).

66. See generally Calmore, _Fair Housing v. Fair Housing: The Problem with Providing Increased Housing Opportunities Through Spatial Deconcentration_, 14 CLEARINGHOUSE REV. 7 (1980); Lev, _HUD Site and Neighborhood Selection Standards: An Easing of Placement Restrictions_, 22 URB. L. ANNUAL 199 (1981).

67. Calmore, *supra* note 66, at 15.

68. 42 USCA 5301(c)(6).

69. *Id.*

70. Calmore, *supra* note 66, at 7-8.

71. Note, *Symbolic Gestures and False Hopes: Low Income Housing Dispersal After Gautreaux and the Housing and Community Development Act*, 21 ST. LOUIS L. J. 759 (1978).

72. 43 Fed. Reg. 2363 (Jan. 16, 1978).

73. Community Devel. Digest, Sept. 11, 1979, at 8.

74. *Id.* at 9.

75. Housing Affairs Letter, Oct. 26, 1979, at 7.

76. Vernarelli, *Integration and Section 8 New Construction*, HUD Division of Housing Assistance Research, April 1981.

77. *Id.*

78. Johnson, *NAACP Parley Ties Black Survival to Ability to Move to Suburbs*, N.Y. Times, July 11, 1971, at 43, col. 4.

79. U.S. COMM'N ON CIVIL RIGHTS, EQUAL OPPORTUNITY IN SUBURBIA 5 (1974).

80. McDougall, *Gentrification: The Class Conflict Over Urban Space Comes Into the Courts*, 10 FORDHAM URB. L. J. 177, 180 (1981-82).

81. See, e.g., Comment, *Urban Development Action Grants: A Housing-Linked Strategy for Economic Revitalization of Depressed Urban Areas*, 26 WAYNE L. REV. 1469 (1980). For dysfunctional consequences, however, see *Munoz-Mendoza v. Pierce*, 711 F. 2d 421 (1st Cir. 1983).

82. See generally *Gentrification and Displacement Within Cities: A Comparative Analysis*, 61 SOC. SCI. Q. 638 (1980); P. CLAY, NEIGHBOR-HOOD RENEWAL (1979).

83. *Business Ass'n of Univ. City v. Landrieu*, 660 F. 2d 867, 874 n. 8 (3d Cir. 1981).

84. McDougall, *supra* note 80, at 180.

85. 660 F. 2d 867 (3d Cir. 1981).

86. S. REP. NO. 95-175, 95th Cong., 1st Sess. 8 (1977).

87. McGrew, *supra* note 14.

88. 518 F. Supp. 935 (N.D. Ill. 1981), *aff'd*, 688 F. 2d 529 (6th Cir. 1982).

89. 395 F. 2d 910 (2d Cir. 1968).

90. Id. at 931.

91. 294 F. Supp. 433 (N.D. Cal. 1968).

92. McGhee, Urban Renewal in the Crucible of Judicial Review, 56 VA. L. REV. 816, 874 (1970). See also Note, Judicial Review of Displacee Relocation in Urban Renewal, 77 YALE L. J. 966, 967 (1968).

93. 414 F. 2d 687 (5th Cir. 1969).

94. 387 F. 2d 179 (6th Cir. 1967).

95. See Cohen, The Battle of Jersey City's Redevelopment Project, CITY LIMITS, Aug.-Sept. 1982, at 13; C. HARTMAN, D. KEATING & D. LE GATES, DISPLACEMENT: HOW TO FIGHT IT (1982); C. WEILER, REINVESTMENT DISPLACEMENT: HUD'S ROLE IN A NEW HOUSING ISSUE (1978); Hanson, Applicability of Federal Statutory Remedies in Housing Displacement Cases: How Much Federal Involvement Is Necessary?, 59 U. DET. J. URB. L. 341 (1982); and Roisman, Combatting "Private" Displacement, 13 HOUSING L. BULL 1 (1983).

96. G. GRIER & E. GRIER, URBAN DISPLACEMENT: A RECONNAISSANCE 8 (1978).

97. LeGates & Hartman, Displacement, 15 CLEARINGHOUSE REV. 207, 229 (1981).

98. Id. at 220.

99. Mariano, Nation's Policy on Integration at Crossroads, Washington Post, August 17, 1984, at E3, col. 1.

100. Id.

101. Apparently, the Justice Department is motivated here by its uniform opposition to quotas associated with affirmative action goals and any policy that is not color-blind. See Integration Maintenance Policies Violate Fair Housing Act, Says Justice Official, HOUSING AND DEVELOPMENT RPTR (BNA) 509 (Nov. 18, 1985) (reporting on comments made to the U.S. Civil Rights Comm'n by Assistant Attorney General William Bradford Reynolds).

102. See generally Smolla, In Pursuit of Racial Utopias: Fair Housing, Quotas, and Goals in the 1980's, 58 S. CAL. L. REV. 947 (1985).

103. Note, Benign Steering and Benign Quotas: The Validity of Race Conscious Government Policies to Promote Residential Integration, 93 HARV. L. REV. 938, 939 (1980).

104. See generally Ackerman, Integration for Subsidized Housing and the Question of Racial Occupancy Controls, 26 STAN L. REV. 245 (1974).

105. 484 F. 2d 1122 (2d Cir. 1973), reversing the trial court decision at 354 F. Supp. 941 (S.D. N.Y. 1973).

106. Id. at 1134.

107. Ackerman, supra note 104, at 300 n. 257.

108. Note, supra note 103, at 962.

109. 551 F. Supp 746 (W.D. Pa 1982).

110. Id. at 767.

111. Id. at 769.

112. Id. at 770.

113. Smolla, Racial Occupancy Controls and Integration Maintenance: A Constitutional and Statutory Analysis, paper presented before the U.S. Civil Rights Comm'n Hearings, supra note 11, at 14-15.

114. Id. at 15.

115. Smolla, supra note 102, at 1015-16.

116. Silberman, Beware the Day They Change Their Minds, FORTUNE, Nov. 1965, at 152 (emphasis omitted).

117. Zangrando & Zangrando, Law, the American Value System and the Black Community, 3 RUT-CAM L. J. 32 (1971).

118. Hamilton, The Phenomenon of the Jesse Jackson Candidacy and the 1984 Presidential Election, in THE STATE OF BLACK AMERICA 1985, at 21 (J. WILLIAMS ed.).

119. Calmore, supra note 11, at 237.

120. Id.

121. D. GLASGOW, THE BLACK UNDERCLASS 191 (1980).

122. Id. at 193.

123. Hirsch, The Causes of Residential Segregation: An Historical Perspective, paper presented before the U.S. Civil Rights Comm'n Hearings, supra note 11, at 39.

124. Id.

125. Id.

126. Id. at 40.

127. Id.

128. _Id._ at 41.

129. Phillips & Agelasto, _Housing and Central Cities: The Conservation Approach_, 4 ECOLOGY L.Q. 797 (1975).

130. _Id._ at 880.

131. See generally NATIONAL LOW INCOME HOUSING COALITION, LOW INCOME HOUSING POLICY STATEMENT, "MAKING AFFORDABLE HOUSING A REALITY," HEARING BEFORE THE SUBCOMMITTEE ON HOUSING AND COMMUNITY DEVELOPMENT OF THE COMMITTEE ON BANKING, FINANCE AND URBAN AFFAIRS, HOUSE OF REPRESENTATIVES, Ninety-Eighth Cong., 2d Sess., June 28, 1984, at 4.

132. The personal troubles-public issues discussion is in C. WRIGHT MILLS, THE SOCIOLOGICAL IMAGINATION 8-9 (1959); the personal-political discontent discussion is in Boulding, _Social Justice in Social Dynamics_, in SOCIAL JUSTICE 80-88 (R. BRANDT ed. 1962).

133. C. WRIGHT MILLS, _supra_ note 132, at 226.

PROLOGUE TO A DEBATE

U.S. SOCIAL POLICY: OBSTACLE OR OPPORTUNITY FOR DISADVANTAGED AMERICANS?

The two papers that follow address themselves to the question above and each presents a different perspective. Originally, the authors engaged in a dialogue on this question at a special forum held during the 1985 Annual Conference of the National Urban League in Washington, D.C.

They were later requested by the NUL to revise their presentations and submit them for publication in "The State of Black America-1986." As with their presentations at the Conference, we set before them this proposition:

> Resolved, that the role of the national government--as exemplified in the 1960s and throughout part of the 1970s--in addressing broad social problems such as poverty, unemployment, health and education, and in fostering and implementing policies and programs designed to encourage affirmative action and enhance the enforcement of civil rights laws, was a positive force in improving the status of black Americans.

The opposing views that are presented here capture much of the essence of a debate taking place within the black intellectual community. To those unfamiliar with the history of Black America it might seem that such a debate represents something new. This, however, is not the case. There have been many other debates on social issues. One that comes immediately to mind took place earlier in this century between those who followed Booker T. Washington's emphasis on economics and moral advancement to be achieved through cooperation and conciliation, and those who felt as W. E. B. DuBois did that a more activist position should be taken by black people with a concentration on securing civil and voting rights.

Therefore, this present debate should be seen in its proper historical context. Not as something new, but as part of a continuing exchange of ideas that in the final analysis serves to strengthen Black America.

THE CASE FOR SOCIAL POLICY

By

Bernard E. Anderson

I. INTRODUCTION

Few issues of the past four decades have so absorbed the energies and efforts of the American people as the "problem of the color line." Forty years have passed since the publication of Gunnar Myrdal's American Dilemma, the epochal study of the American race problem by the internationally respected Swedish social scientist. Thirty years have passed since the U.S. Supreme Court's decision in Brown v. Board of Education, which struck down racial segregation in the nation's schools, and sounded the death knell for legal segregation throughout society. And twenty years have passed since the enactment of the Civil Rights Act of 1964, which erected a broad policy framework for the federal government's protection of the basic rights of blacks and other victims of discrimination.

Throughout this period, the nation has groped haltingly, but unmistakably toward its potential as a society that lives up to its ideal of equal opportunity for all. The uneven progress has moved more like a meandering stream than a straight arrow, but the general direction of change has been favorable. While there were always critics who preferred other strategies, a broad consensus emerged among the populace in support of social policy as an essential device for achieving an equal opportunity society.

Social policy is the legislative and administrative law aimed at reducing poverty, broadening economic opportunities and protecting basic rights. Federal, state and local governments have long developed and enforced such policies because in their absence, many members of the population either would be unable to make a productive contribution to society or would be denied the rewards their contribution justifies. The consensus in support of such policy grew over time as national life became more complex, and as national appreciation for the value of pluralism deepened.

A. The "New Conventional Wisdom"

Today, the consensus no longer exists, and social policy faces a serious challenge rooted in conflict over the appropriate role and the duty of government. Some critics say the government tried to do too much in the past; that government has overstepped its bounds, exceeded its legitimate functions, and has become an unhealthy and unnecessary intrusion into the lives of private citizens. The critics say government cannot solve social and economic problems, but indeed, when government attempts to solve such problems, it only makes things worse. To paraphrase the old VISTA slogan, some suggest that whenever government becomes part of the solution, it becomes part of the problem.

Some critics further argue that social and economic problems can only be solved through free enterprise, in an unbridled and unregulated free marketplace, where each individual is motivated by narrow self interest, while government keeps hands off to let it all happen. This suggests that neither the development of social policy nor the promotion of social change are legitimate functions of government.

If this is true, the implications for social and economic progress are enormous, and potentially disastrous both for the black community and for the nation as a whole. It means there is no place for public policy to help reduce economic inequality and to protect equal opportunity in American life. It means replacing government assistance with self-help in a society where the means and resources for going it alone are vastly and unequally distributed. It also means turning away from the egalitarian traditions of our past in favor of a social Darwinistic future.

Charles Murray is a popular spokesman for the new conventional wisdom. In his book "Losing-Ground",[1] he insists that the government-financed programs which evolved from the Great Society have been both destructive and counterproductive. "The complex story," according to Murray, "comes down to this: basic indicators of well-being took a turn for the worse in the 1960s, most consistently and most drastically for the poor. In some cases, earlier progress slowed; in other cases mild deterioration accelerated; in a few instances advance turned into retreat... it is indeed possible that steps to relieve misery can create misery. The most troubling aspect of social policy toward the poor in late twentieth-century America is not how much it costs, but what it has bought."

According to Murray, government-financed programs have "bought" increases in social pathology: increases in crime, teenage unemployment, teenage pregnancies, abortions, poverty, households headed by single mothers, and so on. Since the interventions of the Federal Government are responsible for creating such social ills, Murray believes the nation will be healthier when we abolish welfare, food stamps, medicaid, and the whole array of cash grants and services to the poor along with the bureaucratic structures they have created.

B. The Role of Black Conservatives

Murray is not alone in his denunciation of social policy. During the past few years a group of black conservatives has emerged as prominent critics of social policies designed to help the disadvantaged.[2] The black conservatives differ among themselves in their analysis of race in contemporary America, and in their policy prescriptions, but their common aversion to a significant role for government in addressing the remaining problems of racial inequality in American life is a unifying theme. Indeed the attention and prestige now accorded to black conservatives by the mainstream print and electronic media tends to lend a legitimacy to some criticisms of social policy that otherwise might be dismissed out of hand.

C. Government Protects the Public Interest

When thinking about the connection between government and the social progress of racial minorities today, it is not only helpful, but essential to remember that the role of government as protector of the national interest was accepted from the beginning of the Republic and has been reaffirmed on numerous occasions since then. The national interest is served by policies designed to make social conditions more just, and the distribution of important social goods and opportunities more equal and fair. To be sure, the government has not always acted in ways that reflect such values, but the overarching goal, expressed in the American Creed, has always been the standard by which government actions are measured.[3/]

D. Social Policy and Self-Help

It is fashionable to suggest that since the legal stucture of discrimination has now been dismantled, black people must turn their attention to their own community, and through self-help and individual initiative, address the remaining problems of inequality.[4/] But to affirm the role and responsibility of government to act in favor of enhancing the life opportunities of racial minorities does not in any way demean or negate individual initiative or self-improvement. Quite the contrary, the reaffirmation demonstrates a strong commitment to individual initative and a determination to exercise it.

No one familiar with the history of black people in America will ever suggest that they have not spent many years, much energy, and enormous resources engaged in self-help.[5/] Black churches are widely known for their Men's Day, Women's Day, Usher's Day, Children's Day -- almost every day but judgment day. Black fraternities, sororities, and other social organizations are often the despair of their members for the demands on time and money to address community problems. No black professional association of any size or significance ever holds a meeting at which the agenda is not overcrowded with discussions on "how to help the black community." Black people would not have survived in America without an inordinate devotion to self-help.

But there is more to self-help and individual initiative than "picking yourself up by your own bootstraps." Self-help and individual initiative are also expressed and fulfilled when black leadership and black people act as the conscience of America, to keep the nation from turning its back on the promise of opportunity expressed in the American Creed. As stated by Roger Wilkins, "while government cannot be our salvation, it must be our ally."

Self-help as a device for social progress is not the issue. The important point is the balance between self-help and other strategies at this time.[6/] The essence of American democracy has been the use of state authority by different groups to enjoy the benefits of a pluralistic society and to protect the rights and opportunities of its populace. Those who would urge black people now, in the name of self-help and individual initiative, to abandon efforts to pressure government into acting

-155-

on their behalf are really advocating a dangerous, self-defeating strategy in which the power of the state would be used to protect and extend the interest of virtually every group except the black population.

II. DOES SOCIAL POLICY HELP?

It seems almost an article of faith today to hear that government assistance, in fact, is harmful and ineffective even if well intentioned. [7/] According to this view, the inequities of social policy consist not only in its intrusion into the private lives of individuals, but also in its failure to produce positive results.

To say all government efforts to improve the lives of minorities, the poor and disadvantaged were total, counterproductive failures is pretentious, academic hogwash. No one of sound mind and honest opinion would portray all programs developed under social policy as perfect, but there is no question that some social programs of the last two decades helped reduce poverty, helped increase job opportunities, and helped broaden the participation of black and other minorities in American life.

It is not possible to provide a complete review of the impact of social policy, but it might be helpful to provide evidence on three social policy issues of broad public concern: the rate of poverty, youth unemployment, and affirmative action.

A. Poverty

The official poverty rate, based on data from the Census Bureau, declined sharply from 1965 to the early 1970s, remained stable in the mid-70s, then began to climb higher in 1978. As late as 1982, while 15.0% of all Americans lived below the poverty line, the rate of poverty for the black population was 36%, compared with only 12% among white persons.

A careful examination of the evidence suggests that economic growth contributed significantly to the reduction in poverty during the late 1960s, but public assistance cash grants distributed during the war on poverty also played an important role. In fact, according to economists at the Institute for Research on Poverty at the University of Wisconsin, cash transfers accounted for about half the reduction in poverty between 1967 and 1969. [8/] The elderly benefited more than younger groups from the increase in cash transfers, but policies designed to increase the income of poor families clearly achieved a measure of success, at least until recent years.

In the absence of all government benefits, stimulated by public concern about poverty during the past two decades, there certainly would have been more Americans living below the poverty line.

Much of the public concern today is focused on poverty among black households headed by women. Since 1960, the number of such families more than tripled; and now, half of all black families with children are headed by women. In 1983, almost seven out of ten children living in such families were poor.

Some have suggested that public welfare, especially to females with dependent children (AFDC) is responsible for the increase in the number of black families headed by women. But a review of the evidence does not support that conclusion.

Since 1972, the fraction of all children living in a female headed household increased, while the fraction of children in homes collecting AFDC remained unchanged. It is hard to see how AFDC is responsible for more single parent families when the number of children in the program remained constant when family structures changed the most.

If not AFDC, then what is responsible for the growing number of black female single parents? While changing values and attitudes, and behavior might help explain this development, the diminished employment opportunities among young black men played a major role.

There is a close correlation between increases in black households headed by single mothers and the decrease in job opportunities for black males. As Professor William J. Wilson of the University of Chicago wrote in a recent paper "Despite the existence of evidence suggesting that the increasing inability of many black men to support a family is the driving force behind the rise of female headed families, in the last 10 to 15 years welfare has dominated explanation of the increase in female headed households."[9]

Since 1960, the number of black families headed by women has more than tripled. But something else has been happening at the same time. The labor force participation rate for black men declined from 83% in 1960 to 61% in 1983. The decline was most dramatic for young black men aged 16 to 19; only two of five had jobs, or were seeking work last year.

In the last eight years alone the number of black families headed by women increased by 700,000 -- and so did the number of black males unemployed or out of the labor force. More than half of black men aged 16 to 24 looked for work but did not find it during the recession year of 1982. Persistent joblessness has long been a problem for the group and has continued through the current recovery. The record clearly shows that structural unemployment and black family structure are closely interrelated.

B. Labor Market Policy

Critics of social policy say structural unemployment is a problem of labor supply rather than labor demand. They say if the total number of jobs exceeds the number of unemployed, then those who are jobless are in that position because they are unwilling to accept the terms offered in the marketplace. This is considered a problem of values and behavior, and not an issue the Federal Government can effectively address. Thus, according to the new philosophy, there is no meaningful role for the Federal Government in reducing structural unemployment, except to get out of the way and let the market operate.

Much has been written about the failure of job training programs to increase the employment and earnings of disadvantaged populations. The experience with such efforts has been mixed. Many mistakes were made, and many dollars were wasted in some of the employment and training programs supported during the past two decades.[10/] But a number of valuable lessons were learned along the way, and we know much more now than we did during the past decade about the essential elements of effective jobs programs. Most important, we know that in an expanding economy, well-designed job training and employability development programs can help increase the economic opportunity available to low-income disadvantaged groups.

For example, the youth incentive entitlement pilot project (YIEPP) was a demonstrably successful program.[11/] The entitlement projects were authorized by Congress as part of the Carter Administration's Youth Employment Policy in 1977, and was aimed specifically at testing the link between schooling and employment for disadvantaged youth. The program was targeted to low-income teenagers in 17 selected cities. A guaranteed job at the federal minimum wage was provided so long as the youth remained in (or returned to) school and achieved satisfactory performance in both school and work.

An evaluation of the entitlement program was conducted by the Manpower Demonstration Research Corporation, a New York based social science research organization. During the two and one half years the program was in operation, 76,000 youths worked in program jobs. Most participants were young minorities, enrolled in school, and members of welfare dependent families. Few had ever held an unsubsidized job, and most had never participated in other federally assited job training programs.

More than half of the eligible youths in each area participated in the program, and the communities showed they could deliver on a job guarantee. Most important, school year employment more than doubled for black youth, reversing the 25-year gap between black and white youth employment rates. Youth wages increased sharply for program participants, especially during the school year.

The entitlement program is not the only example of successful youth employment programs. Important and valuable lessons also have been learned from a series of school to work transition programs supported jointly by the private sector and the Federal Government. During the past five years, the Jobs for Americas Graduates program has operated in almost 100 high schools in a dozen cities in eight states. Two-thirds of the students who participated in the program were minorities.

Seventy percent of the participants were successfully placed in jobs, or further education within three months after high school graduation. Equally important, the benefits of program participation were greatest for minority youth with marginal academic records.

C. Affirmative Action

The assault on social policy also redefines the purpose of civil rights law, and the protection of basic rights. In this view, civil rights are color blind, neutral, and vested solely in the individual. Civil rights legislation, according to proponents of the new social policy, must guarantee the right of each individual to be free of discrimination, but must never be applied to groups or to individuals as members of groups. Thus, the premise of affirmative action is rejected and opposed under the new social policy.

The redefinition of civil rights laws ignores the experience of history and present reality. Individuals are not discriminated against in isolation or solely because of individual characteristics, but rather because of their membership in and identification with groups. The identification and protection of certain groups suffering the effects of past and current discrimination is what affirmative action is all about.

Racial quotas have been imposed only in cases in which the courts have found discrimination. In keeping with the constitutional requirement that courts find a remedy to correct the denial of basic rights, racial quotas have been used at times to assure nondiscriminatory behavior. Even conservative judges, such as Justice Powell in the Bakke case, recognize the legitimate use of race as a criterion for distributing public benefits when there is a history of past discrimination.[12/] Affirmative action in all other instances means no more (and no less!) than taking special pains to remove all vestiges of discrimination by making sure qualified minorities and women are included in the relevant applicant pool, and are seriously considered for available positions when employment, education, housing, and other distributional opportunities are dispensed.

According to the critics, affirmative action is not only wrong in concept, but also, it does not work. They say no minorities and women get jobs they would not have had in the absence of affirmative action, and any minorities and women hired in the environment of affirmative action will never know whether the decision was based on merit, or influenced by the individual's membership in the protected group.

The evidence does not support this claim. According to a study conducted, but unpublished by the U.S. Department of Labor in 1983, employment and promotion for minorities in companies doing business with the Federal Government was significantly higher than in businesses without Federal Government contracts. Between 1974 and 1980, the rate of minority employment grew by 20% among the contractors compared to only 12% in other companies. In addition, 22% of the minorities in the contractor firms were in lower-paying service or unskilled jobs, compared to 39% in companies without federal contracts.

This evidence is confirmed by research conducted by Professor Jonathan Leonard of the University of California.[13/] After a carefully designed, exhaustive review of data from the Office of Federal Contract Compliance, Leonard concluded, "In the contractor sector, affirmative action has increased the demand relative to white males for black males by 6.5%, for non-black minority males by 11.9%, and for white females by 3.5%." While acknowledging the administrative deficiencies in the enforcement of the executive order on government contracting, this study, nonetheless, shows rather conclusively that affirmative action has a positive impact on the employment opportunities of protected groups. A reexamination of Leonard's findings by two economists, who in the past had been skeptical about the impact of affirmative action failed to refute the evidence. Indeed, the verification study concluded that affirmative action among government contractors had strong positive effects, especially for college graduates.[147]

III. CONCLUSION

This brief review of the impact of social policy provides only an introduction to the body of evidence that suggests government initiatives in support of equal opportunity often have been successful. The challenge now is to build upon, and expand those policies and programs shown to be effective, and abandon those that are not.

Despite the social and economic progress achieved during the past two decades, many disparities between the status of black and other communities remain, and real equal opportunity and economic security for many black people remains only a distant dream. There is a major role for government in addressing such problems, not alone, but in cooperation with the black community, and with other enlightened segments of society.

Racial inequality in American life was nurtured and enforced by government in the past, and can only be corrected through strong social policy at this time. The debate over self-help versus government action is unfortunate because it diverts attention from the serious political and organizational effort now required to attack the remaining remnants of inequality. Self-help by the black community will not reduce structural unemployment, increase a quality housing stock, raise academic test scores, or improve health care for poor black children or the elderly. Such problems require the resources of the state deployed with care, intelligence, commitment, and compassion working, in part, through voluntary organizations within the black community. The framework for such cooperation must be expressed in a social policy unabashedly aimed at reducing racial inequality in American life. Only then will the nation live up to its creed as a society committed to equal opportunity for all.

: : :

FOOTNOTES

1. Murray, Charles, "Losing Ground" (New York: Basic Books, 1984), pp. 3-15.

2. Council on A Black Economic Agenda, "Policy Statement," January 15, 1985.

3. Hamilton, Charles V. and Hamilton, Dona C. "Social Policies, Civil Rights, and Poverty," Institute For Research on Poverty, Conference Paper, December 6-8, 1984.

4. Loury, Glenn, "Internally Directed Action for Black Community Development," Review of Black Political Economy Summer-Fall, 1984, pp. 31-46; and Jeffrey Howard and Ray Hammond, "Rumors of Inferiority," New Republic, September 1985.

5. Franklin, John Hope, "Values and Traditions, in the Black Community," unpublished paper, March 6, 1985.

6. Committee for Policy for Racial Justice, "A Policy Framework for Racial Justice," published by Joint Center for Political Studies, November 1983.

7. Williams, Walter, "The State Against Blacks" (New York: McGraw-Hill 1983).

8. Gottschalk, Peter and Danniger, Sheldon "Macroeconomic Conditions, Income Transfer, and the Trend in Poverty," in Lee Bawden (ed.) "An Assessment of Reagan's Social Welfare Policy." (Washington: Urban Institute Press, 1984).

9. Wilson, William J and Neckerman, Kathryn "Poverty and Family Structure," Institute for Research on Poverty Conference Paper, February 1985.

10. Perry, Charles R and Anderson, Bernard E. al., The Impact of Government Manpower Programs (Philadelphia, University of Pa. Press, 1975); and National Research Council, Youth Employment and Training Programs: The YEDPA Years (Washington: National Academy of Sciences, 1985).

11. Gueron, Judith M. "The Youth Incentive Entitlement Pilot Projects: Lessons from a Job Guarantee," Manpower Demonstration Research Corp., New York, May 1984.

12. For an argument in favor of preferential treatment consistent with a broadly defined public interest and beyond the constitutional requirement for the protection of basic rights, see Richard Wasserstrom, "A Justification of Preferential Treatment Programs," Rockefeller Foundation Conference Paper, October 1983.

13. Leonard, Jonathan S. "The Impact of Affirmative Action on Employment," National Bureau of Economic Research, Working Paper No. 1310, March 1984.

14. Welsch, Finis and Smith, James "Affirmative Action and the Labor Market," Journal of Labor Economics, Vol. 2, No. 2, 1984.

BEYOND CIVIL RIGHTS

By

Glenn C. Loury*

I. INTRODUCTION

My theme will be the limitations of civil rights strategies for effectively promoting the economic and social progress of minorities. By a "civil rights strategy" I mean two things: First, that the cause of a particular socio-economic disparity be identified as racial discrimination; and second, that the advocates seek such remedies for the disparity as the courts and administrative agencies provide under the law. It has by now become a common theme in commentary on racial inequality in American society to observe that not all problems of blacks are due to discrimination, nor can they be remedied via civil rights or, more broadly, through racial politics [Loury, 1985]. I will reiterate this theme here.

More than this, however, I want to suggest that the inappropriate specification of a particular obstacle to minority progress as a civil rights matter can have significant costs. Evoking civil rights remedies for circumstances to which they are not suited can obviate the pursuit of alternative, more direct and effective approaches to the problem. Such activity uses scarce resources which might otherwise be applied-the time and attention of those engaged directly in the advocacy, but also the goodwill and tolerance of those expected to respond. Finally, I will argue that the broad application of the civil rights method to every instance of differential achievement by blacks can be positively harmful in attaining the long sought goal of fully equal status in the society-and threatens if continued successfully to make it literally impossible for blacks to be genuinely equal in American society.

I should make clear at the outset that I continue to believe there is an important role for civil rights law enforcement, and for those organizations which have played such a crucial part in the historic struggle for civil rights in this country. I do not believe racism has disappeared from American life, nor that appeals to conscience, based upon the history of injustice to which blacks have been subject, no longer have a place in our public life. Yet, it is obvious, given the American political and philosophical tradition, that the reach of civil rights law is and will remain insufficient to eliminate all socially and economically relevant discriminatory behavior. In light of this fact (to be elaborated below), it is important for blacks to augment this historically important approach to the problem of racial inequality.

I begin by noting that there are enormously important contractual relationships into which people enter, as a result of which their social

---

*This paper was presented to the Annual Conference of the National Urban League, Washington, DC, July 1985. A version of it latter appeared in The New Republic, October 7, 1985.

and economic status is profoundly affected, but among which racial discrimination is routinely practiced. Choice of marital partner is the most obvious. People discriminate here by race with a vengeance. A black woman does not have an opportunity equal to that of a white woman to become the wife of a given white man. Indeed, though this inequality in opportunity cuts both ways, since white men are on the whole better-off financially than black men, one could imagine calculating the monetary cost to black women as a class of the fact that white men engage in discrimination of this sort. A class action suit might be filed on their behalf, seeking redress for the "damages" which result. Yet, of course, this is absurd. In large part, its absurdity derives from our acceptance, in principle as well as in fact, of an individual's right to engage in discrimination of this sort.

The point is of much more general applicability. Voluntary associations among individuals of all sorts (residential communities, friendship networks, business partnerships) are the result of mutual choices often influenced by racial criteria, but which lie beyond the reach of civil rights laws. A fair housing law cannot prevent a disgruntled resident from moving away if the racial composition of his neighborhood changes. Busing for school desegregation cannot prevent unhappy parents from sending their children to private schools. Withdrawal of university support for student clubs with discriminatory selection rules cannot prevent student cliques from forming along racial lines. Application of the non-discrimination mandate has, in practice, been restricted to the domain of impersonal, public, and economic transactions (employment, credit, housing, voting rights), but has not been allowed to much interfer with personal, private, and intimately social intercourse.

Yet, the fact that such exclusive social "clubs" do form along group lines has important economic consequences. An extensive literature in economics and sociology documents the importance of family and community background as factors influencing a child's latter life success [Datcher, 1982]. Studies have shown that access to the right "networks" can beneficially affect the outcome of job search in the labor market [Datcher, 1983]. Indeed, it has been theoretically demonstrated that, under plausible assumptions, when social background influences offspring's opportunities to acquire human capital, and when two groups of equal innate capabilities start with unequal economic status, then elimination of racial discrimination in the economic sphere but not in patterns of social attachment is generally insufficient to bring about eventual equalization of economic outcomes [Loury, 1977; Loury, 1981]. There are, thus, elemental limits on the degree of economic equality between the races which one can hope to achieve through the use of civil rights laws. These limits derive from the fact that the anti-discrimination principle has been, as a matter of historical fact, restricted in its application to a limited domain of personal interactions.

Moreover, it is possible to question the ability of civil rights strategies to reduce group disparities in those areas to which they have been freely applied--education and employment, for example. Elsewhere I have argued that some important part of group economic disparity is due to the nature of social life within poor black communities [Loury, 1984; Loury, 1985].

With upward of three-fourths of children born out-of-wedlock in some inner-city ghettos, with black high school drop-out rates of better than 40% (measured as the fraction of entering freshmen who do not eventually graduate) in Chicago and Detroit, with 40% of murder victims in the country being blacks killed by other blacks, with fewer black women graduating from college than giving birth while in high school, with black women ages 15-19 being the most fertile population of that age group in the industrialized world, with better than two in five black children dependent on public assistance, and with these phenomena continuing space notwithstanding two decades of civil rights efforts—it is reasonably clear that civil rights strategies alone cannot hope to bring about full equality [Wilson, 1984; see also Wilson, 1978]. This is not to deny that, in some basic sense, most of these difficulties are related to our history of racial oppression. I only suggest (as, for example, Eleanor Holmes Norton has argued [Norton, 1985]) that they have by now taken on a life of their own, and cannot be effectively reversed by civil rights policies.

II. EDUCATION

Further illustration of this point is provided by reference to the field of higher education. In the past (and not too distant past at that), there were severely limited opportunities for minorities to participate in higher education, as student or faculty, especially at the elite institutions. Nonetheless, many distinguished black scholars, scientists, inventors, jurists, writers and teachers had overcome the obstacles of racism to contribute to the common intellectual life of their country. Yet, in decades past, these men and women of genius learned and practiced their academic crafts under the most difficult conditions. Even after black scholars studied at the great institutions, their only possiblities for employment were at the historically black colleges, where they faced large teaching loads and burdensome administrative duties. Their accomplishments were often acknowledged by their white peers only grudgingly, if at all.

Today, opportunities for advanced education and academic careers for blacks abound. Major universities throughout the country are constantly searching for qualified black candidates to hire as professors, or admit to study. Most state colleges and universities near black population centers have made a concerted effort to reach those in the inner-city. Almost all institutions of higher learning admit blacks with lower grades or test scores than white students. There are special programs funded by private foundations to help blacks prepare for advanced study in medicine, economics, engineering, public policy, law and other fields. Special scholarship and fellowship funds have been set up for black students throughout the country.

Yet, with all these opportunities, and despite some improvement, the number of blacks advancing in the academic world is distressingly low. The percentage of college students who are black, after rising throughout the 1970's, has actually begun to decline. And while the proportion of doctorates granted to blacks has risen slightly over the last decade, it is still the case that the majority of black doctorates are earned in the field of education [The College Board, 1985]. Despite constant pressure to hire black professors and strenuous efforts to recruit them, the percentages of blacks on elite university faculties has remained constant or fallen in the past decade [New York Times, Jan. 28, 1984].

Meanwhile, other groups traditionally excluded are making impressive gains. Asian-Americans, though less than 2% of the population, make up 6.6% of U.S. scientists with doctorates; they constitute 8% of the student body at Harvard, 7.5% at Yale, and 9% at Stanford [Bell, 1985]. Women have also made progress: The fraction of doctorates going to women has risen from less than one-seventh to nearly one-third in the last decade [New York Times, Jan. 28, 1984]. At Harvard's Graduate School less than 3% of the students are black, but more than 30% are women. Less than 2% of Harvard professors at all ranks are black, but more than 25% are women [Affirmative Action Report of Harvard University, 1985].

No doubt, blacks continue to experience some discrimination at these institutions: But it is not a credible assertion to anyone who has spent time in an elite university community that these institutions are racist in character, and deny opportunities to blacks whose qualifications are outstanding. A case could be made that just the opposite is true--that these institutions are so anxious to raise the numbers of blacks in their ranks that they overlook deficiencies when making admissions or appointment decisions involving blacks. But for my purpose it only need be accepted that this state of affairs, in which black representation languishes at what, for many campus communities are politically unacceptable levels, does not admit a viable civil rights oriented solution. It would be very difficult to make the case that, upon finding and eliminating the racially discriminatory behavior of faculty and administrators, this circumstance would reverse itself.

One obvious reason for skepticism about the efficacy of a civil rights strategy here would seem to be the relatively poor academic performance of black high school and college students. Black performance on standardized college admissions tests, though improving, still lags far behind whites. In 1982, on the mathematics component of the SAT, the median white score was 484, while the median black score was 369. There were only 205 blacks in the entire country who scored above 700, though 3,015 Asian Americans achieved this distinction [College Board, 1983]. And, as Robert Klitgaard has shown convincingly, post admission college performance by black students is less than that of whites, even when controlling for differences in high school grades and SAT scores [Klitgaard, 1985].

These differences in academic performance are not just limited to poor blacks, or to high school students. On the SAT exam mentioned earlier, blacks from families with income in excess of $50,000 per year still scored 60 to 80 points below comparable whites [College Board, 1983]. On the 1981 Graduate Record Exam, taken by virtually all college seniors seeking to pursue advanced studies in the humanities and sciences, the gap between black and white students median score on the quantitative mathematics component of this test was 171 points [Educational Testing Service, 1982]. At Harvard College there is a significant and disturbing difference in the grades earned by black and white students. According to professors at the Harvard Law School there have only been a few black students graduated in the top half of their class in the last five years. Klitgaard [1985, chp. 8] found that black law school admittees in the late

1970's had median scores on the Law School Aptitude Test at the eighth percentile of the overall distribution of scores among law students.

It is clearly a matter of great concern that such substantial differences in educational results exists. One imagines that social background and limited past opportunities for blacks play an important role in accounting for these test score differences. It is also possible that the psychological effects on blacks of the "Rumors of Inferiority" which have circulated in American society about the intellectual capabilities of black people partly explains this disparity [Howard and Hammond, 1985]. Arguably, the government should be actively engaged in seeking to attenuate them. But it seems equally clear that this is not a civil rights matter--that it cannot be reversed by seeking out and changing someone's discriminatory behavior. Moreover, it is possible that great harm will be done if the problem is defined and pursued in those terms. This is illustrated by the example of a recent controversy over racial quotas at the Boston Latin School.

The Boston Latin School is the pride and joy of the city's public school system. It was founded before Harvard, in 1635. It has been recognized for centuries as a center of academic excellence. Boston Latin maintains its very high standards through a grueling program of study, including Latin, Greek, calculus, history, science and the arts. Three hours of homework per night is typical. College admissions personnel acknowledge the excellence of this program. Ninety-five percent of the class of 1985 will go to college: Harvard has accepted 22 Latin graduates for next year's freshman class [Boston Globe, April 22, 1985].

The institution admits its students on the basis of their primary school marks, and performance on the Secondary School Admissions Test. In 1974, when Boston's public schools became subject to court-ordered desegregation, Judge Arthur Garrity considered closing Boston Latin, because at that time the student population had been more than 90% white. Upon consideration though, it was ordered that a racial admissions quota be employed requiring 35% of the entering classes to be black and Hispanic. Of the 2245 students last year, over half were female, 57% white, 23% black, 14% Asian and 6% Hispanic [Boston Globe, April 22, 1985].

Historically the school has maintained standards through a policy of academic "survival of the fittest." Those who were unable to make it through the academic rigors simply transferred to another school. Thus, there has always been a high rate of attrition; it is now in the range of 30-40% [Daniels, 1985]. But, unlike the pre-desegregation era, today most of those who do not succeed at Boston Latin are minority students. Indeed, though approximately 35% of each entering class is black and Hispanic, only 16% of last year's senior class was. That is, for each (non-Asian) minority student who graduates from Latin, there is one who did not. The failure rate for whites is about half as great [Boston Globe, April 22, 1985]. Some advocates of minority student interest have, in the face of this racial disparity, complained of discrimination, saying in effect that the school is not doing enough to assist those in academic difficulty. Yet there is reason to doubt the effectiveness of this "civil rights strategy." Surely one reason for the poor performance of the black and Hispanic students is the racial admissions quota ordered by Judge Garrity a decade ago. To be considered for admissions, whites must score at the 70th percentile or higher on the admission exam, while blacks and Hispanics need only score above the 50th percentile. But the problems of minority students at Boston Latin have not prevented some from advocating that the minority admissions quota be increased.

Attorney Thomas Atkins, former General Counsel of the NAACP, who has been representing the black plaintiffs in this law suit off and on for ten years, proposed to Judge Garrity in the Spring of 1985 that the quota at Boston Latin be raised to roughly 50% black, 20% Hispanic and Asian and 30% white--a reflection of the racial composition of the rest of Boston's public schools. Absent a significant increase in the size of the school, this could only be accomplished by doubling the number of blacks admitted while cutting white enrollment in half. This in turn, under plausible statistical assumptions, would require an approximate doubling of the now 20 point gap in threshold test scores of black and white admittees. Since the additional black students admitted would of necessity be less prepared than those admitted under the current quota, one would expect an even higher failure rate among minorities, were this plan to be accepted. The likely consequence would be that more than three-fourths of those leaving Boston Latin without a degree would be blacks and Hispanics. It is also plausible to infer that such an action would profoundly alter, if not destroy, the academic climate in the school.

This is not simply an inappropriate use of civil rights methods, though it is surely that. We have here an almost wanton surrender of the moral high ground by an advocate who would seek remedy for the failure of Boston's black students to excel from a federal judge! By what logic of pedagogy can these students' difficulty be attributed to racism, in view of the fact that the school system has been run by court order for over a decade? By what calculus of fairness do those fighting for justice arrive at the position that outstanding white students, many from poor homes themselves (80% of Latin graduates require financial aid in college) should be denied the opportunity for this special education so that minority students who are not prepared for it may nonetheless enroll? Responding to black student underrepresentation at Boston Latin as if this were a civil rights problem seems patently unwise. Is there so little faith in the aptitude of the minority young people that the highest standards should not be held out for them? Are their advocates so vindictive about the past that they would risk injuring their own children and inflict gross unfairness on the children of others all in the name of numerical racial balance?

Another example from the field of education illustrates how the use of civil rights methods, when not appropriate to the problem at hand, can have significant "opportunity costs." In 1977 the Ann Arbor public school system was sued by representatives of a class of black parents with children in the primary grades. The school system was accused of denying equal educational opportunity to these children. The problem was that the black students were not learning how to read at an acceptable rate, though the white youngsters were. The suit alleged that, by failing to take into account in the teaching of reading to these children the fact that they spoke an identifiable, distinct dialect of the English language--Black English--the black students were denied equal educational opportunity.

The lawsuit was successful [Glazer, 1981].

As a result, in 1979 the court ordered that reading teachers in Ann Arbor be given special "sensitivity" training so that, while teaching standard English to these children, they might "accommodate" the youngsters' culturally distinct patterns of speech. Ann Arbor's public school system has dutifully complied. A recent discussion of this case with local educators revealed that, as of six years after the initial court order, the disparity in reading achievement between blacks and whites in Ann Arbor persists at a level comparable to that which obtained before the lawsuit was brought. It was their opinion that, though of enormous symbolic importance, the entire process had produced little in the way of positive educational impact on the students.

This is not intended as a condemnation of those who brought the suit, nor do I offer here any opinion on whether promotion of Black English is a good idea. What is of interest is the process by which the problem was defined, and out of which a remedy was sought. In effect, the parents of these children were approached by public interest lawyers and educators active in civil rights, and urged to help their children learn to read by bringing this action. Literally thousands of manhours went into conceiving and trying this case. Yet, in the end only a hollow, symbolic victory was won. Apparently, the federal district judge did not have it within his power to eliminate the disparity between black and white children in rates at which reading competency was acquired.

But it is possbile that, more than simply ineffective, this line of attack on the problem and the advocative instincts from which it sprang caused other viable strategies not to be pursued. One imagines for example that a direct effort to tutor the first and second graders might have made an impact, giving them special attention and extra hours of study through the voluntary participation of those in Ann Arbor possessed of the relevant skills. With roughly 35,000 students at the University of Michigan's Ann Arbor campus (a fair number of whom are black), it would have required that only a fraction of one percent of them spare an afternoon or evening once a week for there to be sufficient numbers to provide the needed services. There were at most only a few hundred poor black students in the primary grades experiencing reading difficulties. And, more than providing this needed aid for specific kids, such an undertaking would have helped to cultivate a more healthy relationship between the university and its community. It could have contributed to building a tradition of direct service that would be of more general value. But none of this happened, in part because the "civil rights approach" was almost reflexively embraced by the parties concerned.

III. AFFIRMATIVE ACTION

Indeed, there is reason to be concerned that the tendency to perceive every instance of differential performance between racial groups as remediable by some affirmative action-like treatment may, if successfully continued, destroy the posssbility of attaining "real" equality of status for black Americans.

The simplest version of this argument is by now very familiar—

affirmative action creates uncertain perceptions about the qualifications of those minorities who benefit from it. If, in an employment situation say, it is known that differential selection criteria are used for different races, and if it is further known that the quality of performance on the job depends on how one did on the criteria of selection, then in the absence of other information it is a rational statistical inference to impute a lower perceived quality of performance to persons of the race which was preferentially favored in selection. Using race as a criterion of selection in employment, in other words, creates objective incentives for customers, co-workers, etc., to take race into account after the employment decision has been made.

More than this, however, the broad use of race preference to treat all instances of "underrepresentation" introduces uncertainty into the process by which individuals make inferences about their own abilities. A frequently encountered question today from a black man or woman promoted to a position of unusual responsibility in a "mainstream" institution is: "Would I have been offered this position if I had not been a black?" Most people in such situations want to be reassured that their achievement has been earned, and is not based simply on the organizational requirement of racial diversity. As a result, the use of racial preference tends to undermine the ability of people to confidently assert, if only to themselves, that they are as good as their achievements would seem to suggest.

It therefore undermines the extent to which the personal success of one black can become the basis of guiding the behavior of other blacks. Fewer individuals in a group subject to such preferences can confidently say to their fellows: "I made it on my own, through hard work, self-application and native ability, and so can you!" And, disturbingly, the broad use of affirmative action as a vehicle for black achievement puts even the "best and brightest" of the favored group in the position of being the supplicants of benevolent whites.

But neither is this the end of the story. Because in order to defend such programs in the political arena--especially at the elite institutions--it becomes necessary to argue that almost no blacks could reach these heights without special favors. This, when examined closely, entails the virtual admission that blacks are unable to perform up to the white standard. Thus, Harvard Univeristy president Derek Bok--arguing in defense of black interests, he thinks--has publicly declared that, without the use of quotas in undergraduate admissions, only 1% of the entering class would be black (though roughly eight times as many would be Asian Americans!) [Bok, 1985]. This practically forces the conclusion that blacks, on the whole, must make up through the use of quotas what they lack in intellectual capabilities.

In New York City, where the last examination for promotion to police sergeant was passed by 10.1% of whites, 4.4% of Hispanics, but only 1.7% of blacks [New York Times, September 4, 1984], the city has agreed to scrap the test and promote its quota of blacks. The test, they say, is illegally discriminatory since fewer blacks passed, and since the city's legal department does not think it could be defended as job-related. Yet, the test was explicitly prepared (at a cost of $500,000 and under a court supervised consent decree), so as only to test job-relevant skills. No one really believes the <u>test</u> was unfair to non-white officers, only the <u>results</u> are questioned. But, after this episode, can anyone be made to believe that blacks are capable of the same results as whites?

The use of racial quotas, deriving from the civil rights approach to problems of racial differences in performance, can have subtle effects on the way in which black people think about themselves. When there is internal disagreement among black intellectuals, for example about the merits of affirmative action, critics of the policy are often attacked as being disingenuous, since they clearly owe their own prominence to the very policy they criticize. The specific circumstances of the individual do not matter in this, for it is presumed that <u>all</u> blacks, whether directly or indirectly, are indebted to civil rights activity for their achievements. The consequence of this is a kind of "socialization" of the individual black's accomplishments. The individual's effort to claim achievement for himself, and thus to secure the autonomy and legitimacy needed to lead and shape the groups' views of its condition, is perceived as a kind of betrayal.

This is, in a subtle but non-trivial way, destructive of black self-esteem. There is nothing wrong, of course, with acknowledging the debt all blacks owe to those who fought and beat Jim Crow. There is everything wrong with a group's most accomplished persons feeling that the celebration of their personal attainments represents betrayal of their fellows.

IV. CONCLUSION

In his recent, highly esteemed comparative history of slavery, <u>Slavery and Social Death</u>, Orlando Patterson defines slavery as the "permanent, violent domination of natally alienated and generally dishonored persons" [Patterson, 1982]. Most discussion of the American slave experience in contemporary policy discourse focuses on the violent character of the institution, its brutalization of the Africans, and its destructive effects on social life among the slaves. There is much debate among historians and philosophers on the precise extent to which this history is related to current-day policy concerns. Less attention is paid nowadays to the <u>dishonored</u> condition of the slave, and by extension of the freedman. For Patterson this dishonoring was crucial. He sees as a common feature of slavery wherever it has occurred the parasitic phenomenon whereby masters derive honor and standing from their power over the slaves, and the slaves suffer an extreme marginality by virtue of having no social existence except that mediated by their masters. Patterson rejects the "property in people" definition of slavery, arguing that relations of respect and standing among persons are also crucial. But if this is so, it follows that emancipation--the ending of the master's property claim--is not of itself sufficient to convert a slave (or his descendant) into a genuinely equal citizen. There remains the intractable problem of overcoming the historically generated "lack of honor" of the freedmen.

This problem, in my judgment, remains with us. It's eventual resolution is made less likely by black's broad, permanent reliance on racial preferences as remedies for academic or occupational under-performance. A central theme in Afro-American political and intellectual history is the demand for respect--the struggle to gain inclusion within the civic community, to become co-equal participants in the national enterprise. This is, of course, a problem which all immigrant groups also faced, and which most have overcome. But here, unlike some other areas of social life, it seems that the black population's slave origins, subsequent racist exclusion, and continued dependence on special favors from the majority uniquely exacerbates the problem.

Blacks continue to seek the respect of our fellow Americans. And yet it becomes increasingly clear that, to win the equal regard of our fellows, black Americans cannot substitute judicial and legislative decree for what is to be won through the outstanding achievements of individual black persons. That is, neither the pity, nor the guilt, nor the coerced acquiescence in one's demands--all of which have been over the last two decades amply available to blacks--is sufficient. For what ultimately is being sought is the freely conveyed respect of one's peers. Assigning prestigious positions so as to secure a proper racial balance--this as a permanent, broadly practiced policy--seems fundamentally inconsistent with the attainment of this goal.

It is a truth worth noting that not everything of value can be redistributed. With respect to personal traits like beauty or intelligence this is readily obvious. But it is no less true for other important nonpecuniary goods like dignity and respect. If, in the psychological calculus by which people determine their satisfaction such status considerations are important, then this observation places basic limits on the extent to which public policy can effect fully egalitarian outcomes. This is especially so with respect to the policy of racially preferential treatment, because its use to "equalize" can actually destroy the good which is being sought on behalf of those initially unequal. It would seem that, where the high regard of others is being sought, there is no substitute for what is to be won through the unaided accomplishments of individual persons.

: : :

REFERENCES

1. Bell, David (1985). "The Triumph of Asian Americans," The New Republic July 15 & 22, 1985, pp. 24-31.

2. Bok, Derek (1985). "Admitting Success," The New Republic February 4, 1985.

3. Boston Globe (1985). "Boston Latin at 350 Faces Challenge of Old Ways vs. New Times," April 22, 1985.

4. College Entrance Examination Board (1983). Profiles, College Bound Seniors, 1982, New York.

5. College Entrance Examination Board (1985). Equality and Excellence: The Educational Status of Black Americans, New York.

6. Daniels, Lee (1985). "The Halls of Boston Latin School," The New York Times Magazine April 21, 1985.

7. Datcher, Linda (1983). "The Impact of Informal Networks on Quit Behavior," Review of Economics and Statistics LXV, No. 3 (August) pp. 491-495.

8. Datcher, Linda (1982). "Effect of Community and Family Background on Achievement," Review of Economics and Statistics LXIV (Feb.) pp. 32-41.

9. Educational Testing Service (1982). "Summary of Data Collected from Graduate Record Examinations Test-Takers During 1980-81." Princeton.

10. Glazer, Nathan (1981). "Black English and Reluctant Judges," The Public Interest (No. 62) Winter.

11. Howard, Jeff and Ray Hammond (1985). "Rumors of Inferiority," The New Republic, September 9, 1985, pp. 17-21.

12. Klitgaard, Robert (1985). Choosing Elites. New York: Basic Books.

13. Loury, Glenn (1977). "A Dynamic Theory of Racial Income Differences," Chap. 8 in P.A. Wallace (ed.) Women, Minorities and Employment Discrimination, Lexington Books.

14. Loury, Glenn (1981). "Is Equal Opportunity Enough?" American Economic Review Papers and Proceedings (May), pp. 122-126.

15. Loury, Glenn (1984). "A New American Dilemma," The New Republic, Dec. 31, 1984, pp. 14-19.

16. Loury, Glenn (1985). "The Moral Quandry of the Black Community," The Public Interest, Spring.

17. New York Times (1984). "Blacks Decrease But Women Increase on University Faculties." June 28, 1984.

18. New York Times (1984). "Koch Defends Sergeants Test and Orders Its Results Used," September 4, 1984, p. A1.

19. Norton, Eleanor (1985). "Restoring the Traditional Black Family," The New York Times Magazine (June 2): 43.

20. Patterson, Orlando (1982). Slavery and Social Death. Cambridge: Harvard University Press.

21. Wilson, William J. (1978). The Declining Significance of Race: Blacks and Changing American Institutions, Univ. of Chicago Press.

22. Wilson, William J. (1984). "The Urban Underclass," Minority Report, L.W. Dunbar (ed.) New York: Pantheon.

CONCLUSION AND RECOMMENDATIONS

The heart of Black America is strong. It has more than its fair share of problems and there are not too many places to which it can turn for a helping hand or even a sympathetic ear. Nevertheless, there is a growing movement within this community that emphasizes doing more for ourselves. And it is not a movement of despair, but rather one of high hopes born out of the conviction that while we cannot change some circumstances, there are many things that we can do to set our house in order.

These are not new sentiments within Black America, but history will record that the watershed of their convergence into something that can properly be described as a national movement took place in the spring of 1984 at a Black Family Summit co-sponsored by the National Urban League and the National Association for the Advancement of Colored People. Out of that Summit, which was attended by representatives of more than 100 national black organizations, came a revitalization of the spirit of Black America, a renewal of faith in the strength of its own institutions, a renewed commitment to achieve equity, excellence and empowerment within Black America.

Looking back, there were some critics who questioned the value of holding such a meeting and who expressed doubts that anything would ever come out of it. They've been answered now. There is hardly a community within Black America in which its various institutions have not stepped forward to deal with a variety of problems that threaten the strength, viability and future growth of these communities.

In light of this, it is difficult to understand why so many people outside the black community, and even a handful inside, persist in instructing this community that it should do more on its own—as if it is not doing anything. The truth is that the black community has long been doing things for itself despite its limited resources. Dr. Bernard Anderson sets the record straight in his paper "The Case for Social Policy."

He states:

> "No one familiar with the history of black people in America will ever suggest that they have not spent many years, much energy, and enormous resources engaged in self-help. Black churches are widely known for their Men's Day, Women's Day, Usher's Day, Children's Day—almost everyday but judgment day. Black fraternities, sororities, and other social organizations are often the despair of their members for the demands on time and money to address community problems. No black professional association of any size or significance ever holds a meeting at which the agenda is not overcrowded with discussions on 'how to help the black community.' Black people would not have survived in America without an inordinate devotion to self-help."

-175-

"But there is more to self-help and individual initiative than 'picking yourself up by your own bootstraps.' Self-help and individual initiative are also expressed and fulfilled when black leadership and black people act as the conscience of America, to keep the nation from turning its back on the promise of opportunity expressed in the American Creed. As stated by Roger Wilkins, 'while government cannot be our salvation, it must be our ally.'"

The statement by Wilkins brings into sharp focus our view of what the proper relationship with government should be. We do not look to government for all the answers, but there are certainly clearly definable areas in which its assistance is indispensible such as hunger, poverty and unemployment. Examining the critical issue of unemployment, Dr. David Swinton earlier described in detail how the end of every recession has found blacks worse off than they were at its beginning, and how they never make up the lost ground. He has further described how black males are securing less and less of the job market and how the income gap between white and black is growing.

In his conclusion, he stated:

"The continuation of current laissez faire policies will likely produce more of the same results that we have experienced for the last decade. We will continue to have a gradual erosion of the economic position of the working class, an increasingly large population of poor and near poor families, and increasing racial inequality in economic status. This is because left to themselves, economic incentives will continue to give signals that will lead to the decline of high wage sectors and expansion of low wage sectors.

"In view of the disproportionately heavy impacts that poor policies have on the black community, black leaders must take the lead role in advocating a more effective national economic policy. In addition to a set of more rational and effective national policies, black leaders are justified in seeking policies to promote equal opportunities and to eliminate the historical disadvantages of blacks in wealth and human capital ownership."

The fact is that there are certain problems that cannot be solved without the assistance of the government and avoiding them today—as the present Administration has done—can only make them that much more difficult to solve in the future.

We are encouraged, however, that not everyone in Washington shares the Administration's apparent aversion to social service programs that help the poor. There are Democrats and Republicans alike who still believe government has a role to play in promoting the welfare of all its people. We listened with interest at our 1985 Annual Conference when Senate Majority Leader Robert Dole said:

"Republicans understand that there are those who must look to the federal government for help in opening the door of opportunity. But we also believe that compassionate governments don't impose double-digit inflation on the poor and give them welfare checks instead of jobs in a healthy private sector. We believe that a rising tide lifts all boats, but we also understand, as Vernon Jordan once said, that some boats are still in the 'drydocks of America's economy' and will remain stranded without the government's help."

Having reviewed 1985, we offer some ideas as to what Black America will be like in 1986. In 1986, the black community will have to fight off continuing threats to past civil rights gains for there is little reason to expect the Administration's offensive against affirmative action, school desegregation, and other key issues to slacken.

Still to be resolved is the fate of Executive Order 11246, and it is with this that the President has one of his last chances, before he leaves office, to take a positive action on behalf of civil rights. It would be best for the nation if the order remained unchanged because it has been demonstrably successful in promoting equal opportunity and it has wide support within the business community.

The implementation of the Gramm-Rudman budget deficit bill, with its mandated cuts in domestic programs and the military, will in all probability produce further attempts to cut or end social programs, especially with the massive federal deficit likely to grow beyond current projections. Fortunately, some of the programs that serve the poor, such as food stamps, have been exempted from cuts, but this still leaves other social programs vulnerable.

The Congress is determined to lower the massive deficit and the Administration is equally determined to continue increases in military spending. Since neither side is willing to raise taxes, that means programs for the poor and domestic programs in general will be the targets for budget-cutting.

So a major challenge in the coming year will be to reorder national priorities, for we can't allow poor people to suffer more--they've already been driven to the wall by earlier cuts in survival programs that helped increase poverty and hunger in this rich land.

The black-white job gap is growing instead of closing, and this intolerable situation has to be met by programs providing work for the jobless and training opportunities for displaced workers and youth.

This will also be a year in which education becomes the major issue in the black community.

Black dropout rates are high and college entrance rates are lower than in past years. The new jobs coming on stream today demand skills,

knowledge and attitudes not found among many poor youth, so it is imperative that the educational system become responsive to the needs of the
black community.

That won't happen through current proposals to undercut public education by vouchers, tuition tax credits, and similar schemes. But it can
happen if the black community harnesses its political power and its vo-
lunteer power to insist on schools that provide quality education for all.

And it can happen if a business community concerned about the need for
a higher skilled and better trained work force joins fully in the struggle
to make the educational system function as well in inner-city ghettos as
it functions in suburban communities.

There are signs that this may happen. A blue-ribbon group of top
business leaders has issued a report calling for massive new resources
for public education, and many individual companies are working to make
the schools more effective.

So 1986 will find a growing community of interest between industry
and the black community, with both having a major stake in making the
schools provide quality education.

The National Urban League's recommendations follow:

1. Under present policies and the nature of the job market, youth unemployment continues at horrendous levels. Congress should take the
   initiative in establishing a National Youth Employment Program that
   includes education, training and work components. Pending development and passage of such a measure, the Youth Incentive Employment
   Act (H.R. 671), the American Conservation Corp. Act (H.R. 99) and
   the Extension of the Targeted Jobs Tax Credit Act (H.R. 983) should
   be passed.

2. A Universal Employment and Training System should be established
   that would guarantee the unemployed productive work and the skills
   training necessary to obtain and hold a job. Such a system would be
   a joint public-private effort that would include rebuilding the de-
   caying infrastructure of the nation such as its roads, bridges, rail
   systems and ports, as well as improving public services. The system
   would train the unskilled and the unemployed and retrain displaced
   workers for jobs in growth industries.

3. Congress should take the initiative in establishing a full employment policy that would have a multitude of elements including macroeconomic policies and tax reforms that stimulate expanded economic
   activity and encourage maximum use of the less skilled and educated
   workers. The policy would require aggressive affirmative action
   programs to ensure that blacks are included in employment gains and
   should include assistance to black business development as well as
   meet the needs of displaced workers, older workers, new entrants into
   the work force, and female headed households.

4. The Job Training Partnership Act should be modified so as to become

more effective through the provision of increased funding, better monitoring to ensure compliance with program targeting, and mandated participation of community based organizations.

5. A joint Congressional Select Committee should be established to examine the defense program from top to bottom and develop a rational, affordable defense program that enhances our security and frees tax revenues to reduce the deficit and to fund programs that serve the needy.

6. The proposed Civil Rights Restoration Act of 1985 should be passed in this session of Congress to restore the broad coverage and protection embodied in Title VI of the Civil Rights Act of 1964, Title IX of the Education Amendments of 1972, Section 504 of the Rehabilitation Act of 1973, and the Age Discrimination Act of 1975.

7. While teen pregnancy is a problem that has to be addressed at the local level there is a role for the national government. To ensure a more concerted national effort to address this problem, Congress should pass the Teenage Pregnancy Block Grant authorizing a two-year grant program to permit state AFDC agencies to operate a two-part teenage pregnancy program geared toward prevention and self-sufficiency. At the local level, community based organizations should be actively involved in the implementation of such programs.

8. Parity in income security for all our children and their families can only be accomplished through the federalization of funding for the Aid to Families With Dependent Children Program thereby assuring that all Americans, no matter where they live, will have access to an equal level of benefits (relative to need) and are subject to the same criteria of eligibility. Congress should therefore seriously examine the great disparity in our current AFDC system and pursue federalization as a reform measure.

9. The Administration's proposal to establish a voucher system in public education poses the possibility that funds for the public schools--through which the overwhelming majority of minority and poor youngsters obtain their education--will be further reduced. Until the government can conclusively demonstrate that a voucher system would meet the goal of quality education for all children, the national thrust should be concentrated on efforts to improve the public schools.

10. Federal outlays for the Aid to Families With Dependent Children Program have decreased each year since passage of the Omnibus Budget Reconciliation Act of 1981 resulting in the accumulated loss of 19% between fiscal year 1981 and 1984. More than two-thirds of AFDC recipients are children and Congress should act to not only reject any further budget cuts in this program but to also restore funding.

11. Congress should pass a tax reform bill that is fair and broadly based, with corporations bearing an equitable share and individuals contributing according to their ability to pay, exempting the poor

and those with incomes insufficient to meet basic human needs.

12. A long term and consistent program for federal support for histori-cally black colleges should be ensured through the reauthorization of the Higher Education Act containing Title III (H.R. 2907) which includes provisions for historically black colleges and universities.

13. Maximum parity in health care coverage for all Americans can be ac-complished through Congressional enactment of a universal comprehen-sive health care plan and through adoption of the cost-containment principles set forth in the Medicare Solvency and Health Care Fi-nancing Act of 1985 (H.R. 1801).

14. In light of the grave disparity in the treatment of black children within the child welfare and juvenile justice systems, Congress should insist on strict enforcement of Title VI of the Civil Rights Act of 1964 with regards to the delivery of child welfare services, and provide at least a $70 million funding of the Juvenile Justice and Delinquency Prevention Act of 1974 to allow continued implementa-tion of its goals.

15. The Fair Housing Act should be amended to provide enforcement powers and to extend the bill's coverage to include families with children.

16. The Section 237 Program which created a special mortgage lending pool for low income families to purchase homes, and provide counseling to these families to reduce the risks associated with lower cash re-quirements should be revised.

17. Congress and the Administration should renew the national commitment made nearly 40 years ago to provide a decent and suitable living environment for all Americans by providing funding to increase the supply of affordable housing and targeting benefits.

18. A massive effort must be undertaken by Black America to increase the achievement level of all black students in the public schools. These schools, through community and institutional activism, must be made to prepare black youngsters to function and prosper in today's eco-nomy. Urban schools must teach, in addition to the 3Rs, higher order thinking skills, problem solving, test competency and computer literacy to all of their students. The community must demand more accountability from the schools.

19. Community based efforts to combat teen pregnancy should be expanded and where possible should concentrate on prevention. Included in any program, however, should be the elements identified by the Mayor's Blue Ribbon Panel on Teenage Pregnancy Prevention in the District of Columbia--(1) parental involvement, (2) male involvement and respon-sibility, (3) greater initiative on the part of the schools in de-veloping relevant curriculum for sex education, (4) job programs for high risk teens, (5) school based health clinics, and (6) day care for teen parents.

20. Black parents must assume a greater role in instilling responsible sexual standards in their children and must become more active in serving as a counterbalance to the sexually permissive messages that reach their children through the various media, including radio, records, and TV videos, and from the streets.

21. The media should devote more attention to the many positive developments taking place within Black America such as the increasing mobilization of community resources to deal with a variety of problems, the success of programs to train the disadvantaged for the job market, individual and institutional achievements, etc. At the same time, the American people must be made aware that some problems within Black America are properly within the province of government including reducing structural unemployment, increasing a quality housing stock for low income families, providing health care for the poor and elderly, and assuring non-discrimination in employment, education, public services, housing, etc.

22. Now representing only 2% of all businesses, black businesses must be increased and developed: The black community bears a responsibility to support all black businesses wherever and whenever possible. Government bears the responsibility of fostering minority small businesses through loan guarantees, technical assistance and the continuation and further development of minority set-aside programs. The private sector bears the responsibility of fostering black business by utilizing more of its services and products.

23. American corporations doing business in South Africa should exert pressure on the U.S. government to step up its efforts to bring about an end to apartheid. The corporations should also exert whatever leverage they have on Pretoria to hasten the downfall of apartheid and should began making plans for withdrawal from that country if apartheid is not dismantled within a reasonable amount of time.

24. In all black institutions including churches, schools, community organizations, youth clubs and social and fraternal groups, much more emphasis must be placed on inculcating in black children a deeper knowledge and understanding of the black past. Race should be a matter of pride with our young people but this can only occur if their elders expose them on a continuing basis to the history and the struggle of black people. This should be done unapologetically, building on the experience of other racial and ethnic groups who have found that a shared history joins a people together.

: : :

CHRONOLOGY OF EVENTS

1985*

AFFIRMATIVE ACTION

Jan. 6:   Reportedly, the Reagan Administration has joined an effort in Congress to reverse a Supreme Court decision in the Grove City College case. The Administration has proposed new language to be included in a civil rights bill that would allow federal funds to be withheld from educational institutions with discriminatory programs whether they were government financed or not. The bill is in response to the court's ruling that federal funding could be withheld only from specific programs guilty of discrimination within such institutions and not the entire institution itself. However, civil rights critics oppose the language charging that it applies only to educational institutions and does not specify all institutions receiving federal funds.

Feb. 1:   Clarence Pendleton, Chairman of the United States Commission on Civil Rights, and Morris Abram, Vice Chairman, say they support the Supreme Court decision that invalidates affirmative action plans that conflict with seniority programs. The Commission adopts a statement approving the high court's decision in the Memphis (TN) firefighters case No. 11784 V. Stotts, which sanctions the layoff of recently hired blacks in favor of more senior employees. Commissioners Mary Frances Berry and Blandina Cardenas dissent.

Feb. 13:   Clarence Thomas, Chairman of the Equal Employment Opportunity Commission, announces a new policy in which the commission will focus on resolving individual cases of discrimination rather than broader complaints against businesses and industries. Critics maintain the move demonstrates the federal government's ever weakening role as an enforcer of civil rights.

Feb. 16:   Special hearings held by an American Bar Association panel on minorities in the legal profession reveal that blacks continue to be underrepresented as students and faculty in law schools, in private law firms and bar groups, and the judicial bench. While the enrollment of blacks in law school has increased by nearly 20% in the last decade, according to the National Law Journal, blacks comprised only 1.5% of all lawyers in the nation's 100 largest law firms in 1984. This is down from a figure of 2.9% just two years ago.

March 1:   In special letters sent to nearly 50 cities and states, the Justice Department asks that they consider modifying existing court orders and consent decrees establishing numerical goals and timetables for hiring minorities and women. The department's rationale for its action is a 1984 Supreme Court decision barring the layoffs of senior white firefighters in Memphis, TN, to preserve the jobs of recently hired blacks. Assistant Attorney General William Bradford Reynolds, head of the department's civil

---

* This chronology is based on news reports. In some instances the event might have occurred a day before the news item appeared.

rights division, contends the ruling applies to hiring and promotion plans as well.

March 7: Civil rights groups boycott a U.S. Commission on Civil Rights hearing on the use of goals, timetables and quotas as remedies to discrimination charging it has already decided to oppose such measures.

March 13: Clarence Pendleton, Chairman of the U.S. Commission on Civil Rights, says he favors the elimination of the commission after full public debate on the "central issue of preferential treatment." Once this occurs (in three to four years he estimates) Pendleton says civil rights monitoring should be the responsibility of the Justice Department and the Equal Employment Opportunity Commission.

March 16: A Justice Department lawyer, Richard J. Ritter, in a sworn statement, charges that the department is contradicting the terms of a consent decree it negotiated in 1981 to facilitate the increased hiring of minorities and women in Birmingham, AL. The Justice Department now contends that the plan is discriminatory and permits the hiring of less qualified minorities rather than "demonstrably better qualified whites."

March 25: A study issued by the Potomac Institute credits affirmative action with nearly doubling the percentages of women, blacks and other minorities in professional and managerial positions between 1970 and 1980. Based upon government statistics, during this period, the number of black officials and managers rose from 1.9% to 4%; women from 10.2% to 18.5% and Hispanics from 1% to 2.2%. Herbert Hammerman, a private consultant who conducted the study, asserts he is convinced the gains would not have occurred without the affirmative action programs.

March 29: The Labor Department and the General Motors Corp. reach a new agreement on the frequency and quantity of information the company will provide on its affirmative action efforts. According to the accord's terms, GM will have to demonstrate the viability of its program by providing more information on hiring and promotions at some 300 major facilities, and will submit to compliance reviews at ten or more sites each year.

April 3: The Justice Department makes public, the names of the 56 cities and states in which it seeks to modify affirmative action plans to end the use of numerical goals and quotas to increase the employment of blacks, women and other minorities. Among the agencies and jurisdictions are the New York State Police, the Los Angeles Police and Fire Departments and the North Carolina Highway Patrol. The Department maintains that such "preferences" are not permissible under Title VII of the Civil Rights Act of 1984.

April 30: A motion is filed in court by the Justice Department to overturn the affirmative action programs of the Indianapolis Police and

Fire Departments. The department's action is the first such effort taken against one of the 56 cities and states it sent letters asking that they voluntarily abandon the use of numerical goals and quotas. Indianapolis officials state that they will oppose the action.

May 2:   The NAACP files suit in U.S. District Court against the Justice Department's effort to force more than 50 cities and states to abandon court-ordered affirmative action plans utilizing race and sex-based quotas and timetables. It calls the effort unconstitutional and asks the court to issue a restraining order barring the department from further action.

May 4:   In a letter to Attorney General Edwin Meese, III, five Democrats on the House Judiciary Committee advise that the Justice Department should "vigorously" enforce affirmative action hiring goals, which "should not be tampered with," in more than 50 jurisdictions nationwide.

May 7:   A report by the House Government Operations Committee recommends that the Justice Department, the Federal Trade Commission and the National Endowment for the Humanities no longer receive federal funds if they continue to refuse to submit goals and timetables for hiring and promoting blacks, minorities and women.

May 8:   A cross-section of civil rights advocates picket the Justice Department with placards protesting its national campaign to dissemble court-ordered affirmative action plans that include hiring and promotion goals and timetables. Rabbi Alexander M. Schindler calls the department's action "an attempt to subvert civil rights enforcement in the United States."

May 10:   A federal judge gives approval for the deletion of hiring goals from affirmative action plans for the city of San Diego. Although the Justice Department filed a motion in court seeking the action, it did so with the consent of city officials who had reached agreement with the department before the Supreme Court ruling in the Memphis firefighters case.

May 21:   Continuing its campaign to overturn hiring and promotion plans containing quotas and numerical goals for the employment of women, blacks and minorities, the Justice Department files five separate motions in pending cases involving the Chicago Police and Fire Departments. The motions challenge remedies contained in court orders settling three separate discrimination lawsuits filed by the Justice Department during previous adminstrations. Chicago officials oppose the department's current stance.

May 25:   According to a survey by the Bureau of National Affairs, many of the 50 states and local governments urged to abandon the use of goals and timetables in their affirmative action plans for public employees, are rejecting the Justice Department's request. Thus far, only three jurisdictions have agreed to join the department's effort: the Arkansas State Police, the police and fire departments in Buffalo, NY and the police force in Wichita Falls, TX.

June 2: Black and Hispanic leaders in San Diego criticize the agreement reached between the city and the Justice Department to dismantle court ordered affirmative action plans utilizing quotas and time-tables. The minority leaders contend that the city has not fully met its goals in hiring and promoting its minorities. The President of the San Diego Urban League, Rudolph Johnson, says while there has been some progress for blacks in the administrative and clerical positions, they have not made similar inroads into management.

June 5: As hearings by the Senate Judiciary Committee begin on his nomination as Associate Attorney General, William Bradford Reynolds announces that the Justice Department will discontinue its legal effort to force jurisdictions to abandon the use of goals and timetables in their affirmative action hiring and promotion plans. Reynolds says that the department will suspend the filing of lawsuits against jurisdictions that refuse to comply until the Supreme Court clarifies whether such measures are legal.

June 25: At the NAACP's 76th Annual Convention, Labor Secretary William Brock asserts that the country will "have to have some form of affirmative action for the foreseeable future." Secretary Brock stresses that he is referring only to those affirmative action plans that fall under his jurisdiction in the enforcement of fair hiring and promotion practices by federal contractors.

July 20: In Buffalo, NY, a federal district judge rules against abolishing the city's numerical goals for hiring minorities in the city's police and fire departments. The judge's ruling is the first of its kind among the more than 50 jurisdictions that the Justice Department has tried to convince to abandon the special measures.

July 24: In a speech to the National Urban League's 75th Annual Conference, Labor Secretary William Brock states his opposition to "absolute numerical quotas," in affirmative action programs. However, Brock continues to express support for the use of goals and timetables in such programs to remedy job discrimination against women, blacks and minorities. Brock's position counters that of William Bradford Reynolds, head of the Justice Department's civil rights division, who remains strictly opposed to the use of quotas, goals or timetables.

Aug. 9: Assistant Attorney General William Bradford Reynolds clarifies his definition of affirmative action as the number of persons recruited to apply for positions at companies charged with discriminatory hiring practices, not the actual number of blacks and minorities hired. According to the report, the definition was set out in an earlier letter to Sen. Edward M. Kennedy (D-Mass.) in which Reynolds claimed that the Reagan Administration has had equal success in hindering job discrimination by requiring companies to actively recruit qualified blacks and minorities.

However, less than half of the 26 cases cited by Reynolds were companies unable to provide substantive data showing that their recruitment efforts were as successful as the use of goals, quotas and timetables in increasing the ranks of their minority employees.

Aug. 15:   Attorney General Edwin Meese and William Bradford Reynolds, head of the Justice Department's Civil Rights division, urge President Reagan to sign a draft executive order rescinding a 1965 order (11246), mandating fair employment and hiring practices through the use of goals and timetables by government contractors. The proposal specifies that the contractors are not required "to utilize any numerical quota, goal or ratio" or to be found in violation of the order, for not using them as remedies to discrimination based on race, sex, or religion.

Aug. 16:   The draft executive order that would no longer require government contractors to use numerical goals and timetables to insure fair hiring and promotion for blacks and minorities is challenged by business organizations. James Conway, associate director of equal opportunity for the National Association of Manufacturers says most of its 13,600 member companies are comfortable with the use of goals and timetables and regard them as "a way of measuring progress."

Sept. 12: Labor Secretary William Brock announces that the Reagan Administration has developed a draft revision of executive order 11246, which will no longer require federal contractors to use numerical goals and timetables in the hiring and promotion of minorities and women. Under the revised order, federal contractors may voluntarily use the measures, but they are not required to by law.

Sept. 18: In a speech to students and faculty at Dickinson College (Carlise, PA), Attorney General Edwin Meese accuses proponents of the use of goals and timetables in affirmative action plans of employing the same kind of reasoning that allowed slavery to exist. He states that the Reagan Administration unequivocally rejects the notion "that affirmative action must mean race-conscious, preferential treatment." Meese adds that the Administration's policy of "nondiscrimination" is being berated as against affirmative action.

Sept. 19: President Reagan is urged to retain Executive Order 11246, requiring federal contractors to set goals and timetables for their affirmative action programs, by a bipartisan group of 125 members of the House and Senate. The executive order also authorizes oversight by the Labor Department's Office of Federal Contract Compliance Programs, and was signed into law by President Johnson in 1965.

Sept. 20: Expanding a Reagan Administration offensive against race and sex-conscious remedies for discrimination in affirmative action programs, Assistant Attorney General William Bradford Reynolds calls federal programs that set aside contracts for minority businesses "offensive" charging they are discriminatory and may be illegal. In a speech to the National Construction Industry Council, Reynolds asserts there is no justification for tolerating or perpetuating the programs at the federal, state or local levels.

Oct. 23: Unable to agree upon a final draft revision of executive order 11246, key administration officials send President Reagan a proposal detailing three different policy options for changing hiring and promotion regulations for federal contractors. The policy options propose either to: issue a new executive order sanctioning the use of voluntary goals and timetables, but providing no legal basis for mandating such measures; to leave the executive order intact, but to prohibit mandatory quotas in Labor Department regulations; or to issue a new executive order explicitly barring mandatory quotas by government contractors without referring to the use of goals and timetables.

Oct. 29: President Reagan postpones a decision on whether to revise Executive Order 11246 on the basis of recommendations presented to him in an options paper developed by key aides and Cabinet officials.

Nov. 1: Assitant Attorney General William Bradford Reynolds claims that the govenment's affirmative action program for federal contractors has prevented "deserving" blacks and women from being hired, in a speech to the Rotary Club in Wilmington, Del.

Nov. 4: In an interview on CBS-TV's "Face the Nation," Clarence Pendleton, Chairman of the U.S. Commission on Civil Rights, predicts that President Reagan will sign an executive order that critics says will severely weaken affirmative action guidelines for federal contractors. Pendleton claims that the use of numerical goals and timetables to ensure fair hiring and promotion practices for minorities and women is discriminatory.

Dec. 4: The Equal Employment Opportunity Commission reports that in FY 1985, it substantially increased its productivity filing 411 lawsuits and recovering $54 million for job discrimination victims. According to the commission's Office of General Counsel, the $54 million reflects the settlement of 204 lawsuits and the resolution of 90 subpoena enforcement actions. The number of cases that were closed increased from 55,343 in the previous fiscal year to 63,567 in FY 1985.

Dec. 23: Federal District Judge Sam Pointer Jr., dismisses the reverse discrimination suit of 14 white firefighters in Birmingham, Ala. who claimed they were denied advancement because of a city hiring and promotion plan favoring less qualified blacks. Judge Pointer ruled that the consent decree accepted by the city and Justice Department in 1981 is valid, and that the firefighters failed to prove the plan violated that agreement.

THE FEDERAL BUDGET

Jan. 1:   Alan Beals, Director of the National League of Cities says in a news conference, that despite "token" budget surpluses, American cities cannot absorb further cuts in federal aid. Beals contends that an estimated $5 to $6 billion surplus for all state and local governments, cited by the Reagan Administration as evidence that they no longer need federal aid, is misleading. He says because the cities are legally bound to operate with balanced budgets, occasional surpluses occur when their economies generate more tax revenue than anticipated.

Jan. 5:   Representative William H. Gray 3rd, a Democrat from Pennsylvania, is elected Chairman of the House Budget Committee, after a solid and steadfast campaign for the prestigious post, which had been sought by a number of other candidates in Congress. Gray, who is black, quit the budget committee in 1981 citing its reluctance to stem cuts in social spending but, rejoined it in 1983 to seek the chairmanship.

Feb. 4:   According to reports, President Reagan's fiscal year 1986 budget proposes nonmilitary spending cuts of $38.8 billion, while military spending would increase by 12.7% to $277.5 billion. More than 25 programs would be eliminated under the $973.7 billion budget package, in which total program spending cuts are $47.5 billion. Among the program cuts are the elimination of revenue sharing (saving $3.4 billion), limits on student financial aid, a $4 billion cut in Medicare, reductions in Medicaid and support for subsidized housing.

Feb. 8:   The President of the U.S. Conference of Mayors, Ernest N. Morial of New Orleans, says that the federal budget proposed by President Reagan, which cuts grants to state and local governments by $20 billion, signals the end of "the historical federal-city partnership" that has helped the nation's urban areas to survive. The Administration's budget proposes the elimination of general revenue sharing funds, urban development action grants and the Economic Development Administration.

Feb. 15: According to reports, while corporate contributions to charity have increased significantly in recent years, they have not been enough to fill the gap in social service programs left by federal budget cuts. While corporate giving increased from $2.5 billion in 1981 to $3 billion in 1983 (latest year for which figures are available), it comprised only 5% of all charitable giving in the nation.

Feb. 20: Marian Wright Edelman, president of the Children's Defense Fund, charges that the Reagan Administration's 1986 budget will provide $5.2 billion less for poor children and families.

March 11: A special survey issued by the U.S. Conference of Mayors reveals that the $20 billion of cuts in grants to the cities and states proposed in the Reagan Administration's FY 1986 budget, will result in an 18% decrease in federal aid. Federal assistance to cities will total only 5.5% of federal outlays compared to 8.5% in 1981. Of 157 cities responding to the survey, 97% say they will have to cut services, while 68% say they will have to increase local revenues. Among the assistance curtailed by the cuts will be housing for the elderly, summer employment for disadvantaged youth and emergency food and shelter programs for the hungry and homeless.

March 15: The Senate Budget Committee passes a FY 1986 budget of $966.1 billion, which includes a freeze on Social Security benefits and wide-ranging cuts in domestic spending.

March 15: In a 40-page report, the Southern Regional Council asserts that federal budget cuts have had the greatest impact on the Southern poor. The SRC says that nearly 36% of the four million people dropped from poverty programs nationwide since 1980 have been Southerners.

April 10: According to the reports, President Reagan agrees to cuts in his defense spending request, to freeze Social Security benefits and to spare the elimination of Job Corps and other programs, in an effort to win Senate passage of his budget calling for $50 billion in deficit reductions for FY 1986.

April 21: According to this report, if the Reagan Administration succeeds in winning all of its proposed domestic spending cuts, the nation's non-profit organizations will have $6 billion less per year to provide services to the handicapped, the poor and the disadvantaged. A budget study by the Urban Institute (based in Washington, D.C.) estimates that if the proposals are accepted, federal assistance to social service agencies will drop 54% below the 1980 level, community development grants will decrease by 60% and higher education institutions will receive 45% less.

May 1: The Senate, in a narrow vote of 50 to 49, approves the Reagan Administration's FY 1986 budget, which increases military spending while reducing or eliminating many domestic programs.

May 17: The House Budget Committee approves its version of the FY 1986 federal budget by a vote of 21 to 12. According to the committee's budget plan, the federal deficit would be reduced by $56 billion in 1986 and by $259 billion over three years.

May 24: In a vote of 258-170, the Democratic-controlled House approves the federal budget for FY 1986 at $967 billion, projecting revenue at $794 billion and a deficit of $173 billion. The plan is geared to reduce the federal deficit by $56 billion in FY 1986 and by $259 billion over three years.

June 12: As the House-Senate conference to develop a compromise on the federal budget for FY 1986 opens, the House Budget Committee Chairman, William H. Gray, III (D-Pa.), in a speech to the American Stock Exchange, says that reduction of the federal deficit is going to require a tax increase.

Aug. 2: After revisions made by a House-Senate Conference Committee of the federal FY 1986 budget, the House votes 309-119 to give its final approval to the $967.6 billion funding measure. The budget cuts $55.5 billion from the federal deficit, while authorizing spending increases for Social Security and defense.

Aug. 16: According to the Congressional Budget Office, the federal budget deficit will not be reduced as substantially as anticipated in the spending cuts voted by Congress. The CBO says that the federal deficit will be reduced by only $203 billion, not the $272 billion that the legislators envision over a three year period.

Sept. 1: A special study commissioned by the Urban Institute reveals that reductions in social spending executed in the first four years of the Reagan Administration have greatly weakened programs serving children, young adults and the hard-core unemployed. The Washington, D.C.-based research organization says that federal spending on 25 programs serving these groups dropped by 11% over all (after adjusting for inflation) from 1981-1984. In specific areas such as job training, the decline was 53% and 18% in the Aid to Families with Dependent Children Program.

Sept. 25: James C. Miller, the nominee for director of the Office of Management and Budget says that he will pursue federal spending cuts with the same intensity of his predecessor, David A. Stockman.

Oct. 20: A number of federal agencies are informed in letters from the Office of Management and Budget that their FY 1987 budget requests exceed ceilings set by President Reagan. According to the report, the agencies had been instructed to keep spending down to levels authorized in his "mid-session review of the 1986 budget."

Oct. 22: Rudolph G. Penner, director of the Congressional Budget Office, warns a House-Senate Conference Committee against passing legislation allowing the president to make "across-the-board" budget cuts in federal programs, to meet budget targets, when large deficits seem inevitable.

Nov. 7: According to a study released by the National Conference of State Legislatures and the National Governors' Association, proposed "balanced budget legislation" (Gramm-Rudman-Hollings), could force cuts in the Medicaid Program of as much as 22% in fiscal years 1987 and 1988. The result could be the loss of $2.3 to $9.7 billion in grants to the states to help pay medical costs for the poor.

Nov. 12: According to the report, the Senate version of the Gramm-Rudman-Hollings deficit-reduction bill will cut $4.9 billion from the Medicare program in FY 1987.

Dec. 12:   The House and the Senate approve the Gramm-Rudman-Hollings
            balanced budget bill in separate votes—271-to-154 in the House
            and 61-to-31 in the Senate. The legislation mandates the
            reduction of the federal budget deficit to zero by the year
            1991, by setting deficit ceilings that decrease in each
            successive year. The deficit ceiling for FY 1987 is $144
            billion, which anticipates budget reductions of $55 billion.
            The President has the authority to impose automatic spending
            reductions if unable to agree with Congress on an acceptable
            plan for reaching the deficit ceiling.

            Later, President Reagan signs the bill into law.

CIVIL RIGHTS

Jan. 16:   President Reagan holds a controversial meeting with 20 black
            educators, businessmen and other officials to discuss the group's
            "agenda for black progress." The group does not include blacks
            from the established civil rights community, fostering charges
            that the president is attempting to bypass traditional black
            leadership. The group, the Council for a Black Economic Agenda,
            is led by Robert L. Woodson.

Jan. 19:   In an interview published in "USA TODAY", President Reagan
            asserts that because of their political commitment to the Demo-
            cratic Party, some black leaders distort his civil rights record
            to "keep their constituencies aggrieved." President Reagan's
            remarks are denounced by the leaders of several black organiza-
            tions, including John E. Jacob of the National Urban League, who
            says the statements reflect a "shocking ignorance" of the role
            of black community institutions.

Jan. 26:   In a unanimous decision, a three-judge panel of the United States
            Court of Appeals for the District of Columbia rules that the
            NAACP Legal Defense and Educational Fund Inc., can continue to
            use the initials of the National Association for the Advancement
            of Colored People.

Feb. 17:   Benjamin L. Hooks, Executive Director of the NAACP, calls on
            President Reagan to meet with his organization to discuss civil
            rights and social issues vital to blacks. Hooks accuses the
            Reagan Administration of "leading the attack on recent civil
            rights gains," and says a recent request to meet with the
            president was denied.

Feb. 21:   According to the report, the NAACP will relocate its headquarters
            in Baltimore as a cost savings measure. The association is nego-
            tiating the purchase of a suitable building for $2 million in
            the city, after being unable to find a location in New York City
            at a similar price. According to a spokesperson, the NAACP has
            rented its offices since its founding in 1909. The move is
            scheduled for sometime at the end of the year.

Feb. 26:   U. S. Civil Rights Commissioners Mary Frances Berry and Blandina Cardenas Ramierez ignite controversy in a written statement asserting that civil rights laws are designed to protect blacks, minorities and women, not white men. The statement, attached to a commission study that hails a Supreme Court decision upholding the seniority of whites over recently hired blacks during layoffs, counters the Reagan Administration contention that race and sex conscious remedies are discriminatory and illegal.

March 4:   Led by the Rev. Joseph Lowery, head of the Southern Christian Leadership Conference, nearly 2,000 people restage the historic Selma to Montgomery march to "resurrect the spirit" of the civil rights movement. The four-day, 50-mile march is also undertaken to register dissatisfaction with President Reagan's civil rights policies according to the Rev. Jesse Jackson, one of the participants. The original march prompted the passage of the Voting Rights Act of 1965.

March 9:   The late Clarence M. Mitchell, Jr., is honored in Baltimore with the renaming of the Court House West, in commemoration of the contributions of the 40-year civil rights advocate for the NAACP. The ceremony is attended by hundreds of friends, supporters and family, among them Supreme Court Justices Thurgood Marshall and William Brennan. City spokesmen say the court house is the first in a major American city to be named in honor of a civil rights leader.

April 8:   According to the report, President Reagan's efforts to court the black middle class and win its support for the Administration's economic and social policies has been largely unsuccessful. The president's views in these areas have been rejected by established black leaders, who, along with their organizations, are still held in high esteem by the black community at large.

May 1:   In a special service, a statue of Martin Luther King, Jr., is dedicated at the Washington Cathedral (Washington, D.C.), as a memorial to his extensive contributions and leadership in the civil rights movement.

May 3:   In a joint hearing by the House Judiciary and Education and Labor Committees, Clarence Pendleton, Chairman of the U.S. Commission on Civil Rights, testifies against legislation designed to reverse the Supreme Court ruling in the Grove City College (Pennsylvania) case. Pendleton claims that the Civil Rights Restoration Act of 1985 would unnecessarily broaden the scope of civil rights enforcement.

May 8:   Confirmation hearings on the promotion of William Bradford Reynolds, head of the Justice Department's civil rights unit, to Associate Attorney General, are postponed. According to the report, Sen. Joseph R. Biden, Jr., (D-Del.) requests the delay to allow civil rights groups and other opponents to prepare their testimony against Reynold's confirmation.

May 26:   According to this report, the U.S. Commission on Civil Rights has appointed a greater number of white men to head its state advisory committees than in the past. Presently, the committees are headed by 46 men and 4 women, as compared to 31 men and 20 women (which included a representative for the District of Columbia), heading the old panels. Of the new chairmen, 36 are white, 9 black, 3 Hispanic and 2 American Indian. On the previous panels the figures were: 15 white, 7 Hispanic, 21 black, 2 Asian-American and 6 American Indian.

June 5:   The Senate Judiciary Committee opens hearings on the nomination of William Bradford Reynolds to the post of Associate Attorney General in the Justice Department. Reynolds, head of the department's civil rights unit, faces sharp questioning from Democratic opponents who contend that his policies have worked against insuring the civil rights of blacks and minorities. The committee will hear testimony from more than 50 witnesses attempting to block the nomination.

June 6:   As Senate Judiciary Committee hearings close, William Bradford Reynolds, head of the Justice Department's civil rights unit, is criticized for his performance in that post by Democrats and Sen. Charles McC. Mathias, Jr., a Maryland Republican. Sen. Mathias says he is disappointed with Reynolds' record on enforcement in fighting housing discrimination and with his refusal to serve as an advocate for blacks and minorities in the civil rights arena. A vote on Reynolds' nomination is expected in the next week.

June 16:   Senator Charles McC. Mathias Jr., (R-Md.) requests that hearings be resumed on the nomination of William Bradford Reynolds because of what he terms "unanswered questions." Reynold's nomination to the post of Associate Attorney General of the Justice Department seems less certain according to Senate aides. Meanwhile, President Reagan defends his nominee as a "tireless fighter against discrimination."

June 19:   Democrats and Republicans on the Senate Judiciary Committee challenge William Bradford Reynolds on numerous discrepencies in his sworn testimony regarding his handling of civil rights cases for the Justice Department. In one instance, Reynolds testified that he conferred with attorneys for blacks challenging election laws in 11 Mississippi counties, all of whom agreed with him that the department should not file suit in the cases. In fact, Reynolds met with only one attorney, who filed an affidavit with the committee stating that he repeatedly urged Reynolds to file suit against the counties.

June 21:   A vote on the nomination of William Bradford Reynolds to become Associate Attorney General in the Justice Department is postponed for a week by the Senate Judiciary Committee. The action is taken after it becomes evident that Reynolds will not win the unanimous endorsement of the Senate Judiciary Committee. Republican Senator Arlen Specter of Pennsylvania, says he will vote against Reynolds, who he accuses of consistently having "placed himself above the law," in the enforcement of civil rights.

June 23:   William Bradford Reynolds sends a memorandum to key Senate Judiciary Committee members rebutting, point-by-point, charges that he has not enforced civil rights laws on behalf of blacks and minorities. According to an official close to him, the memorandum is designed to counter what Reynolds perceives as a "character assassination" and a "witch hunt." Critics contend that Reynolds testimony on his performance in office during his tenure has been misleading.

June 28:   William Bradford Reynold's nomination to the post of Associate Attorney General of the Justice Department is rejected by the Senate Judiciary Committee. According to several committee members, Reynold's nomination is rejected because of his lax enforcement of civil rights laws and misleading statements about his handling of cases in sworn testimony. Republican Senators Arlen Specter of Pennsylvania and Charles McC. Mathias, Jr., of Maryland sided with Democrats in a 10-8 vote against the nomination. In addition, a number of the senators say Reynolds should resign his post.

July 7:   According to this report, White House officials are trying to force a vote by the full Senate, on the nomination of William Bradford Reynolds as Associate Attorney General of the Justice Department. Senate Majority Leader Robert Dole (R-Kan.) is reportedly determining how many Republicans might approve a discharge petition forcing the nomination to the floor to "help" President Reagan push Reynolds for the post.

Aug. 9:   In an interview on ABC-TV's "Good Morning America," Attorney General Edwin Meese, III, brands civil rights organizations that successfully blocked the appointment of William Bradford Reynolds as Associate Attorney General, "a very pernicious lobby." Meese, who led a White House attempt to force a vote on the nomination by the full Senate, which failed, called the defeat a "tragedy."

Sept. 19: A survey conducted by the Center for Media and Public Affairs purports to have found a "surprising divergence" of opinion between black leaders and the constituencies that they represent. The differences are supposedly revealed in a broad range of questions on issues such as affirmative action, racial progress and busing among others. Benjamin L. Hooks, Executive Director of the NAACP, disputed the reliability of opinion surveys, asserting that a black person is more likely to respond to what a question asks, while black leaders respond to what a question means. The survey was conducted by telephone in May through July, in a nationwide random sample of 600 blacks. The same questions were reportedly asked of black leaders of several prominent black organizations.

Sept. 20: The head of the U.S. Commission on Civil Rights, Clarence Pendleton, accuses a House subcommittee chairman of racism for repeated questions about why more blacks, minorities and women have not been appointed to the commission's state advisory panels. Rep. Don Edwards (D-Calif.), who is white, chairs the Judiciary subcommittee and expresses his concern over a "noticeable decrease" in the numbers of minorities and women serving on the new panels. Rep. Edwards says Pendleton's statements show he is unqualified to head the commission.

Sept. 30: Black leaders and political analysts question the validity of a poll conducted by the Center for Media and Public Affairs. Eddie Williams, head of the Joint Center for Political Studies, says an earlier poll conducted in 1984 by his organization and the Gallup group found marked differences. While 77% of the black respondents in the American Enterprise Institute Poll (which sponsored the center's survey) said they opposed preferential treatment for blacks in hiring, only 27% did so in the JCPS poll. Williams contends that such a dramatic shift in opinion in one year's time is unlikely.

Oct. 14: According to this report, the effectiveness of the U.S. Commission on Civil Rights is being tested by an ideological split on the meaning of equality, and civil rights principles, among its commissioners. Reportedly, their differences are based on whether securing civil rights for blacks and minorities means strictly encouraging the promotion of equal opportunity. Opponents on the commission contend that the federal government should play a substantial role in targeting anti-discrimination programs and efforts to "disfavored" (blacks, Hispanics and women) groups.

Nov. 5: William Bradford Reynolds, Assistant Attorney General of the Justice Department's civil rights division, claims that the Reagan Administration's civil rights policies are based on the same policies advanced by Dr. Martin Luther King and other prominent civil rights leaders of the 60's. In a speech to the Wilmington Rotary Club, Reynolds asserts that today's civil rights leaders have "distorted and twisted" these policies by favoring "discriminatory" quotas.

Dec. 1: In Montgomery, Ala., on the 30th Anniversary observation of the day Rosa Parks refused to give up her seat on a bus to a white passenger, an action credited with launching the civil rights movement, Mrs. Parks declares, "I certainly wouldn't change anything in my fight for freedom."

Dec. 11: According to the report, the U.S. Commission on Civil Rights will investigate charges that a school desegregation study that it commissioned, is itself biased against findings on the use of busing to achieve integration. The decision to investigate is made after Gary Orfield, the head of the $475,000 study resigns alleging technical incompetence and possible conflicts-of-interest among researchers associated with anti-busing proponets.

EDUCATION/DESEGREGATION

Jan. 12:   According to this report, although black student scores on the Scholastic Aptitude Test are improving at a faster rate than whites, they still fall substantially below national averages. While black students have gained three points on the verbal and four points on the mathematical portions of the test, their average scores, 342 (verbal) and 373 (math) were below the national averages of 426 and 471 respectively.

Feb. 17:   According to a report released by the National Center for Education Information (a private organization), in the last 15 years, the number of poor children from broken homes has increased among the nation's school-age population. Among its findings, the report says that 23% of the children under the age of 6 are poor, and that the number of female-headed households has doubled since 1970. The report also finds a correlation between the students' achievement levels and the income of their households, with poor children failing to attain the same academic success as more affluent students.

March 8:   Facing a $1 million budget deficit, officials at Fisk University launch an emergency fund drive seeking $1000 contributions from some 9,600 alumni. If successful, the drive will only cover costs for the current academic year. The total deficit is nearly $5 million. A committee of outside consultants tries to develop a plan to eliminate the deficit and increase the historically black college's revenue.

March 22:   In a speech at the Joint Center for Political Studies Annual Dinner, a black economist, Andrew Brimmer, asserts that black economic progress is being hindered not by discrimination, but by the black community's lack of education and marketable skills. Brimmer contends that although discrimination is still a factor, "Certain problems are not a matter of circumstance but a matter of choice for black people," citing high teenage pregnancy rates and black youth joblessness caused by frustrated job search efforts.

April 21:   According to a study co-authored by William Labov and Wendell A. Harris, a black researcher, marked differences in the English spoken by blacks and whites is increasing the likelihood of misunderstandings between the races. The authors contend that the differences may lead to "a permanent division between black and white," and the isolation of the black poor in large urban centers. The three-year study, "Segregation of Black and White Vernaculars," is funded by the National Science Foundation.

May 2:   The Ford Foundation announces it will provide $9 million in fellowships to support doctoral studies for blacks and minorities. The action is undertaken to increase the number of minorities pursuing graduate studies as well as their presence on college and university faculties.

May 4: According to the report, the percentage of financial aid granted to minorities attending public and private colleges dropped significantly in the 1983-84 academic year. A report prepared by the American Association of State Colleges and Universities reveals that overall student aid dropped by 2.3% in that year, as more older white working students received student aid to attend school. Furthermore, the decline in aid for black students is even more substantial, at 12.4%, in the 1981-82 academic year.

May 6: The Federal Government and the state of Maryland reach tentative agreement on a plan to desegregate the state's public colleges and universities according to a spokesman in the Maryland attorney general's office. The plan resolving the dispute dating from 1970, commits the state to a five-year effort. White enrollment at traditionally black colleges will be increased to 19% and black enrollment at predominantly white schools will reach 15% from 11%.

May 13: Citing his commitment to Christianity, Shaw Divinity School awards the Rev. Sun Myung Moon an honorary doctor of divinity degree. According to school officials, a $30,000 donation from Moon's Unification Church did not influence their decision to award the honorary degree. Shaw is a private, predominantly black school.

July 17: Officials of the U.S. Department of Education say that while Virginia has made significant efforts to desegregate its public colleges and universities, greater effort is required, particularly in desegregating its predominantly black colleges.

July 29: According to an analysis by the American Council on Education, students from low-income families can now expect to assume at least one-half of the financial burden for their college educations. The ACE (a higher education lobby) says students from families earning less than $15,000 annually will have to work, secure loans or other monetary sources to meet their college expenses.

Aug. 1: Dr. Laval S. Wilson, 47, is selected by a vote of 9 to 4, as superintendent of the Boston school system, the first black to be chosen for the post. Reportedly, several members of the board characterized Laval as an effective administrator. He will oversee a school system whose student population is 48% black, 28% white and 24% other minorities, and which has been strained by racial discord for more than a decade.

Aug. 31: The Justice Department eases school desegregation standards, no longer requiring actual results as proof that the terms of court-ordered consent decrees have been met. Instead, the department says school districts can be released from such obligations when they have "fully and in good faith" followed the measures outlined in the desegregation plan. However, school officials must still demonstrate that they have not intentionally segregated schools while under the supervision of the court.

Sept. 19:   According to a report by the National Assessment of Education Progress, the reading ability of black and Hispanic children has improved markedly in the last four years. The report said that black 9-year-olds improved their basic skill with the percentage of those unable to read at the elementary level dropping from 30% to 16%. The percentage of black 17-year-olds reading at advanced levels increased from 7% to 16%. However, the figure for white 17-year-olds is 45%, nearly three times that of blacks.

Sept. 24:   In New York City, the College Board announces that minority students achieved the highest gains on the Scholastic Aptitude Test (SAT) in a single year. While the average scores for blacks were 346 on the verbal portion and 376 on the math, higher than previous years, they still lagged behind the white averages by more than 100 points. Further, there were 2,000 fewer blacks taking the college entrance examination in 1985 than in the previous year.

Sept. 26:   The Justice Department files a brief in Federal District Court in Mobile charging that the city has failed to meet the requirements of a consent decree for the desegregation of its public schools. The department's civil rights division requests that the court require the school district to submit a remedial plan to remedy segregation in the system. The Board of School Commissioners had attempted to free the system from the provisions of a 1971 desegregation consent decree.

Oct. 27:   According to this article, educational officials nationwide cite a growing decline in the numbers of minority students attending college for reasons ranging from finances to educators' newer emphasis on educational excellence, rather than the issue of minority access and equity. Bureau of the Census data reveal that the number of black high school graduates going on to college declined to 27% in 1983 from 33.5% in 1976.

Oct. 30:   Recommending that the United States Commission on Civil Rights terminate "this misbegotten study," the director of a federal desegregation study resigns charging that it is biased against busing and technically flawed. The director, Gary Orfield (a University of Chicago professor), charged that the study relied on a limited set of research questions that heavily focused on the exodus of whites from public schools, and "showing no concern for the effects of desegregation on black and Hispanic children."

Nov. 14:   Secretary of the U.S. Department of Education, William J. Bennett, introduces the Reagan Administration's educational voucher plan designed to enable some five million poor children to attend private or public schools outside their own districts.

Nov. 21:   Federal District Court Judge Leon Sand rules that the city of Yonkers (NY), "illegally and intentionally" segregated its public schools and housing on the basis of race, in a 600-page decision. The judge cites the pattern of segregation as having existed since 1949, resulting from deliberate actions taken by city and school officials.

Dec. 11:   A group of black educators, politicians and community leaders
            form "The Select Committee on the Education of Black Youth,"
            established to promote an alternative public school curriculum
            to help reduce the high dropout rates and decreased college
            attendance of black youth. The curriculum designed to improve
            the self-image of black youth, will stress language skills
            (reading, writing and speaking) and is called "Foundation for
            Learning."

POLITICS

Jan. 7:   After a year in office, Philadelphia's Mayor Wilson Goode is
            given high marks for his handling of city "crises" and for his
            progress in other areas, by business and community leaders. Among
            the Mayor's accomplishments are the successful settlement of an
            impending transit strike and securing City Council approval for
            a prison construction project and a convention center plan.

Jan. 28:   A survey by the U.S. Census Bureau reveals that an increase in
            overall voter turnout is due to increased voting by blacks, women
            and the elderly. According to its findings, the percentage of
            voting blacks rose from 51% to 56%, and among blacks over the age
            of 65, those voting constituted 68%, up from 65% in 1980.

Feb. 7:   The U.S. Bureau of the Census reports that in the elections of
            November 1984, 10.3 million or 56% of some 8.4 million eligible
            blacks voted. Reportedly, this is a substantial gain in black
            voters as compared to 1980 when 8.3 million (50%) of some 16.4
            million blacks cast ballots in 1980. The 1984 black voting rate
            is the highest proportion in 16 years according to the bureau.
            The largest gain in voters was among young black adults.

Feb. 11:   Former presidential candidate, Jesse L. Jackson, cautions blacks
            to reassess their loyalty to the Democratic Party, charging that
            its leaders are trying to win white male votes by "proving they
            can be tough on blacks." Jackson denounces the election of Ronald
            W. Burris, another black as vice chairman of the party over the
            candidate of its Black Caucus, Mayor Richard G. Hatcher of Gary,
            Ind. Jackson accuses the party chairman, Paul G. Kirk, Jr., of
            having tried to build stature in the party through his opposition
            to the caucus nominee.

March 19:   Following the defeat of its candidate for the vice chairmanship
            of the Democratic Party, the National Black Leadership Roundtable
            announces a new process designed to ensure that blacks chosen for
            key party posts, provide "genuine representation of black in-
            terests." According to NBLR president, Del. Walter E. Fauntroy
            (D-D.C.), the process will be used when there is a question of
            whether one black candidate is receiving support outside the
            black community over another black in a race, "for the purpose
            of limiting black leverage."

March 22:   According to the Joint Center for Political Studies, there are

286 black mayors in the nation. The center reports that their ranks have more than doubled since 1975, when there were only 135. Further, last year's elections produced the largest number of black mayors (31) elected in a single year. A senior research associate attributes the gains to Jesse Jackson's presidential candidacy and an increase in black voter registration.

March 24: Patricia Roberts Harris, former Cabinet secretary, diplomat and lawyer, dies of cancer at 60, in Washington, D.C. Harris was the first black women to serve in the presidential Cabinet, first as secretary of Housing and Urban Development and then as secretary of Health, Education and Welfare (now Health and Human Services) during the Carter Administration.

April 18: Mayor Lionel Wilson, 70, the first black mayor of Oakland, is reelected to a third term. Wilson defeated seven other candidates with 60% of the 54,000 votes cast. His nearest opponent, City Councilman Wilson Riles Jr., garnered only 32.5%. The total number of registered voters in the city is 204,000.

May 9: One of Michigan's most influential black politicians, William Lucas, chief executive of Wayne County, the largest and most powerful in the state, announces he will change his party affiliation to Republican. At a news conference, Lucas claims he is making the switch because despite black loyalty to the Democratic Party, "its proposed solutions have kept us poor and stripped many of us of our dignity." Reportedly, Lucas' move could put him in line for the Republican gubernatorial nomination in 1986.

May 14: In Philadelphia, a state police helicopter drops an incendiary bomb on a house occupied by members of the group MOVE, after a day long siege involving gunfights with police. The fire engulfs nearly 60 other homes in two blocks of the western Philadelphia neighborhood. Mayor Wilson Goode, in a City Hall news conference states that as mayor, he accepts "full and total responsibility," for the outcome of the action.

May 16: Philadelphia's Mayor Wilson Goode says that if the outcome of the bombing of a house occupied by the group MOVE, which resulted in the deaths of 11 people, including four children, could have been known, he would not have approved the action. In a news conference, Goode says that police and fire officials had a "well thought-out plan," stating that the fire was an accident and that there was no intent to destroy the MOVE house.

May 17: Criticism continues to mount over Mayor Goode's approval of a bomb's use to destroy a bunker atop the MOVE house. The armed confrontation with police ended in a fire, which was the probable cause of death for 10 of the 11 persons who died in the house, according to the city's medical examiner. Meanwhile, residents who lost their homes in the fire file a $10 million lawsuit against the city charging that it procrastinated in taking action against the group for over three years.

May 18:   After a tour of the area with Mayor Wilson Goode, Housing and Urban Development Secretary Samuel Pierce announces that a $1 million federal grant will be given to Philadelphia to rebuild the two blocks destroyed by fire in a police assault against the group MOVE. Criticism of the Mayor's and the police and fire commissioners handling of the situation grows as inconsistencies in their accounts of the confrontation become evident.

May 20:   In a commencement speech at the predominantly black Talladega College (AL), Sen. Gary Hart (D-Colo.) urges the Democratic Party to crusade for "equality of economic opportunity," targeted to younger, upwardly mobile blacks. Hart calls the decision by some Democrats in the party to retreat from our historic commitment to social justice," "politically unacceptable" and "morally intolerable."

May 20:   City Officials in Philadelphia declare a day of prayer and mourning for the 11 victims who died during a fire and police assault on the headquarters of the group, MOVE. A number of special religious services featuring sermons, prayer and offerings are held throughout the city. In an appearance on CBS' "Face the Nation," Mayor Goode says the group was "bent on absolute destruction."

May 21:   The "Concerned Philadelphians for Civil Liberties," says it will seek a grand jury investigation of a confrontation staged between police and the group MOVE, that resulted in 11 deaths. The move by the group of prominent blacks, questions the leadership of Mayor Wilson Goode and the actions of the city's police and fire commissioners in the conflict.

June 9:   The Joint Center for Political Studies reports that while blacks have made impressive gains in winning elective office at all levels of government, black elected officials only constitute 1.2% of the 490,800 elective offices in the nation. According to the center, an increase brought the total number of black officials to 6,056 at the start of 1985. Further, 85% of the increase came from the South. Black elected officials continue to come from black majority districts, where the black electorate is crucial to their victory.

June 12:   In Birmingham, the president of the Greene County chapter of the Southern Christian Leadership Conference and four other people are indicted on vote fraud stemming from a Justice Department investigation. A lawsuit filed by the Southern Poverty Law Center on behalf of the defendants, charges Attorney General Edwin Meese, III and department officials with trying to intimidate and punish blacks in poor, rural Alabama counties for supporting Democratic candidates.

June 30:   Despite earlier warnings from Jesse L. Jackson to reassess their ties to the Democratic Party, key members of its black caucus are cautiously supporting the party's new thrust. Reportedly, DNC Chairman Paul G. Kirk Jr., has demonstrated a greater willingness to meet with blacks and make some concessions. Kirk agreed to withdraw a proposal that would have excised seats on the DNC's executive committee for blacks, Hispanics and women. Party officials are trying to forge an image of the DNC as focusing less on so-called "special interests" while adhering to its historic commitment to social justice.

June 30: An audience of more than 3,000 delegates to the National Association for the Advancement of Colored People Convention boo Republican Party Chairman Frank J. Fahrenkopf when he chides blacks for being the only voting bloc to support the Democratic ticket in the presidential election. NAACP executive director Benjamin L. Hooks interrupts Fahrenkopf's speech to ask the crowd to stop, but, reportedly the mood remains tense.

July 22: At the opening of the National Urban League's 75th Annual Conference, John E. Jacob, President, warns the Republican Party that if it wants to win more black votes and hold on to the White House in the 1988 presidential election, it must not continue to "operate as if black people don't exist." Jacob calls for greater communication between the White House and black leadership, stating that the process has disintegrated because of President Reagan's charge that black leaders have misled black voters by distorting his civil rights record in order to keep their jobs.

July 23: In a speech at the National Urban League 75th Annual Conference, Senate Majority Leader Robert Dole (R-Kan.) declares that the Republican Party needs the support of blacks and exhorts them "to join the internal debate" to change things they don't like about it. Dole states that the GOP is moving toward becoming the majority party, which can occur more quickly "if inroads are made in the black vote." However, the Democratic Chairman of the House Budget Committee, William Gray of Pennsylvania asserts in another conference speech that the GOP is moving in the wrong direction on civil and human rights issues.

July 27: The Justice Department and the NAACP Legal Defense and Education Fund, in a joint effort, obtain a consent decree requiring Bessmer, Ala., to change its system of government from a three member commission to a mayor-city council configuration. The town had been accused of deliberately trying to dilute black voting strength through the old system, which reduced the percentage of blacks in the city from 61% in 1950 to 51% by 1980. The former system also reduced the proportion of voting age blacks to 47%. The new system goes into effect in 1986.

Aug. 24: A civil suit is filed against the Darlington County (SC) system of at-large council elections by the Justice Department, which charges that it discriminated against blacks in violation of the Voting Rights Act. State Representative Warren Arthur says that although the county is 40% black, not one black has won election to the county council since its inception.

Aug. 25:   In a public hearing sponsored by the Democratic Party's Fairness
            Commission, former presidential candidate Jesse Jackson urges the
            party to abandon at-large and runoff elections and other rules
            that he says "favors the big shots over the long shots and the
            slingshots." The hearing will determine what changes, if any,
            will be made in the delegate selection rules for the 1988 presi-
            dential candidates, Jackson contends discriminates against
            minorities.

Sept. 18:   In testimony before the bi-partisan Commission on National Elec-
            tions (a privately financed organization), Jesse Jackson asserts
            that ensuring that blacks and other minorities participate fully
            in the political process is more important than altering rules
            to make presidential campaigns shorter and less expensive.

Oct. 9:   A special commission set up by Mayor Wilson Goode to investigate
            the circumstances leading up to the confrontation between Phila-
            delphia police and members of MOVE, attracts few residents to its
            hearings. However, police detective George Draper, who has moni-
            tored the group for several years and is one of the department's
            top experts on it, testifies that he was never consulted about
            plans for the assault.

Oct. 12:   Mayor Wilson Goode, testifying before the special commission he
            appointed on the MOVE confrontation, says that his administration
            adopted a "conscious" hands off policy concerning numerous com-
            plaints of violations of health, housing and safety codes at the
            group's house. Goode says the decision was designed to avoid
            the sort of confrontation that police previously had with the
            group, in which an officer was killed in 1978.

Oct. 15:   In continuing hearings of a special commission investigating the
            May 13 MOVE confrontation, Mayor Wilson Goode testifies that his
            orders to extinguish a fire that engulfed the group's house and
            61 others in two blocks, were disobeyed. During 6-1/2 hours of
            testimony, Goode maintains that he was misinformed and misled by
            subordinates to whom he had delegated authority to make crucial
            decisions on handling the crisis.

Oct. 18:   Police Commissioner Gregore J. Sambor testifies that he informed
            Mayor Wilson Goode of a police plan to use explosive devices to
            drive members of the group MOVE from their row house. Sambor
            says the mayor was informed of a plan to blast small holes into
            the walls of the house to fire tear gas inside, two days before
            the attempt took place. Goode has maintained that he was not
            told details of the assault plan by the police commissioner, and
            did not know of plans to drop a bomb on the roof of the house
            until 17 minutes before it occured.

Oct. 19:   In his second day of testimony, Police Commissioner Gregore J.
            Sambor says that the fire in the MOVE house was allowed to burn
            because he was assured by the city's fire commissioner that it
            could be controlled.

Oct. 24: In the tenth day of hearings of a special commission investigating the MOVE confrontation, police bomb squad commander, Lieut. Frank Powell, refuses to testify about his dropping of a bomb on the house's rooftop bunker. Police have acknowledged that the bomb, which contained an explosive compound believed to be incapable of causing extensive damage or threats to life, also contained a very powerful military explosive, C-4. Powell cites his constitutional right barring incrimination in refusing to testify.

Oct. 31: Philadelphia Fire Commissioner William C. Richmond says he accepts "full responsibility" for the delay in fighting a fire caused by a bomb dropped on a roof-top bunker of the MOVE house, that resulted in the deaths of 11 persons.

Nov. 1: One of the survivors of the fire that killed 11 members of MOVE, Michael Moses Ward ("Birdie Africa"), testifies that adults in the house tried to help four children escape, but were driven back by police gunfire. Ward, 13, says a second attempt to escape was made when fire and smoke became heavy and they were unable to breathe, after spending 13 hours huddled under wet blanklets.

Nov. 2: Jame R. Pheland, an explosives expert, testifies that the bomb used to destroy the bunker atop the MOVE house, was three times more powerful than Philadelphia police have acknowledged. Phelan also testifies that the bomb's design was wrong, that it was used incorrectly and if sought, his advice would have been not to use a bomb.

Nov. 3: An expert pathologist, Dr. Ali Z. Hameli, the chief medical examiner for Delaware, contests the findings of Philadelphia's medical examiner that the deaths of four children in the MOVE house were accidental. Hameli says the dead children should be classified as homicide victims because their deaths "were the consequences of the measured and deliberate acts of and interactions," between adults in the house and city officials in the confrontation. Hameli also contends that five children were victims, not four, as originally determined by the city's medical examiner.

Nov. 7: Sen. L. Douglas Wilder wins election as Lt. Governor in Virginia, reportedly the first black to be nominated to statewide office by a major party in the South since reconstruction. Wilder captures 44% of the white vote in the race, in which opponents played up his race and attacked his support of a state holiday memorializing Martin Luther King, Jr. Wilder says the key to his success is his ability to "speak for more than just a narrow constituency," during his 15-year legislative career.

Nov. 14: Philadelphia Police Commissioner Gregore J. Sambor resigns, stating that he has lost the confidence and backing of Mayor Wilson Goode over his handling of a confrontation between police and the group MOVE.

Dec. 4:   According to the report, Mayor Coleman Young is awarded a 43.8% pay increase by Detroit's Elected Officials Compensation Commission, which will increase his salary to $115,000 if not rejected by two-thirds of the City Council.

Dec. 5:   U.S. Solicitor General Charles Fried argues before the Supreme Court against a lower court ruling overturning a North Carolina redistricting plan it found illegal under amendments to the Voting Rights Act of 1982. Fried asserts that blacks have been elected in significant numbers in the state, and should not be guaranteed seats on the basis of their percentage in the population.

RACE RELATIONS

Jan. 13:   In New York, Hazel N. Dukes, president of the State Conference of Branches of the National Association for the Advancement of Colored People, announces a five-point program designed to fight racism and attacks on civil and human rights.

Feb. 24:   In a keynote speech at the annual convention of the Nation of Islam in Chicago, Rep. Gus Savage (D-Ill.), declares that blacks will not achieve liberation or receive power from Congress, and the only way to achieve those goals is "not integration...but (getting) our rock—not small, individual pieces of rock."

Feb. 25:   Libyan leader, Col. Muammar el-Qaddafi, urges black servicemen to leave the military and to form their own army to create an independent and separate black state, in a 40-minute speech via satellite to the Nation of Islam Annual Conference.

March 4:   According to the report, the appeal of Nation of Islam leader Louis Farrakhan has widened among American blacks as evidenced by some 15,000 people attending his speech at the nation's annual convention in Chicago.

March 9:   A Belvoir, Va. restaurant owner is sentenced to 30 days in jail for refusing to serve black customers. The restauranter, Roy E. McKoy, 61, had faced a maximum penalty of six months in jail and a $1000 fine. McKoy's refusal to serve blacks was his third violation of a federal court order directing him to do so 17 years ago.

March 24:   Judge John Feikens, the chief Federal district judge in Detroit, is cleared of charges alleging he made "racially patronizing and biased" remarks about black elected officials and their administrative abilities. The Judicial Council of the Sixth Circuit rules 8-4 in a vote that the judge's remarks were "untrue and regrettable," but not indicative of an intent to "denigrate" black people as a whole.

March 26:   A trial seeking $48 million in damages for the fatal shootings of five anti-Klan demonstrators by six Ku Klux Klansmen and

American Nazis, who were acquitted of state murder charges, opens in Winston-Salem, N.C. The suit by the plaintiffs (families of the dead and those injured in the 1980 shootings) names 61 defendants including the Klansmen and Nazis, the Greensboro police, the City of Greensboro and several agents of the FBI and the United States Bureau of Alcohol, Tobacco and Firearms.

April 23:   In Austin, the Texas Legislature proposes that the state celebrate Martin Luther King's birthday on the same day that it honors Confederate war heroes, the third Monday in January. Supporters of each holiday oppose the proposal to combine the two.

April 29:   Greensboro police officers give conflicting testimony on their roles in handling an outbreak of violence and shooting during a march staged by anti-Klan demonstrators in 1979. Five demonstrators were killed because of confusion over the exact point of origin of the march and its route, according to some of the officers. Five other officers testify that the starting point of the march was known.

May 2:   (Combined Reports) The Chairman of the Reagan Administration's Copyright Royalty Tribunal denies having written any portions of a racially controversial book, "Foundations of Sand" although she is credited in it as a co-author. Marianne Mele Hall claims her role was merely that of editor of the book that cites American blacks as "preserving their jungle freedoms...avoidance of personal responsibility and their abhorrence of the work ethic."

May 4:   Minister Louis Farrakhan, leader of the Nation of the Islam, announces that a $5 million loan received from the Libyan leader, Muammar el-Qaddafi will be used to establish a toiletry firm.

May 5:   The former police chief of Greensboro, N.C., testifies that he knew of plans by Ku Klux Klansmen and American Nazis to confront anti-Klan demonstrators, but decided on a "low-visibility" strategy for police anyway.

May 7:   According to Lawrence Hafstad, 81, the co-author of a racially controversial book, Marianne Mele Hall, chairman of the Copyright Royalty Tribunal, "generally supported" it and helped to have it published.

May 8:   A Federal jury finds eight defendants in a $48 million civil suit liable for damages in the death of only one of five shooting victims of an anti-Klan march back in 1979 in Greensboro, N.C. Although the jury cites the "wrongful death" of Dr. Michael Nathan and the liability of five Klansmen and Nazis, two Greensboro police officers and a police informer, it rejects charges of a conspiracy against the demonstrators.

May 10:   Warith Deen Muhammad, son of the late Elijah Muhammad, founder of the Nation of Islam, disbands the organization that he inherited and later renamed the "American Muslim Mission." In a five-city simultaneous telephone hookup from Chicago, Muhammad

announces the decision urging his followers to join the international Muslim community.

May 13:   Following the resignation of Marianne Mele Hall, chairman of the
           Copyright Royalty Tribunal, because of controversy about her role
           in the authorship and publication of a book opponents labeled
           racist against blacks, the future of the tribunal is in question.

June 6:   A six-member Federal jury awards almost $400,000 to three plain-
           tiffs in a $48 million dollar civil lawsuit against 20 Klansmen
           and American Nazis, 20 Greensboro, N.C. police officers and the
           city of Greensboro and four federal agents. Damages were awarded
           for the "wrongful death" of Dr. Michael Nathan against two of the
           police officers, five Klansmen and Nazis and a police informer.
           Nathan was one of five demonstrators slain in the 1979 anti-Klan
           march.

July 29:   According to the report, Louis Farrakhan, leader of the black
           Muslim movement, the Nation of Islam, is drawing a diverse group
           of supporters among blacks inspired by his calls for black eco-
           nomic self-sufficiency. In a recent Washington, D.C. appearance,
           more than 10,000 blacks including professionals, students, ar-
           tists, educators and government workers, turn out to hear a
           speech at the Washington Convention Center.

Sept. 16: In California, Jewish leaders score black Muslim leader Louis
           Farrakhan for asserting that blacks, not Jews, are God's chosen
           people in a speech attended by some 17,000 people at the Forum
           sports arena.

Sept. 26: A Federal grand jury indicts nine Ku Klux Klan members in North
           Carolina charging them with conspiracy to violate the civil
           rights of interracial families through a series of shootings and
           cross-burnings.

Oct. 5:   Rabbi Marvin Hier charges that black Muslim leader Louis
           Farrakhan has ties to a former state leader of the Ku Klux Klan.

Oct. 19:   In Louisiana, Susie Guillory Phipps is denied a change in her
           racial classification from black to white because she fails to
           provide sufficient proof of her race, according to the Fourth
           Circuit Court of Appeals. The fair-skinned Phipps had discovered
           her racial classification when she applied for a passport several
           years ago.

Nov. 2:   Los Angeles' Mayor Tom Bradley says that he made a mistake in
           not repudiating Louis Farrakhan before the black Muslim minister
           delivered a recent speech in the city, containing "strong, dan-
           gerous currents of anti-Semitism." Bradley asserts that Farrakhan
           broke a commitment made to the city's black leadership to refrain
           from such oratory.

Nov. 12:   A group of lawyers seek a new trial for Wayne B. Williams, con-
           victed of two of 23 murders of Atlanta children in 1982, in a 31-

page petition claiming the defendant was denied the opportunity to present an adequate defense. The lawyers say important evidence implicating the Ku Klux Klan, was not provided to the defense before the start of the trial.

Nov. 17:   In settlement of a "wrongful death" lawsuit, Mary Nathan, the wife of slain anti-Klan demonstrator Dr. Michael Nathan, is given a check for $351,500 by the city of Greensboro. Nathan is the only plaintiff to receive the award in the judgment against two city police officers, a police informer and five Klansmen and American Nazis. Nathan indicates the award payment will be shared among the spouses of four other demonstrators who were killed and others who were injured at the demonstration.

Nov. 23:   A state of emergency is declared in the Elmwood section of Southwest Philadelphia by Mayor Wilson Goode, after two nights of demonstrations by whites in front of the newly bought homes of black and interracial families in the neighborhood.

Nov. 25:   In an effort to ease racial tension between blacks and whites in the Elmwood area of Southwest Philadelphia, Operation PUSH scraps a demonstration to protest the harrassment of new black and interracial homeowners by whites.

Nov. 26:   Despite offers of protection from city officials in Philadelphia, a black family decides to move out of their recently purchased home, after vandalism and demonstrations by residents in the predominantly white neighborhood.

Dec. 1:   Philadelphia police arrest 34 people demonstrating in violation of a state of emergency imposed by Mayor Wilson Goode in a predominantly white neighborhood where new black and interracial homeowners were picketed. Mayor Goode says the demonstration by "outsiders" was an attempt to inflame tensions among blacks and whites.

Dec. 2:   Thirty-four people arrested for violating a state of emergency in the Elmwood section of Philadelphia by demonstrating, are released pending a court hearing. The demonstrators claim to be members of the International Committee Against Racism and the Communist Progressive Labor Party.

SOUTH AFRICA

(This section briefly highlights some of the year's events involving key black American leadership, the Congress, anti-apartheid advocates and others to end South Africa's racial segregation policies. It is not a definitive account of the many important events that have occurred.)

Jan. 4:   The Rev. Jesse Jackson, after a half hour audience with Pope John Paul II in Rome, says he has asked the Pope to speak out against apartheid. Jackson says he has urged the Pope to focus world attention on the problems of blacks in South Africa, as he did for the banned trade unionist movement Solidarity, in Poland.

Jan. 10: (Combined reports) On a special tour of South Africa, Sen. Edward M. Kennedy (D-Mass.) meets with Winnie Mandela, the wife of jailed black nationalist leader Nelson Mandela. Sen. Kennedy's request to meet with Mr. Mandela is rejected by South African authorities, who claim the visit "could prejudice a Government decision" on his possible release.

Earlier in the tour, Kennedy is jeered by demonstrators from the Azanian People's Organization (a black consciousness group) who assert his trip is designed to garner favor for a U.S. Presidential bid.

Feb. 4: In Johannesburg, South Africa, Desmond M. Tutu, the 1984 winner of the Noble Peace Prize, is enthroned as the city's first black Anglican bishop. In an hour-long speech, Tutu implores the ruling white minority to attempt to understand the aspirations of the black majority.

March 12: The Rev. Jesse Jackson and his two sons, Jesse Jr., 20, and Johnathan, 19, are arrested in an anti-apartheid demonstration in front of the South African Embassy.

March 23: The Chairman of the Congressional Black Caucus, Rep. Mickey Leland (D-Tex.), calls President Reagan an "apologist for apartheid" charging that he defended the actions of white and black South African police who fired on a funeral procession killing 18 people.

April 4: In Johannesburg, Bishop Desmond M. Tutu leads a procession of 30 clergymen through the city's downtown area to police headquarters to protest the detention of an Anglican priest and other apartheid opponents without trial.

April 25: Key Republican Senators on the Foreign Relations Committee introduce a bill that imposes economic sanctions on South Africa within a two-year period if apartheid is not dismantled in South Africa. The bill is sponsored by committee Chairman Richard Lugar of Indiana, and requires the President to impose the sanctions if that timetable is missed. The action by the Republican senators marks a significant break with the administration's policy of "constructive engagement."

May 25: Breaking with a ten-year policy against disinvestment, Harvard University President Derek Bok calls for strong economic sanctions against South Africa, in testimony before the Senate Banking, Housing and Urban Affairs Committee.

June 27: Coretta Scott King and two of her children, Bernice 22, and Martin Luther King III, 27, are arrested for demonstrating in front of the South African Embassy in protest of that government's policy of racial segregation—apartheid.

July 12: In a vote of 80 to 12, the Senate approves legislation imposing economic sanctions on South Africa to encourage its government to abandon apartheid. The bill voted by the Senate bans new bank loans to the South African Government, bans the sale of computers to agencies enforcing apartheid (like the police), and bans the sale of goods used in nuclear production.

July 23:   (Combined reports) John E. Jacob, President of the National Urban League, and other top officials of that organization are among 43 demonstrators arrested outside the South African Embassy in Washington, D.C., in a protest of that Government's racial policies. Also arrested is the "colored" (mixed race) South African anti-apartheid leader, the Rev. Allan Boesak.

The NUL-sponsored demonstration draws some 1,500 people.

Aug. 2:   The House gives final approval to a bill imposing economic sanctions on the South African Government by a vote of 380 to 48. The bill, worked out by a House-Senate conference committee, bans the importation of the South African Krugerrand gold coin, prohibits new bank loans by the United States and the sale of nuclear technology, as well as computer sales in excess of $100,000. The Reagan Administration remains opposed to the legislation.

Aug. 21:   After a five-and-a-half day tour of South Africa, the Rev. Jerry Falwell calls the 1984 Nobel laureate, Bishop Desmond Tutu, a "phony" asserting that Tutu does not speak for black South Africans.

Aug. 24:   Moral Majority leader Rev. Jerry Falwell apologizes for calling Anglican Bishop Desmond Tutu, the 1984 Nobel Prize winner, a phony. Falwell, after severe and widespread public criticism for the statement, claims his choice of words was poor and that he was not "impugning" Tutu as a person or a minister.

Aug. 28:   The Rev. Allan Boesak is arrested by South African police in an area of Capetown, just one day before he is to lead a march to demand the release of Nelson Mandela, the jailed black nationalist.

Sept. 10: In a reversal of his policy of "constructive engagement," stressing the use of diplomacy to urge the dismantling of apartheid, President Reagan imposes limited economic sanctions against South Africa via Executive Order. The order calls for most but not all of the sanctions proposed in pending Congressional legislation.

Sept. 28: In two separate anti-apartheid rallies, demonstrators are urged to escalate their protest tactics to pressure South Africa to end its system of racial segregation. The Congressional Black Caucus leads a march of hundreds of demonstrators through downtown Washington that ends in a rally and candle light vigil during its 15th Annual Legislative Weekend.

Oct. 29:   In a speech before the General Assembly's Special Committee Against Apartheid at the United Nations, Bishop Desmond Tutu accuses President Reagan of racism for actions that he says support South African apartheid.

Nov. 6:   The Rev. Allan Boesaks' passport is withheld by the South African Government, preventing him from traveling to the United States to accept the Robert F. Kennedy humanitarian award.

Nov. 21:   According to the report, a black, William A. Keyes, 32, is a lobbyist for the South African Government. Keyes is trying to convince black American anti-apartheid advocates that their efforts are misguided. Keyes asserts, "One-man, one-vote, is the principal question only for activists outside South Africa."

Dec. 30:   A spokesman for the U.S. State Department, Charles E. Redman, denounces the arrest of Winnie Mandela by the South African police for attempting to return to her home in the black township of Soweto. Mandela, wife of jailed black nationalist Nelson Mandela, has been banned and forced to live in another black township in Brandfort for eight years.

: : :

APPENDIX

AMERICA'S BLACK POPULATION: 1980 TO 1984

The black population has continued its progress in the areas of education, health, homeownerships and in the income levels of married-couple
families. Yet, in other areas, blacks have shown little progress. They
have experienced high rates of unemployment, sharp increases in divorce
and separation, substantial rises in the number of families maintained by
women and in the number of persons living in poverty. In addition, wide
gaps remained or worsened between blacks and whites in most social and
economic areas. Outlined below are some basic facts--

- In 1984, the black population numbered 27.7 million and
  comprised 12% of the total population. The black population
  has increased by 1 million since the decennial census of
  1980. Most of the growth can be attributed to natural increase although immigration from abroad has been of some
  importance in recent years.

- The age distribution of the black population differs substantially from that of the white population; blacks are
  much younger. In 1984, the median age of 26 years for
  blacks was about 6 years younger than the average of 32
  years for whites.

- The importance of education in the black community is
  reflected in the continued progress in this area by young
  black adults 25 to 34 years old. In 1984, 79% of young
  black adults were high school graduates compared to only
  53% in 1970. The comparable figures for whites were 88%
  and 76% for those years.

- Some variations in the level of schooling completed are
  evident between black young adults living in the South and
  the North and West. The proportion of blacks in the South
  completing high school still remains below those completing
  school in the North and West; however, since 1970, the
  educational differential has narrowed. In 1970, the percentage of Southern blacks 25 to 34 years old who were high
  school graduates was 13 percentage points below the figure
  for blacks in the North and West. By 1984, 76% of Southern
  blacks had completed school compared to 82% of those in the
  North and West -- a difference of only 6% percentage points.

- Although the majority of black families still have both a
  husband and wife present, the percentage of black families
  maintained by women has risen sharply in recent years. By
  1984, 43% of black families were maintained by women. The
  percentages of white families maintained by women has also
  increased but the increase has not been as pronounced.

- Between 1970 and 1984, black families maintained by women increased 113% compared to only 5% for husband-wife families. During the same period, white families maintained by women increased by about 62% and husband-wife families by about 13%.

- The lack of improvement in the median income level of black families is partly due to the proportion of black families maintained by women and the low incomes received by these families. In 1984, the median income of black families maintained by women was only $8,650, a drop of about 20% since 1980.

- In black married-couple families, the median income was $23,420 in 1984 compared to $30,060 for white husband-wife families.

- Inflation and a periodically recessionary economy has contributed to the increase in, poverty level. The number of black persons below the poverty level rose from 8.6 million in 1980 to 9.5 million in 1984. Among whites, 23.0 million were poor in 1984.

- The poverty rate for blacks has been consistently higher than that for whites. The black poverty rate was 33.8% in 1984, not significantly different from the 1980 rate of 32.5%. The poverty rate for whites was 11.5% in 1984.

- About 31% of all black families (2.1 million) had incomes below the poverty level in 1984. Black female householders accounted for 73% of all poor black families.

- The dramatic change in the number of families maintained by women has been evident not only in the South but in the North and West.

- As a consequence of the increase in families maintained by women, the number of black children living with both parents dropped sharply between 1970 and 1984 (from 58 to 41%) while the percentages in one-parent situations increased. The proportion of white children living with both parents has also declined since 1970; however, in 1984, 81% of white children still lived with both parents.

- Since 1960, unemployment rates for blacks have been consistently double those for whites. In 1984, the jobless rate for blacks was 15.9% and 6.5% for whites. Black teenagers, however, have had the highest rates and sharpest increases in these rates among all component groups in both the black and white population. In 1984, black teenage unemployment was 40%.

• After adjusting for inflation, the median cash income of black families did not change between 1980 and 1984 -- $15,430 versus $15,980; however, the income gap between black and white families increased from 1980 to 1984. In 1980 black family income was 58% of white family income ($15,980 versus $27,610). By 1984, the gap had widened to 56% ($15,430 versus $27,690).

Prepared by:
Racial Statistics Branch
Population of the Census
Washington, DC 20233

BLACK-OWNED BUSINESSES

The number of black-owned businesses increased by more than 100,000—47%—between 1977 and 1982, according to the Commerce Department's Census Bureau.

The first report from the 1982 Survey of Minority-Owned Business Enterprises shows a total of 339,239 black-owned businesses, up from 231,203 in 1977.

Gross receipts for black firms rose from $8.6 billion in 1977 to $12.4 billion in 1982. Nearly half had receipts under $5,000 while 1,129 companies had receipts of $1 million or more.

Service industries and retail trade businesses comprised 68% of black firms and 59% of their gross receipts.

Categories accounting for the largest dollar volume of receipts for black businesses were automotive dealers and service stations ($1.3 billion); miscellaneous retail ($993 million); food stores ($883 million); eating and drinking places ($675 million); and health services ($595 million).

The following table shows data for the 10 cities with the largest number of black-owned firms for 1982, comparable statewide totals, and city proportions of their state totals:

City	City		State		Percent City to State	
	Firms (no.)	Receipts ($1,000)	Firms (no.)	Receipts ($1,000)	Firms	Receipts
New York, NY	17 350	641 187	25 560	918 568	68	70
Los Angeles, Calif	12 197	459 754	44 658	1 619 839	27	28
Chicago, Ill	10 328	766 829	16 214	1 056 793	64	73
Houston, Tex	10 019	283 724	29 927	888 794	33	32
District of Columbia	8 966	268 488	(X)	(X)	(X)	(X)
Detroit, Mich	6 798	272 405	12 270	470 329	55	58
Philadelphia, Pa	5 017	215 337	10 289	395 768	49	54
Dallas, Tex	4 883	134 357	29 927	888 794	16	15
Baltimore, Md	4 077	241 024	15 601	540 256	26	45
Oakland, Calif	3 633	181 179	44 658	1 619 839	8	11

Sole proprietorship accounted for 95% of black firms, 3% were partnerships, and 2% were corporations.

About 10% or 38,631 firms had paid employees, about two-thirds of which employed one to four persons.

Data in the report cover number of firms, gross receipts, number of paid employees, and annual payroll. These data are presented by geographic area (the nation, states, selected metropolitan areas, counties, and cities), industry, size of firm, and legal form of organization of firm.

OTHER AVAILABLE TITLES IN "THE STATE OF BLACK AMERICA" SERIES

THE STATE OF BLACK AMERICA-1985-- "The Phenomenon of the Jesse Jackson Candidacy and the 1984 Presidential Election," Dr. Charles V. Hamilton, Columbia University; "Modern Technology and Urban Schools," Dr. Robert E. Fullilove, III, University of California at Berkeley; "Blackening In Media: The State of Blacks In the Press," Dr. Samuel L. Adams, University of Kansas; "Aged Black Americans: Double Jeopardy Re-Examined," Dr. Jacquelyne Johnson Jackson, Duke University; "Blacks In the Labor Movement," Dr. Lenneal J. Henderson, Howard University; "The Black Family Today and Tomorrow," Dr. James D. McGhee, Research Department, National Urban League, Inc.; "The Potential Problems of Black Financial Institutions," Dr. William D. Bradford, University of Maryland. $17.00

THE STATE OF BLACK AMERICA-1984-- "The High-Tech Revolution and its Implications for Black America," Dr. Charles L. Betsey, University of the District of Columbia and Dr. Bruce H. Dunson, Prairie View A&M University; "The State of Urban Education," Dr. Faustine Jones-Wilson, Howard University; "The Black Vote--The Sleeping Giant," Dr. Dianne Pinderhughes, Dartmouth University; "Ceremonies in Civil Rights: A Thirty Year Retrospective on the Law and Race" Dean Derrick A. Bell, University of Oregon; "Is There An Economic Recovery in Black America?," Denys Vaughn-Cooke, Former Senior Research Associate/Economist, NUL; "A Profile of the Black Single Female-Headed Household," Dr. James McGhee, Director of Research, National Urban League. The introduction is written by John E. Jacob, President, NUL. $15.00

THE STATE OF BLACK AMERICA-1983-- "Blacks in the Military," Dr. Alvin J. Schexnider; "The Mental Health Status of Black Americans," Dr. Alvin F. Poussaint; "The Economic Status of the Black Population," Dr. David H. Swinton; "Education," Dr. Mary Berry; "Changing Demographics in Black America," Dr. James McGhee; "The Status of Black Women," Dr. Barbara Jones; "Blacks in Business," Dr. Lenneal J. Henderson; "The Black Vote in 1983," Dr. Charles V. Hamilton. The introduction is by John E. Jacob, NUL President. $14.00

COMPLETE SET OF THE
STATE OF BLACK AMERICA--

This set contains all seven volumes of "The State of Black America" issued from 1976 through 1982. $150.00

(Except for the editions described above, all other annual editions of "The State of Black America" are out of print and can only be obtained by purchasing the complete set.)

Orders should be addressed to:
The Communications Department
The National Urban League
500 East 62nd Street
New York, NY 10021
Please include $1 for the cost of
handling and postage for each publication.

ACKNOWLEDGEMENTS

The National Urban League acknowledges with sincere appreciation the contributions of the authors of the various papers appearing in this publication and the special contributions of NUL staff including Cynthia Gresham, Ollie Wadler, Farida Syed, Vernice Williams and Faith Williams of the Communications Department; Washington Operations, the Research Department, and the Program Departments.

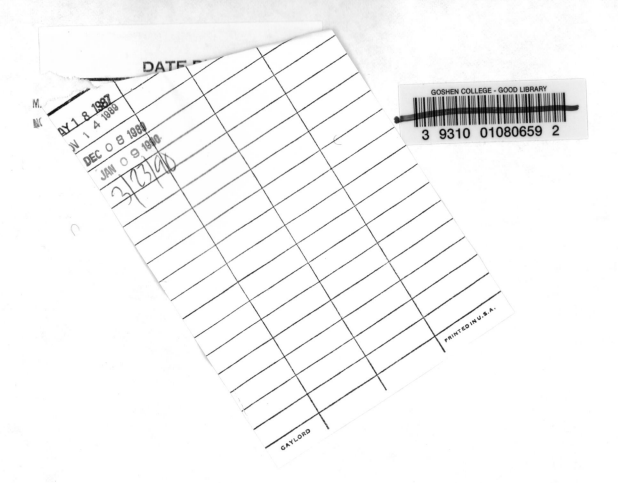